WONDER WOMAN

LAND OF THE DEAD

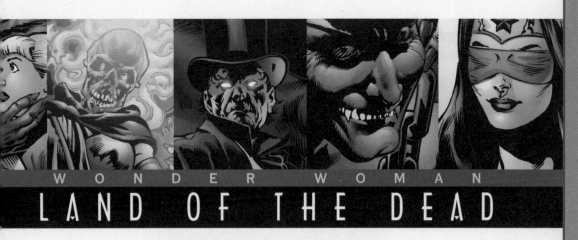

WONDER WOMAN
LAND OF THE DEAD

GREG RUCKA   GEOFF JOHNS WRITERS

DREW JOHNSON   JUSTINIANO

RAGS MORALES   SEAN PHILLIPS PENCILLERS

MICHAEL BAIR   RAY SNYDER   MARK PROPST   LIVESAY

WALDEN WONG   SEAN PHILLIPS INKERS

RICHARD & TANYA HORIE   JAMES SINCLAIR COLORISTS

TODD KLEIN   PAT BROSSEAU LETTERERS

WONDER WOMAN CREATED BY WILLIAM MOULTON MARSTON

WONDER WOMAN: LAND OF THE DEAD

Published by DC Comics. Cover and compilation copyright © 2006 DC Comics.
All Rights Reserved.

Originally published in single magazine form in WONDER WOMAN #214-217, FLASH #219
Copyright © 2004, 2005 DC Comics. All Rights Reserved. All characters, their
distinctive likenesses and related elements featured in this publication are trademarks
of DC Comics. The stories, characters and incidents featured in this publication are
entirely fictional. DC Comics does not read or accept unsolicited submissions of
ideas, stories or artwork.

DC Comics, 1700 Broadway, New York, NY 10019
A Warner Bros. Entertainment Company
Printed in Canada. First Printing.
ISBN: 1-4012-0938-6
ISBN 13: 978-1-4012-0938-4

Cover art by J.G. Jones
Special thanks to Robin Riggs

OUR STORY SO FAR...

DIANA OF THEMYSCIRA (HOME OF THE AMAZONS), AND THE HERO ALSO KNOWN AS WONDER WOMAN, CAME TO "MAN'S WORLD" YEARS AGO. ACTING AS AN AMBASSADOR OF PEACE, SHE HOPED TO TEACH A VIOLENT WORLD THE WAYS OF HER JUST AND HARMONIOUS CIVILIZATION. A THEMYSCIRAN EMBASSY WAS EVENTUALLY SET UP IN NEW YORK, AND A LARGE STAFF RUNS IT SO THAT DIANA CAN CONCENTRATE ON THE IMPORTANT WORK OF BRINGING UNITY.

ON MOUNT OLYMPUS, ARES HAS STIRRED UP MISCHIEF IN ZEUS'S LOVE LIFE. THE WAR GOD EMPLOYED HIS SON EROS TO MANIPULATE ZEUS'S EMOTIONS. HERA CAUGHT HER HUSBAND GAZING AT THE AMAZON ARTEMIS THROUGH A VIEWING POND. IN AN UNEXPECTED JEALOUS RAGE, HERA KICKED AT THE POND, CAUSING MUCH DAMAGE TO THE ISLAND OF THEMYSCIRA. SOON AFTER, THE OLYMPIAN WOMEN BEGIN GATHERING IN PRIVATE TO DEAL WITH THEIR OUT-OF-TOUCH AND LUSTFUL LEADER, ONCE AND FOR ALL.

MEANWHILE, THE GORGON SISTERS STHENO AND EURYALE ARE REUNITED WITH THEIR LONG-DEAD SISTER MEDOUSA. REVIVED BY THE WITCH CIRCE, MEDOUSA IS NOW READY TO TAKE VENGEANCE ON HER ENEMY ATHENA BY KILLING ATHENA'S FAVORITE: WONDER WOMAN. WITH CIRCE'S ENCHANTMENTS, MEDOUSA ARRIVES AT THE EMBASSY AND IS OVERWHELMED BY THE CHANGES MADE IN MAN'S WORLD OVER THE LAST THREE MILLENNIA. CIRCE SUGGESTS THAT MEDOUSA GAIN AN ALLY, VERONICA CALE — A PHARMACEUTICAL CEO WITH AN AXE TO GRIND.

DIANA IS CONCERNED OVER U.S. PRESIDENT JONATHAN HORNE'S MILITARY ACTIONS TARGETING THE ISLAND OF THEMYSCIRA, WHICH, AFTER HERA'S OUTBURST, HAD CRASHED TO EARTH OFF THE EAST COAST OF THE U.S. WHEN HE INVITES HER TO A STATE DINNER, SHE ACCEPTS, HOPING TO RECEIVE A COMMITMENT OF AID RATHER THAN A HEIGHTENED STATE OF CONFLICT.

IN WASHINGTON FOR THE STATE DINNER, DIANA IS UNAWARE THAT MEDOUSA IS ALSO IN THE CAPITAL. DURING A PRIVATE TALK WITH PRESIDENT HORNE, THE AMAZON LEADER PHILLIPUS REFUSES A TREATY, PREFERRING TO REMAIN A NEUTRAL REPUBLIC. HORNE, THOUGH, IS CONCERNED THAT A NATION WITH A MARTIAL CULTURE, NOW RESTING SOME 90 MILES OFF THE CAROLINA COAST, PRESENTS A POTENTIAL THREAT TO U.S. SOVEREIGNTY. THE DISCUSSION IS INTERRUPTED BY THE ARRIVAL OF MEDOUSA, WHO CALLOUSLY TRANSFORMS AND KILLS SEVERAL SECRET SERVICE AGENTS. THE AMAZONS PROTECT THE PRESIDENT, BUT NOT BEFORE DIANA IS BITTEN BY THE SNAKES ATOP MEDOUSA'S HEAD. THE GORGON FLEES THE WHITE HOUSE, HEADED FOR THE EMBASSY WITH A WOUNDED DIANA IN PURSUIT.

AT THE SAME TIME, PALLAS ATHENA INFORMS ARES THAT HE WILL BE INVOKED, FOLLOWING SELDOM-USED TRADITION, AND HE CONCLUDES THAT A COUP AGAINST ZEUS IS ABOUT TO UNFOLD, ENGINEERED BY ATHENA. HE ASSURES HER THAT HE WILL COME WHEN CALLED.

MEDOUSA ARRIVES AT THE EMBASSY JUST IN TIME TO ATTACK FERDINAND, WHO IS WITH DR. ANDERSON. DIANA INTERVENES AND THE TWO BATTLE SAVAGELY THROUGHOUT THE EMBASSY, WITH MEDOUSA THREATENING THE INHABITANTS, EVEN TRANSFORMING YOUNG MARTIN GARIBALDI, THE SON OF ONE OF THE EMBASSY STAFFERS, TO STONE. ENRAGED, DIANA PUMMELS MEDOUSA UNTIL THE GORGON INVOKES THE ANCIENT CALL TO ARMS, SUMMONING ARES. DIANA AGREES TO FOLLOW OLYMPIAN LAW AND DRESSES IN FULL ARMOR, READY TO ENGAGE HER OPPONENT.

DIANA HEADS TO YANKEE STADIUM TO DO BATTLE AS THE EVENT IS TELEVISED AROUND THE GLOBE, VIA A SPELL FROM CIRCE. AT A KEY MOMENT IN THE CONTEST, MEDOUSA INTENDS TO TURN HER GAZE TO THE CAMERAS AND THOSE WATCHING FROM HOME WILL BE TRANSFORMED TO STONE, MORE VICTIMS IN A WAR OF THE GODS.

THE BATTLE IS FIERCE, WITH INJURIES ENDURED BY BOTH COMBATANTS. WHEN IT APPEARS

MEDOUSA IS READY TO WIN, DIANA CONFOUNDS HER BY REMOVING HER HELMET AND REVEALING THAT SHE HAD BEEN FIGHTING BLINDFOLDED, UNAFFECTED BY THE GORGON'S GAZE. STILL, THE FURIOUS MEDOUSA WEARS DIANA DOWN, STRIPPING HER OF ARMOR AND BLINDFOLD. UNDAUNTED, DIANA STAGGERS ACROSS THE OUTFIELD AND GRASPS ONE OF THE SNAKE HEADS SHE SEVERED FROM MEDOUSA'S HEAD, THEN DRIPS ITS POISON INTO HER EYES, BLINDING HERSELF. RISING AGAIN, AXE IN HAND, SHE TAKES ONE FINAL SWING, AND MEDOUSA'S HEAD FLIES ACROSS THE FIELD.

THE GORGON'S SISTERS RUSH TO AVENGE MEDOUSA, BUT THEY ARE TURNED ASIDE BY THE WINGED HORSE PEGASUS, WHO SPRINGS TO LIFE FROM MEDOUSA'S BLOOD AS IN ANCIENT LEGEND, AND WHO COMES TO TRANSPORT DIANA BACK TO THE EMBASSY. AS THE WOUNDED PRINCESS HEADS TO MANHATTAN ON PEGASUS, THE AMAZONS LEARN OF DIANA'S INJURY, AND CARRISA AND IO RUSH TO THE EMBASSY TO OFFER AID. CALE, CONTENT WITH DIANA'S BLINDING, THINKS SHE'S FREE OF THE GORGONS ONLY TO FIND HERSELF IN CIRCE'S THRALL, A PAWN THE WITCH WILL USE TO FREE HER DAUGHTER, LYTA, FROM THE AMAZONS.

DIANA, ACCEPTING HER SIGHTLESS CONDITION, RESTS IN HER ROOM UNTIL SHE IS AWAKENED BY ATHENA. THE GODDESS REVEALS THAT MEDOUSA HAD TO BE STOPPED, HER GAZE HAD TO BE KEPT FROM NEARLY 50 MILLION PEOPLE, AND IF THE PRICE WAS THE LIFE OF MARTIN GARIBALDI, THEN SO BE IT.

SOON AFTER, TO PROVE THAT HER SKILLS ARE UNDIMINISHED, DIANA SPARS WITH THE ENTIRE JUSTICE LEAGUE AT THE WATCHTOWER ON THE MOON. AS THE TEST IS EVALUATED AND DIANA HEADS TO MARTIN'S MEMORIAL SERVICE, THE GODDESSES OF OLYMPUS MAKE THEIR MOVE AGAINST ZEUS, WHO IS FAR MORE AWARE THAN THEY HAD ANTICIPATED. HE AWAKENS HIS PROTECTOR, THE BEHEMOTH BRIAREOS.

ZEUS'S CHAMPION IS CALLED TO BATTLE A WARRIOR CHOSEN BY THE GODDESSES, AND THEY SUMMON DIANA. ASTRIDE PEGASUS, DIANA WAGES A TERRIBLE CONFLICT WITH THE GIANT, ENDURING GREAT PHYSICAL PAIN BUT REFUSING TO RELENT. WHEN ZEUS DENIES HER MERCY, THE DIE IS CAST. PEGASUS BRINGS DIANA A BAG, WHICH IS REVEALED TO CONTAIN MEDOUSA'S HEAD, ITS ENCHANTMENTS STILL POTENT. BRIAREOS, TURNED TO STONE, COLLAPSES TO THE FLOOR OF THE THRONE ROOM. PALLAS ATHENA ASSUMES THE THRONE OF OLYMPUS, SENDING ZEUS OFF WITH HERA. SHE RECEIVES AN OATH OF ALLEGIANCE FROM THE ASSEMBLED GODS AND THEN OFFERS DIANA A GIFT. DIANA ASKS THAT MARTIN BE RESURRECTED, BUT ATHENA ADMITS SHE CANNOT DO SO YET. AT THE SAME TIME SHE WARNS OF A COMING STORM — THE GROWING CABAL OF POWERFUL VILLAINS UNITING TO CHALLENGE HER FELLOW CHAMPIONS OF JUSTICE.

BELOW OLYMPUS, IN DARK TARTARUS, ARES VISITS WITH HADES, POSEIDON AND ZEUS. HE IS ASKED TO JOIN THEM IN THE COMING BATTLE TO RETAKE OLYMPUS, A WAR AMONG GODS THAT WILL NO DOUBT SPILL FROM THE HEAVENS TO MAN'S WORLD, AS WELL...

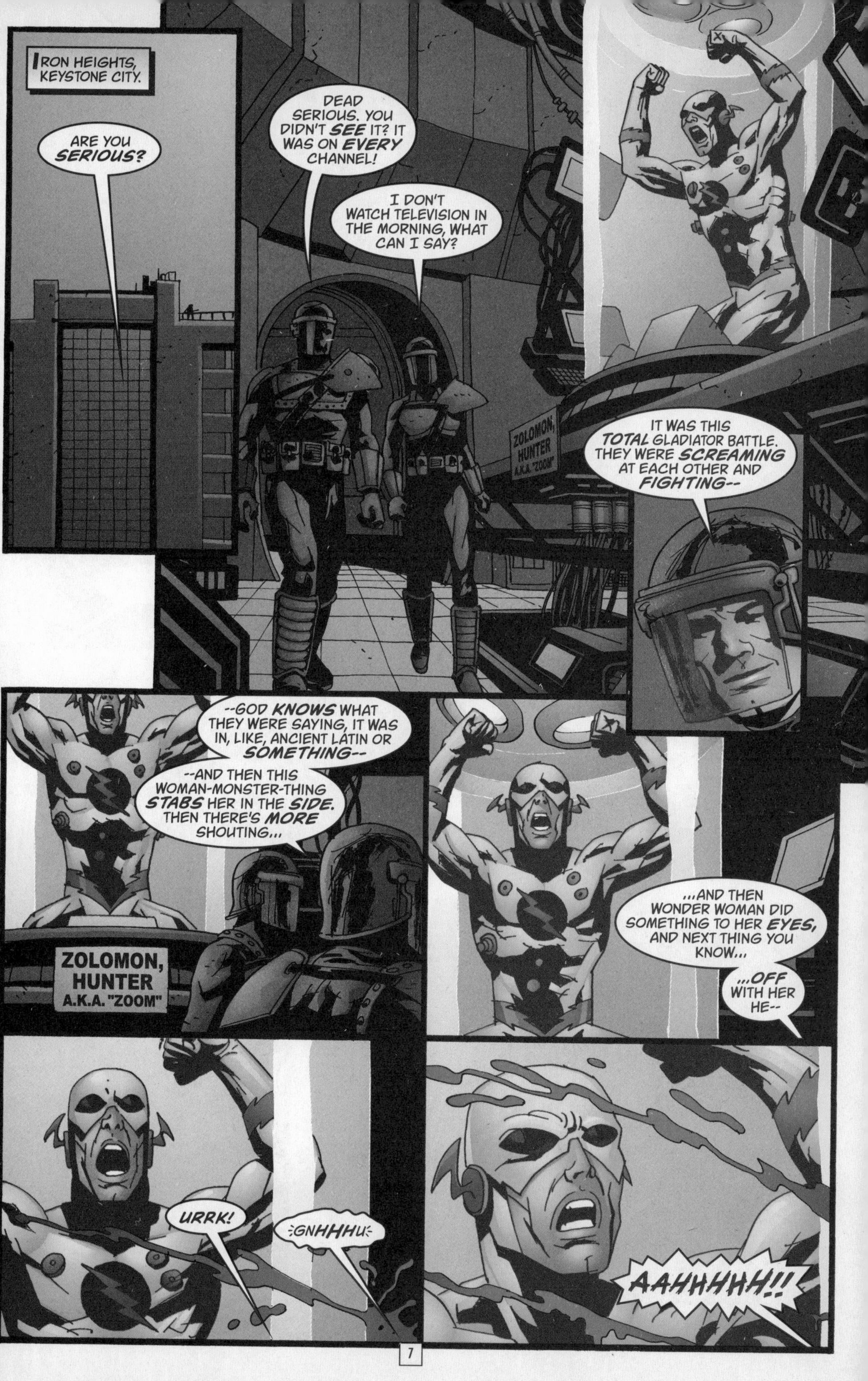
IRON HEIGHTS, KEYSTONE CITY.
ARE YOU SERIOUS?
DEAD SERIOUS. YOU DIDN'T SEE IT? IT WAS ON EVERY CHANNEL!
I DON'T WATCH TELEVISION IN THE MORNING, WHAT CAN I SAY?
ZOLOMON, HUNTER A.K.A. "ZOOM"
IT WAS THIS TOTAL GLADIATOR BATTLE. THEY WERE SCREAMING AT EACH OTHER AND FIGHTING--
--GOD KNOWS WHAT THEY WERE SAYING, IT WAS IN, LIKE, ANCIENT LATIN OR SOMETHING--
--AND THEN THIS WOMAN-MONSTER-THING STABS HER IN THE SIDE. THEN THERE'S MORE SHOUTING...
ZOLOMON, HUNTER A.K.A. "ZOOM"
...AND THEN WONDER WOMAN DID SOMETHING TO HER EYES, AND NEXT THING YOU KNOW...
...OFF WITH HER HE--
URRK!
GNHHHU
AAHHHHH!!

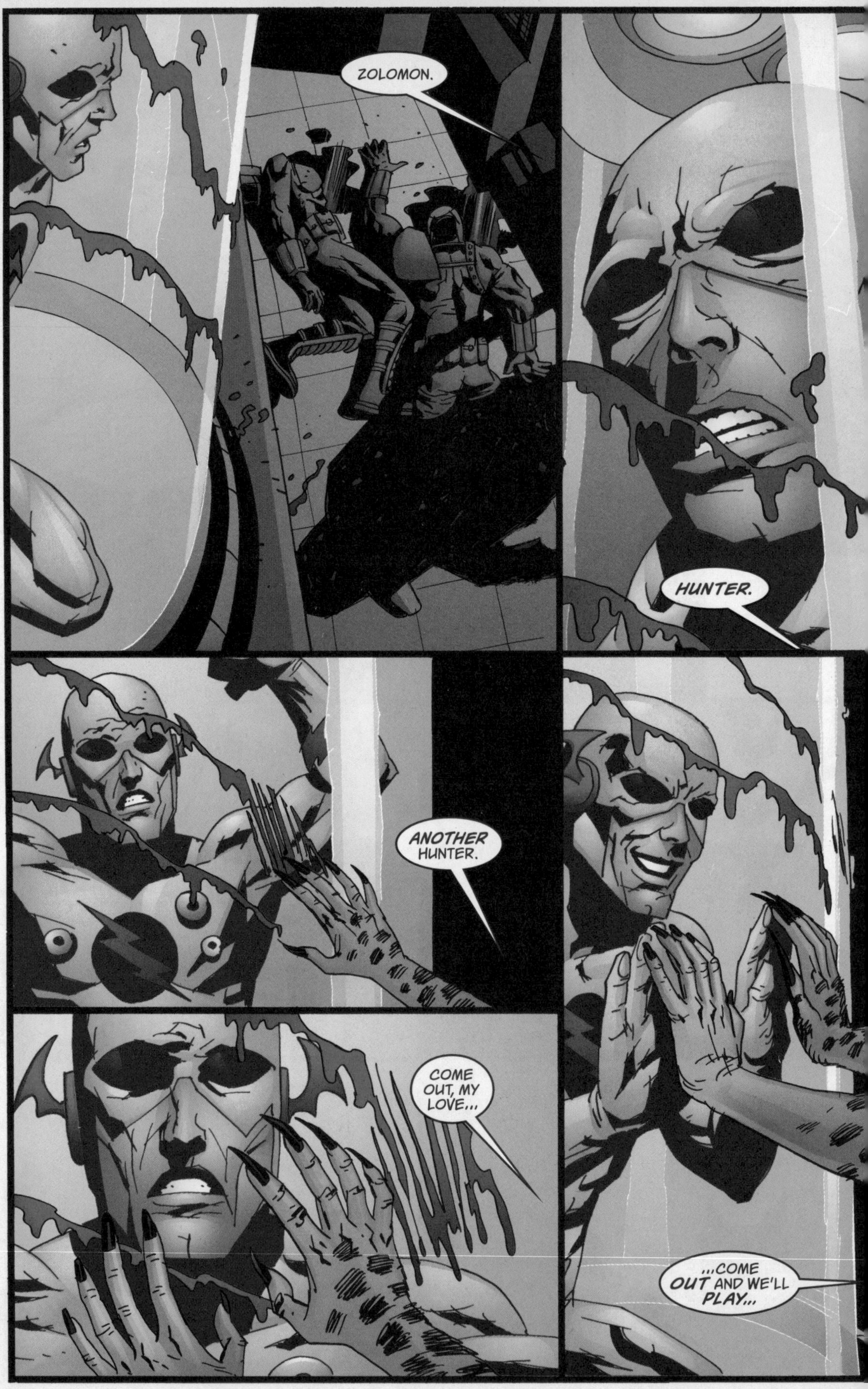

ZOLOMON.
HUNTER.
ANOTHER HUNTER.
COME OUT, MY LOVE...
...COME OUT AND WE'LL PLAY...

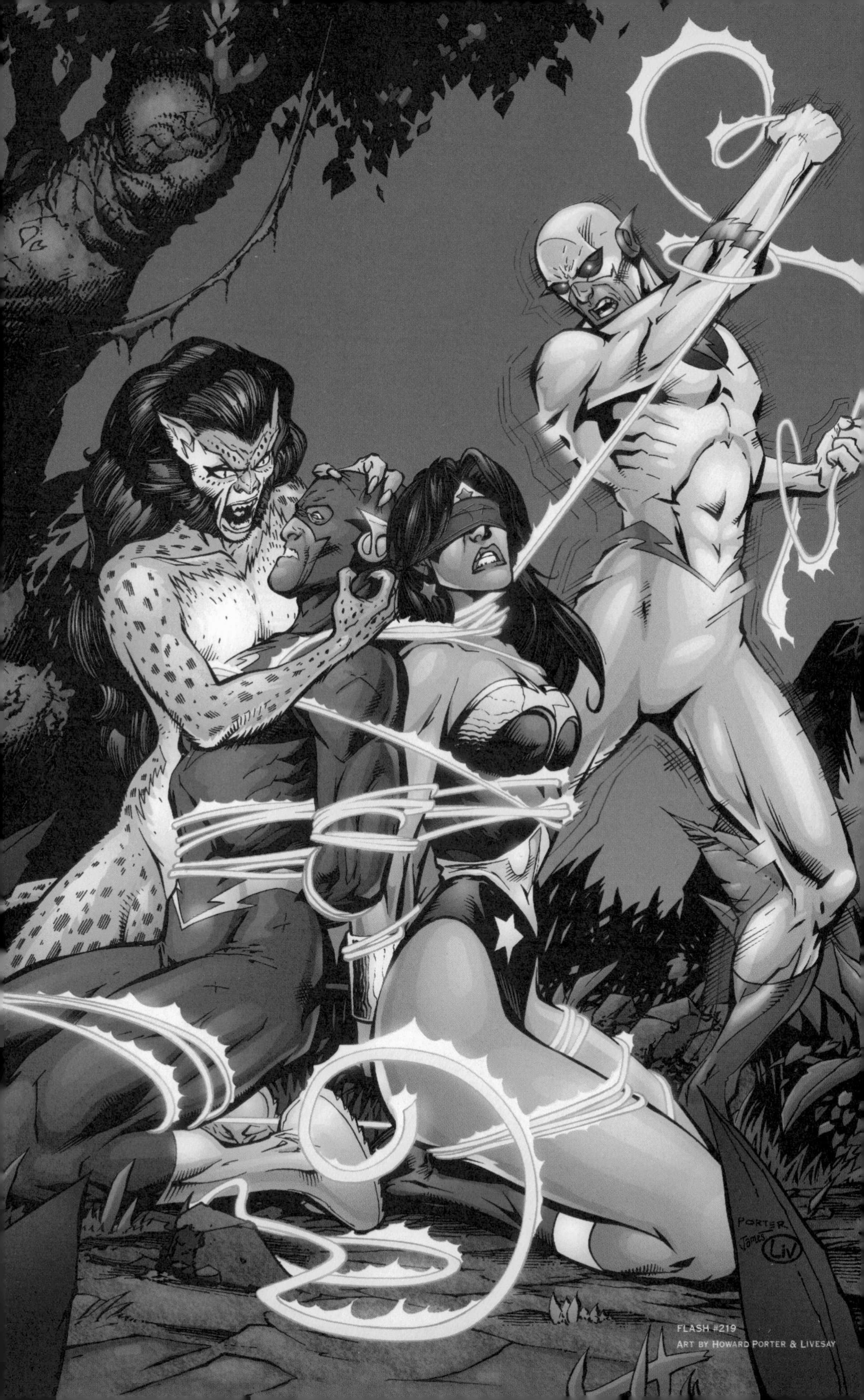
PORTER
James
LiV

FLASH #219
ART BY HOWARD PORTER & LIVESAY

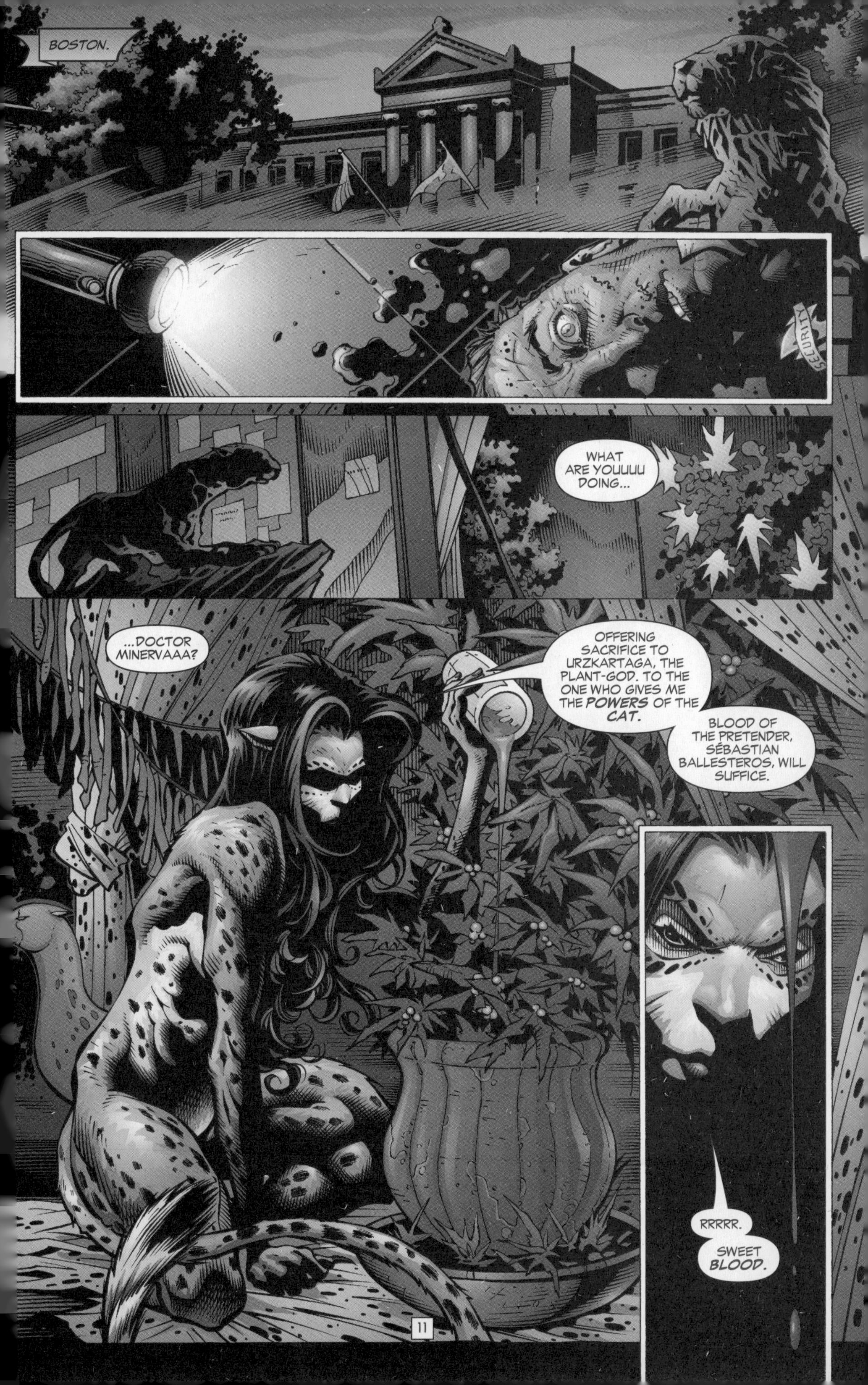

BOSTON.
SECURITY
WHAT ARE YOUUUU DOING...
...DOCTOR MINERVAAA?
OFFERING SACRIFICE TO URZKARTAGA, THE PLANT-GOD. TO THE ONE WHO GIVES ME THE POWERS OF THE CAT.
BLOOD OF THE PRETENDER, SÉBASTIAN BALLESTEROS, WILL SUFFICE.
RRRRR.
SWEET BLOOD.

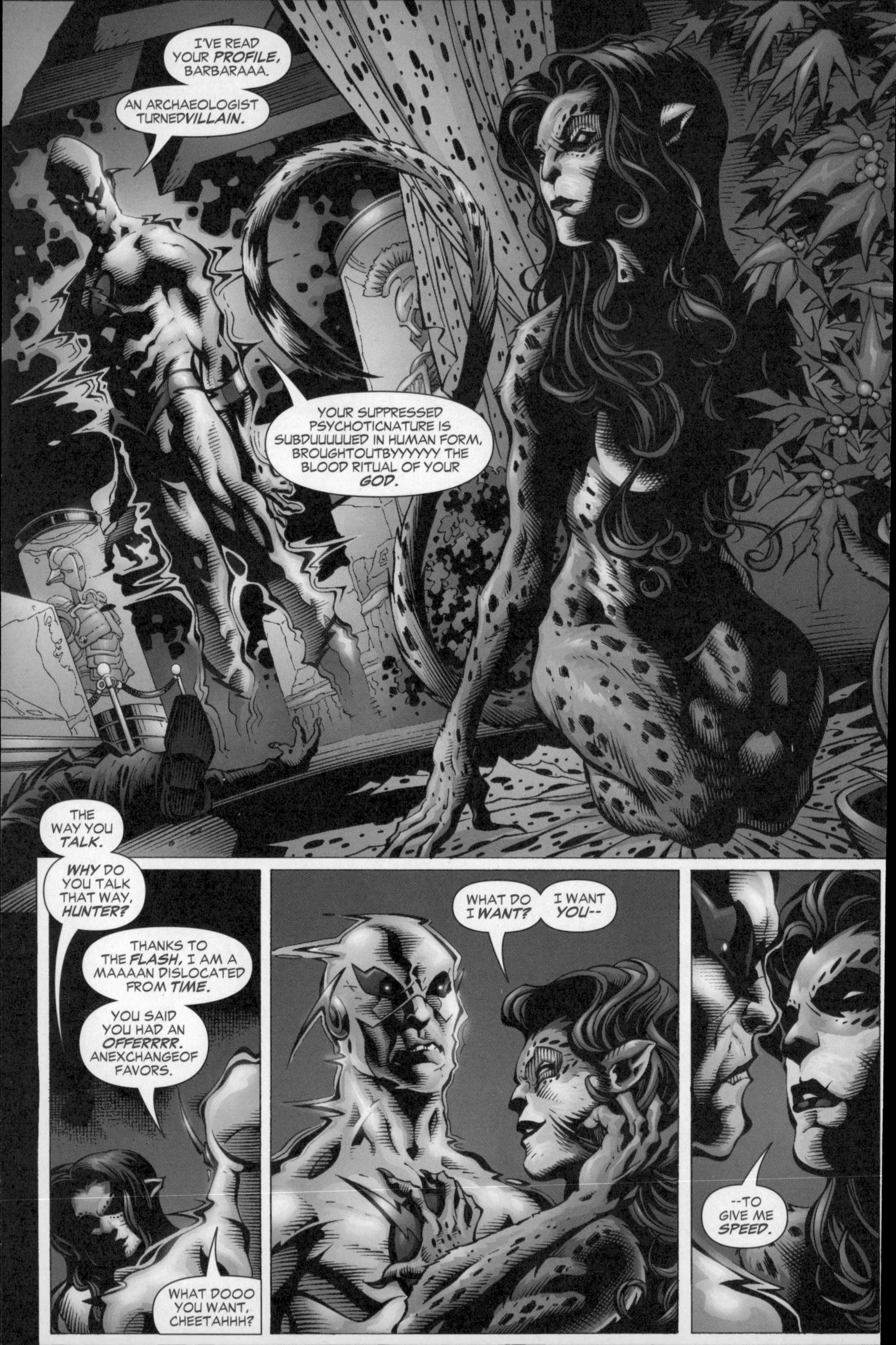
I'VE READ YOUR PROFILE, BARBARAAA.
AN ARCHAEOLOGIST TURNEDVILLAIN.
YOUR SUPPRESSED PSYCHOTICNATURE IS SUBDUUUUUED IN HUMAN FORM, BROUGHTOUTBYYYYYY THE BLOOD RITUAL OF YOUR GOD.
THE WAY YOU TALK.
WHY DO YOU TALK THAT WAY, HUNTER?
THANKS TO THE FLASH, I AM A MAAAAN DISLOCATED FROM TIME.
YOU SAID YOU HAD AN OFFERRRR. ANEXCHANGEOF FAVORS.
WHAT DOOO YOU WANT, CHEETAHHH?
WHAT DO I WANT?
I WANT YOU--
--TO GIVE ME SPEED.

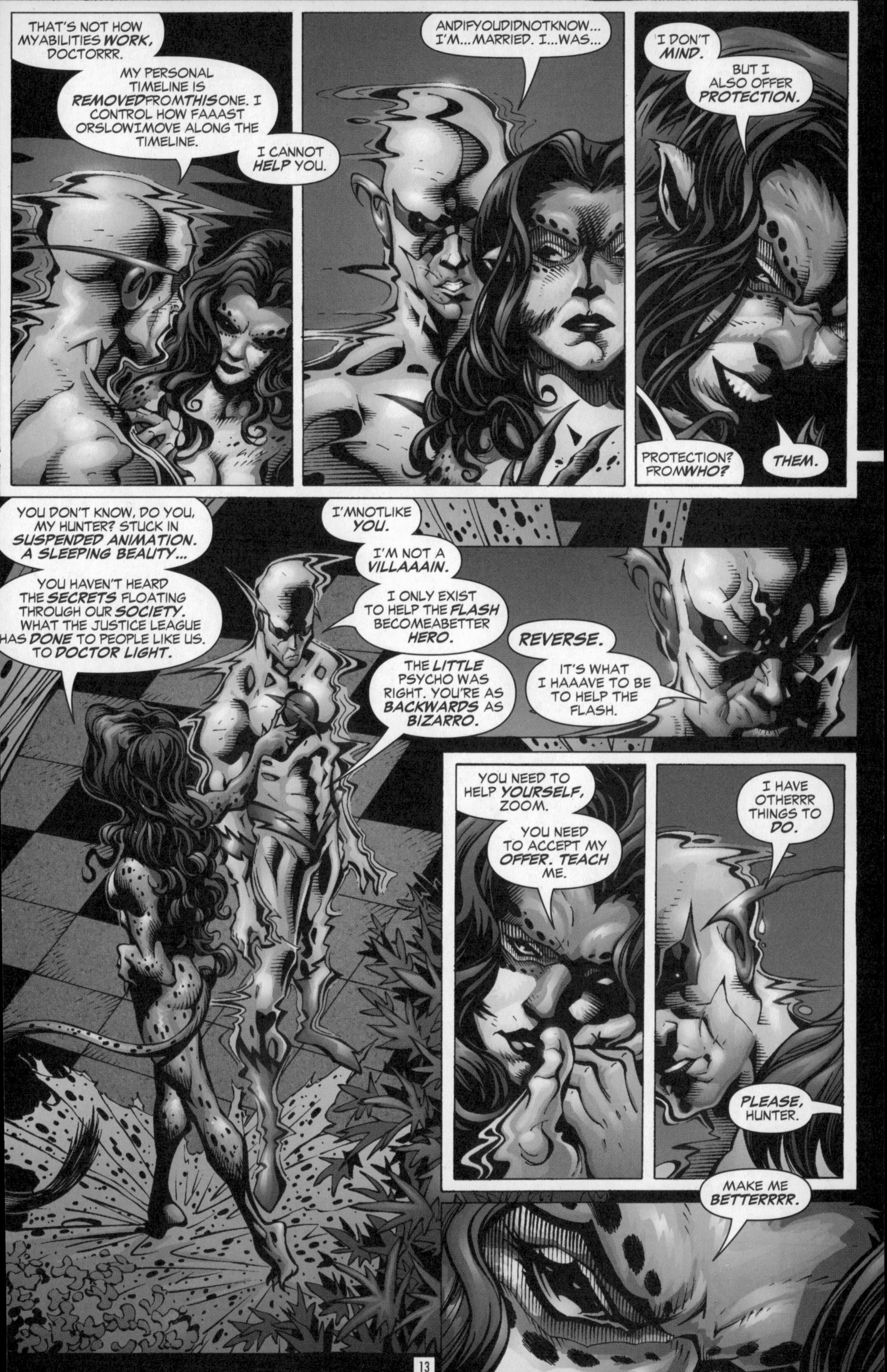
THAT'S NOT HOW MYABILITIES WORK, DOCTORRR.
MY PERSONAL TIMELINE IS REMOVEDFROMTHISONE. I CONTROL HOW FAAAST ORSLOWIMOVE ALONG THE TIMELINE.
I CANNOT HELP YOU.
ANDIFYOUDIDNOTKNOW... I'M...MARRIED. I...WAS...
I DON'T MIND.
BUT I ALSO OFFER PROTECTION.
PROTECTION? FROMWHO?
THEM.
YOU DON'T KNOW, DO YOU, MY HUNTER? STUCK IN SUSPENDED ANIMATION. A SLEEPING BEAUTY...
YOU HAVEN'T HEARD THE SECRETS FLOATING THROUGH OUR SOCIETY. WHAT THE JUSTICE LEAGUE HAS DONE TO PEOPLE LIKE US. TO DOCTOR LIGHT.
I'MNOTLIKE YOU.
I'M NOT A VILLAAAIN.
I ONLY EXIST TO HELP THE FLASH BECOMEABETTER HERO.
THE LITTLE PSYCHO WAS RIGHT. YOU'RE AS BACKWARDS AS BIZARRO.
REVERSE.
IT'S WHAT I HAAAVE TO BE TO HELP THE FLASH.
YOU NEED TO HELP YOURSELF, ZOOM.
YOU NEED TO ACCEPT MY OFFER. TEACH ME.
I HAVE OTHERRR THINGS TO DO.
PLEASE, HUNTER.
MAKE ME BETTERRRR.

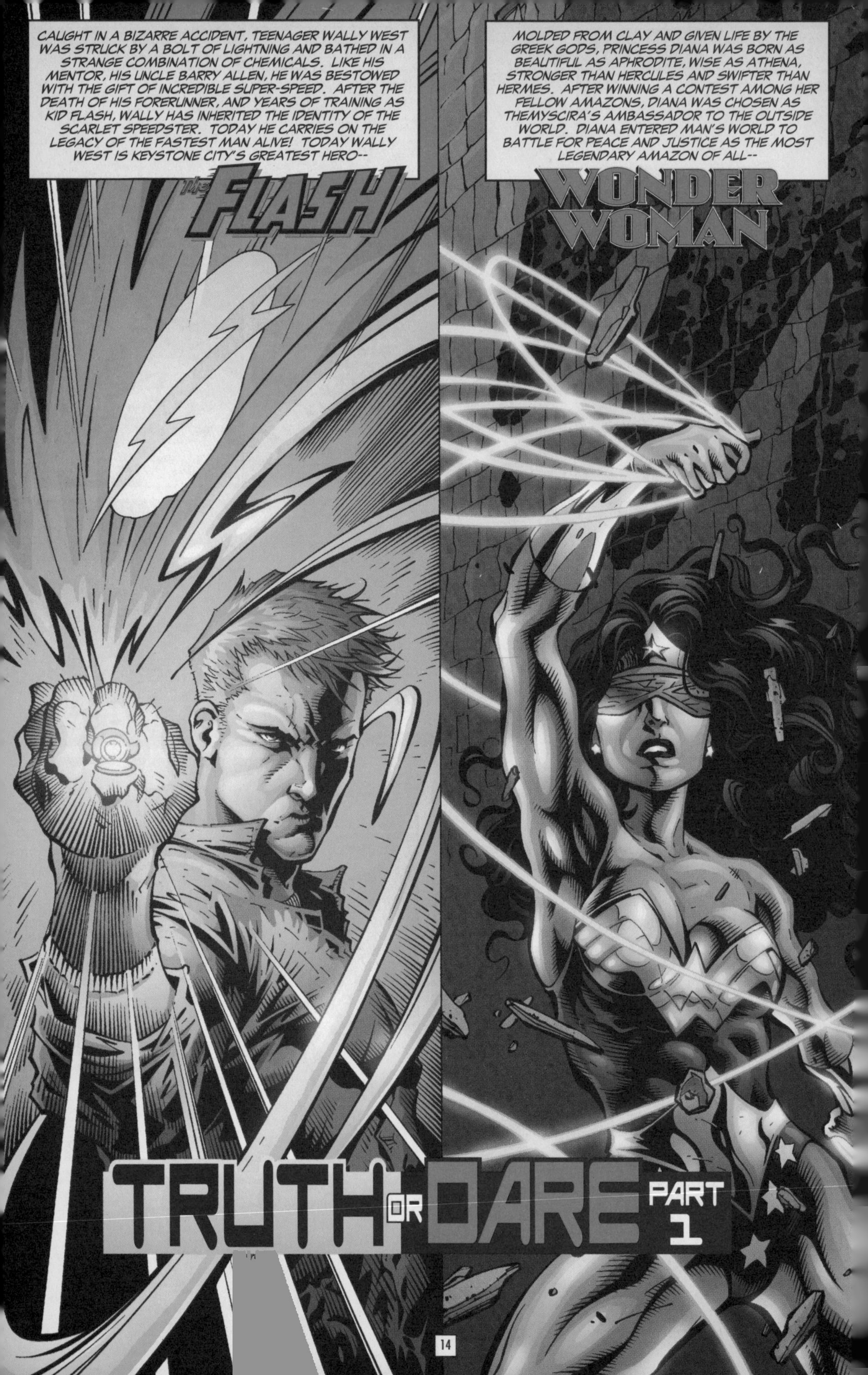

CAUGHT IN A BIZARRE ACCIDENT, TEENAGER WALLY WEST WAS STRUCK BY A BOLT OF LIGHTNING AND BATHED IN A STRANGE COMBINATION OF CHEMICALS. LIKE HIS MENTOR, HIS UNCLE BARRY ALLEN, HE WAS BESTOWED WITH THE GIFT OF INCREDIBLE SUPER-SPEED. AFTER THE DEATH OF HIS FORERUNNER, AND YEARS OF TRAINING AS KID FLASH, WALLY HAS INHERITED THE IDENTITY OF THE SCARLET SPEEDSTER. TODAY HE CARRIES ON THE LEGACY OF THE FASTEST MAN ALIVE! TODAY WALLY WEST IS KEYSTONE CITY'S GREATEST HERO--
THE FLASH
MOLDED FROM CLAY AND GIVEN LIFE BY THE GREEK GODS, PRINCESS DIANA WAS BORN AS BEAUTIFUL AS APHRODITE, WISE AS ATHENA, STRONGER THAN HERCULES AND SWIFTER THAN HERMES. AFTER WINNING A CONTEST AMONG HER FELLOW AMAZONS, DIANA WAS CHOSEN AS THEMYSCIRA'S AMBASSADOR TO THE OUTSIDE WORLD. DIANA ENTERED MAN'S WORLD TO BATTLE FOR PEACE AND JUSTICE AS THE MOST LEGENDARY AMAZON OF ALL--
WONDER WOMAN
TRUTH OR DARE PART 1

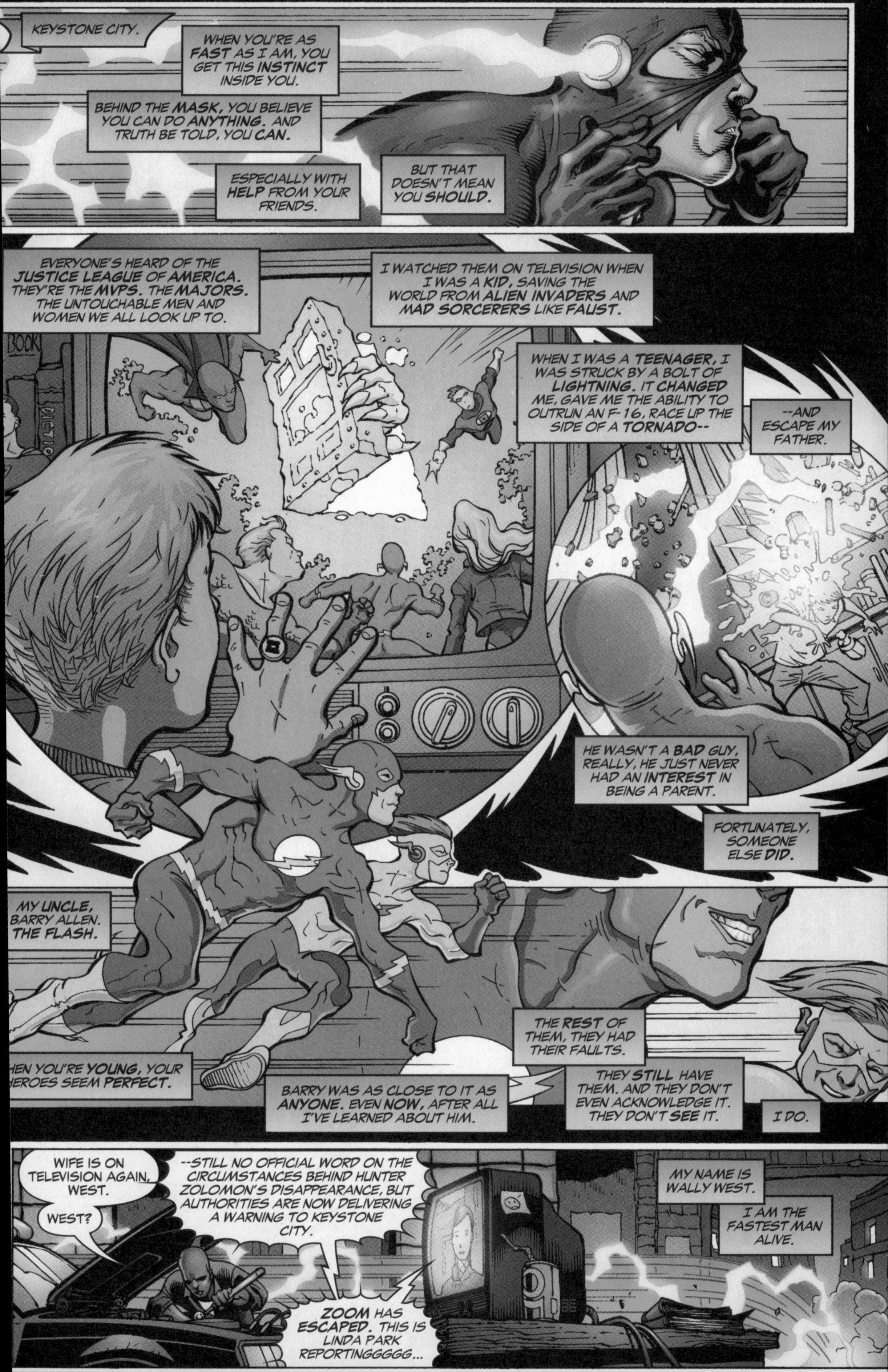
KEYSTONE CITY.
WHEN YOU'RE AS FAST AS I AM, YOU GET THIS INSTINCT INSIDE YOU.
BEHIND THE MASK, YOU BELIEVE YOU CAN DO ANYTHING. AND TRUTH BE TOLD, YOU CAN.
ESPECIALLY WITH HELP FROM YOUR FRIENDS.
BUT THAT DOESN'T MEAN YOU SHOULD.
EVERYONE'S HEARD OF THE JUSTICE LEAGUE OF AMERICA. THEY'RE THE MVPS. THE MAJORS. THE UNTOUCHABLE MEN AND WOMEN WE ALL LOOK UP TO.
I WATCHED THEM ON TELEVISION WHEN I WAS A KID, SAVING THE WORLD FROM ALIEN INVADERS AND MAD SORCERERS LIKE FAUST.
WHEN I WAS A TEENAGER, I WAS STRUCK BY A BOLT OF LIGHTNING. IT CHANGED ME, GAVE ME THE ABILITY TO OUTRUN AN F-16, RACE UP THE SIDE OF A TORNADO--
--AND ESCAPE MY FATHER.
HE WASN'T A BAD GUY, REALLY, HE JUST NEVER HAD AN INTEREST IN BEING A PARENT.
FORTUNATELY, SOMEONE ELSE DID.
MY UNCLE, BARRY ALLEN. THE FLASH.
HEN YOU'RE YOUNG, YOUR HEROES SEEM PERFECT.
BARRY WAS AS CLOSE TO IT AS ANYONE. EVEN NOW, AFTER ALL I'VE LEARNED ABOUT HIM.
THE REST OF THEM, THEY HAD THEIR FAULTS.
THEY STILL HAVE THEM. AND THEY DON'T EVEN ACKNOWLEDGE IT. THEY DON'T SEE IT.
I DO.
WIFE IS ON TELEVISION AGAIN, WEST.
WEST?
--STILL NO OFFICIAL WORD ON THE CIRCUMSTANCES BEHIND HUNTER ZOLOMON'S DISAPPEARANCE, BUT AUTHORITIES ARE NOW DELIVERING A WARNING TO KEYSTONE CITY.
ZOOM HAS ESCAPED. THIS IS LINDA PARK REPORTINGGGGG...
MY NAME IS WALLY WEST.
I AM THE FASTEST MAN ALIVE.

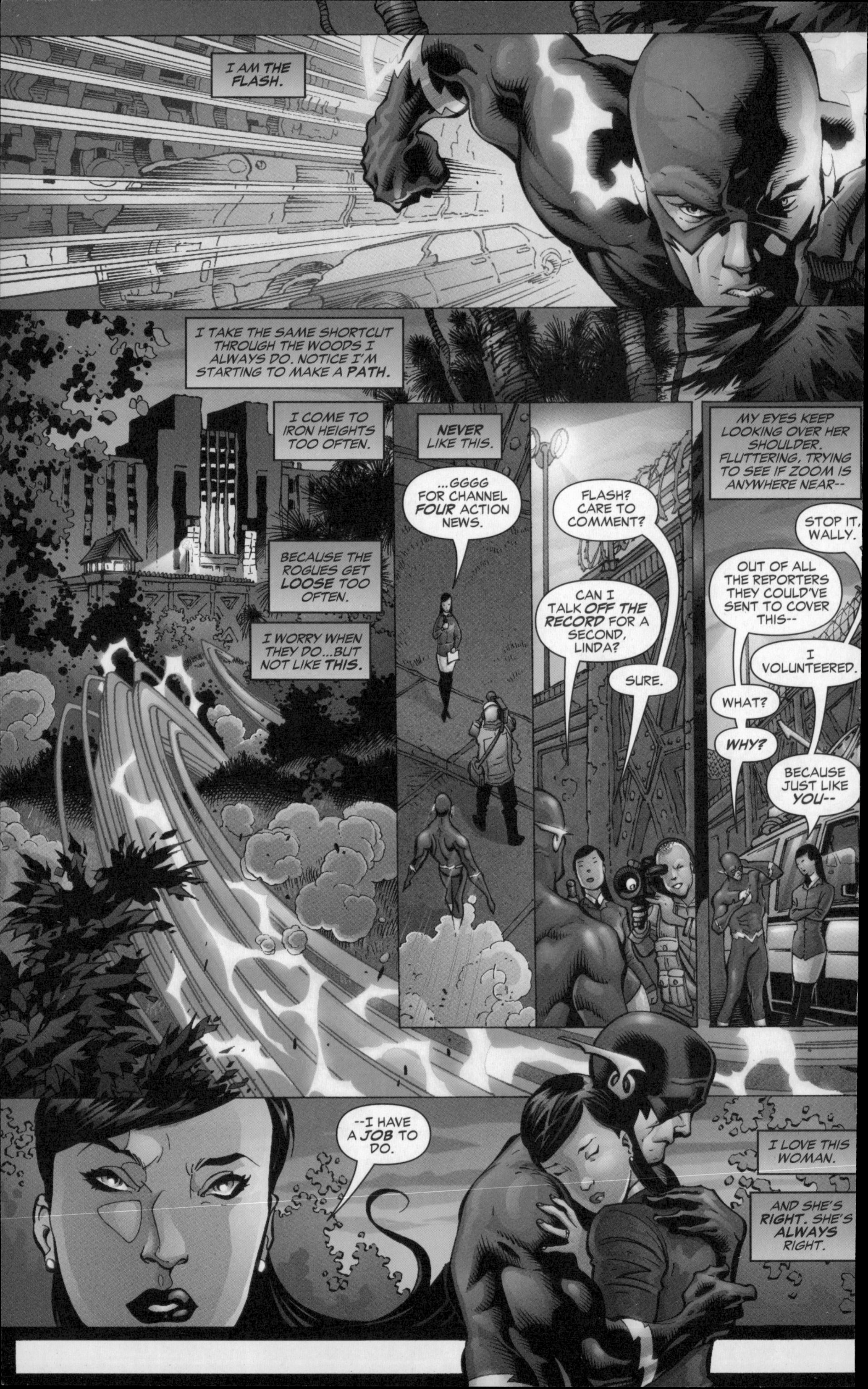
I AM THE FLASH.
I TAKE THE SAME SHORTCUT THROUGH THE WOODS I ALWAYS DO. NOTICE I'M STARTING TO MAKE A PATH.
I COME TO IRON HEIGHTS TOO OFTEN.
BECAUSE THE ROGUES GET LOOSE TOO OFTEN.
I WORRY WHEN THEY DO...BUT NOT LIKE THIS.
NEVER LIKE THIS.
...GGGG FOR CHANNEL FOUR ACTION NEWS.
FLASH? CARE TO COMMENT?
CAN I TALK OFF THE RECORD FOR A SECOND, LINDA?
SURE.
MY EYES KEEP LOOKING OVER HER SHOULDER. FLUTTERING, TRYING TO SEE IF ZOOM IS ANYWHERE NEAR--
STOP IT, WALLY.
OUT OF ALL THE REPORTERS THEY COULD'VE SENT TO COVER THIS--
I VOLUNTEERED.
WHAT?
WHY?
BECAUSE JUST LIKE YOU--
--I HAVE A JOB TO DO.
I LOVE THIS WOMAN.
AND SHE'S RIGHT. SHE'S ALWAYS RIGHT.

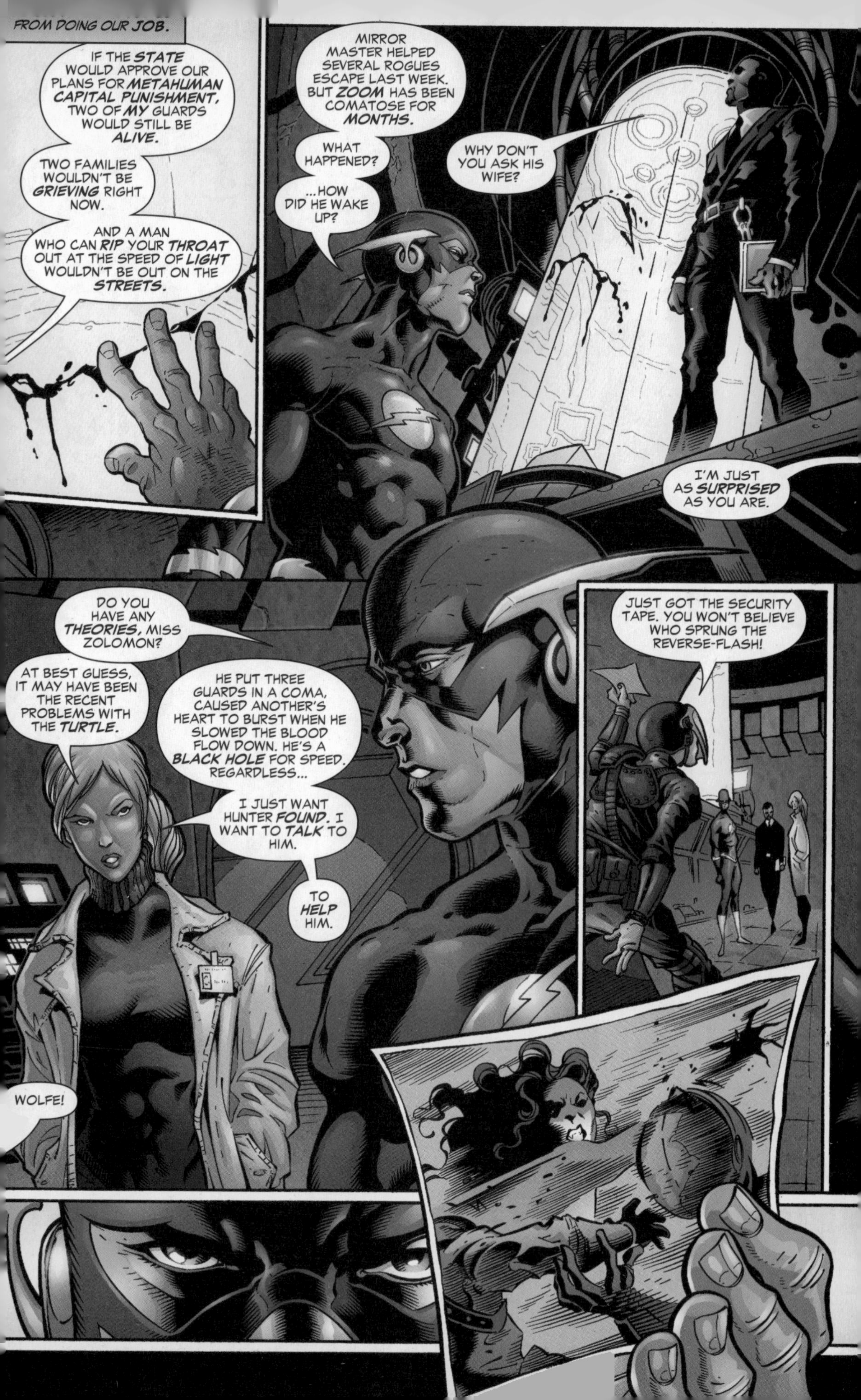
FROM DOING OUR JOB.
IF THE STATE WOULD APPROVE OUR PLANS FOR METAHUMAN CAPITAL PUNISHMENT, TWO OF MY GUARDS WOULD STILL BE ALIVE.
TWO FAMILIES WOULDN'T BE GRIEVING RIGHT NOW.
AND A MAN WHO CAN RIP YOUR THROAT OUT AT THE SPEED OF LIGHT WOULDN'T BE OUT ON THE STREETS.
MIRROR MASTER HELPED SEVERAL ROGUES ESCAPE LAST WEEK. BUT ZOOM HAS BEEN COMATOSE FOR MONTHS.
WHAT HAPPENED?
...HOW DID HE WAKE UP?
WHY DON'T YOU ASK HIS WIFE?
I'M JUST AS SURPRISED AS YOU ARE.
DO YOU HAVE ANY THEORIES, MISS ZOLOMON?
AT BEST GUESS, IT MAY HAVE BEEN THE RECENT PROBLEMS WITH THE TURTLE.
HE PUT THREE GUARDS IN A COMA, CAUSED ANOTHER'S HEART TO BURST WHEN HE SLOWED THE BLOOD FLOW DOWN. HE'S A BLACK HOLE FOR SPEED. REGARDLESS...
I JUST WANT HUNTER FOUND. I WANT TO TALK TO HIM.
TO HELP HIM.
JUST GOT THE SECURITY TAPE. YOU WON'T BELIEVE WHO SPRUNG THE REVERSE-FLASH!
WOLFE!

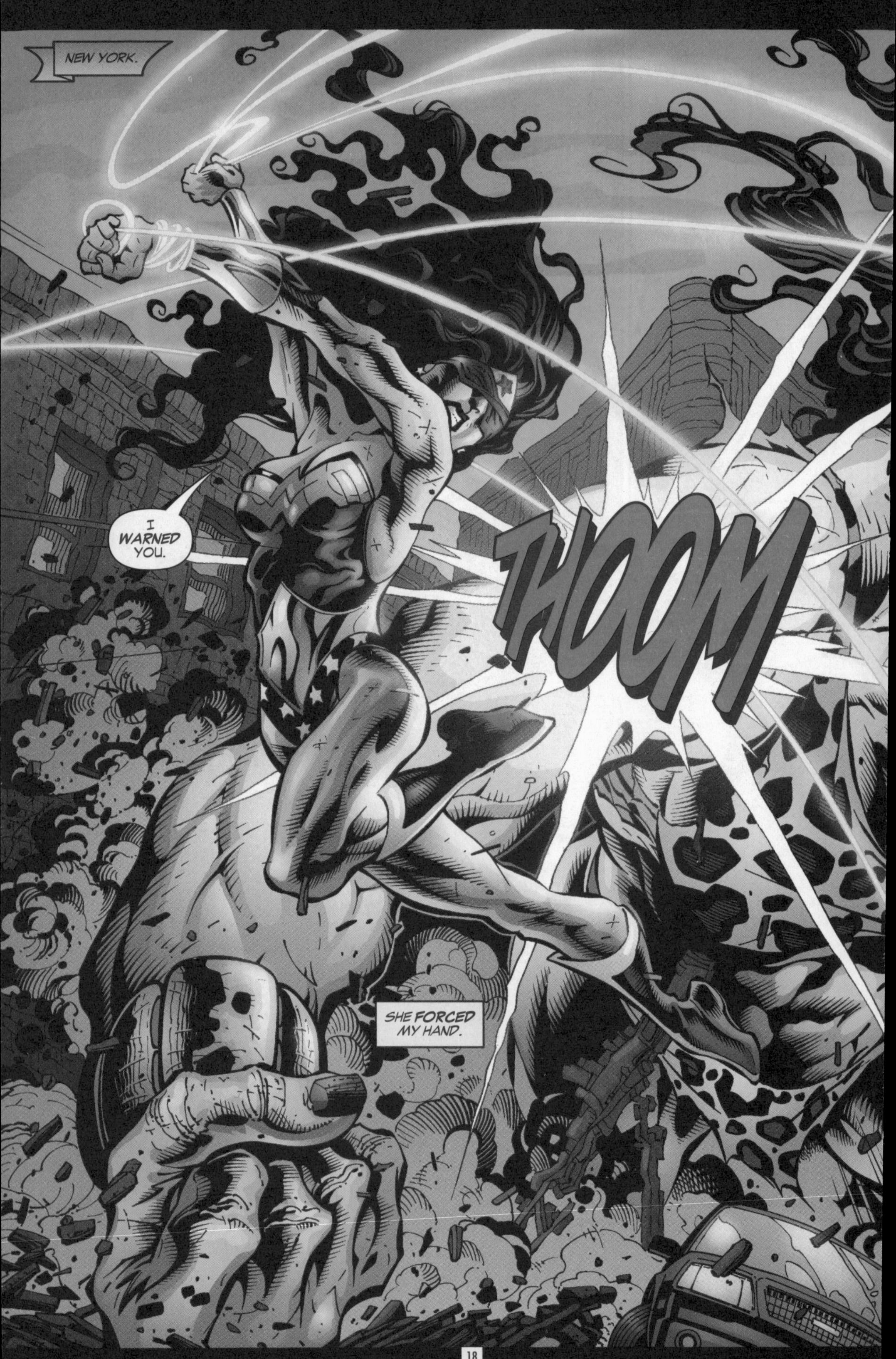
NEW YORK.
I WARNED YOU.
THOOM
SHE FORCED MY HAND.

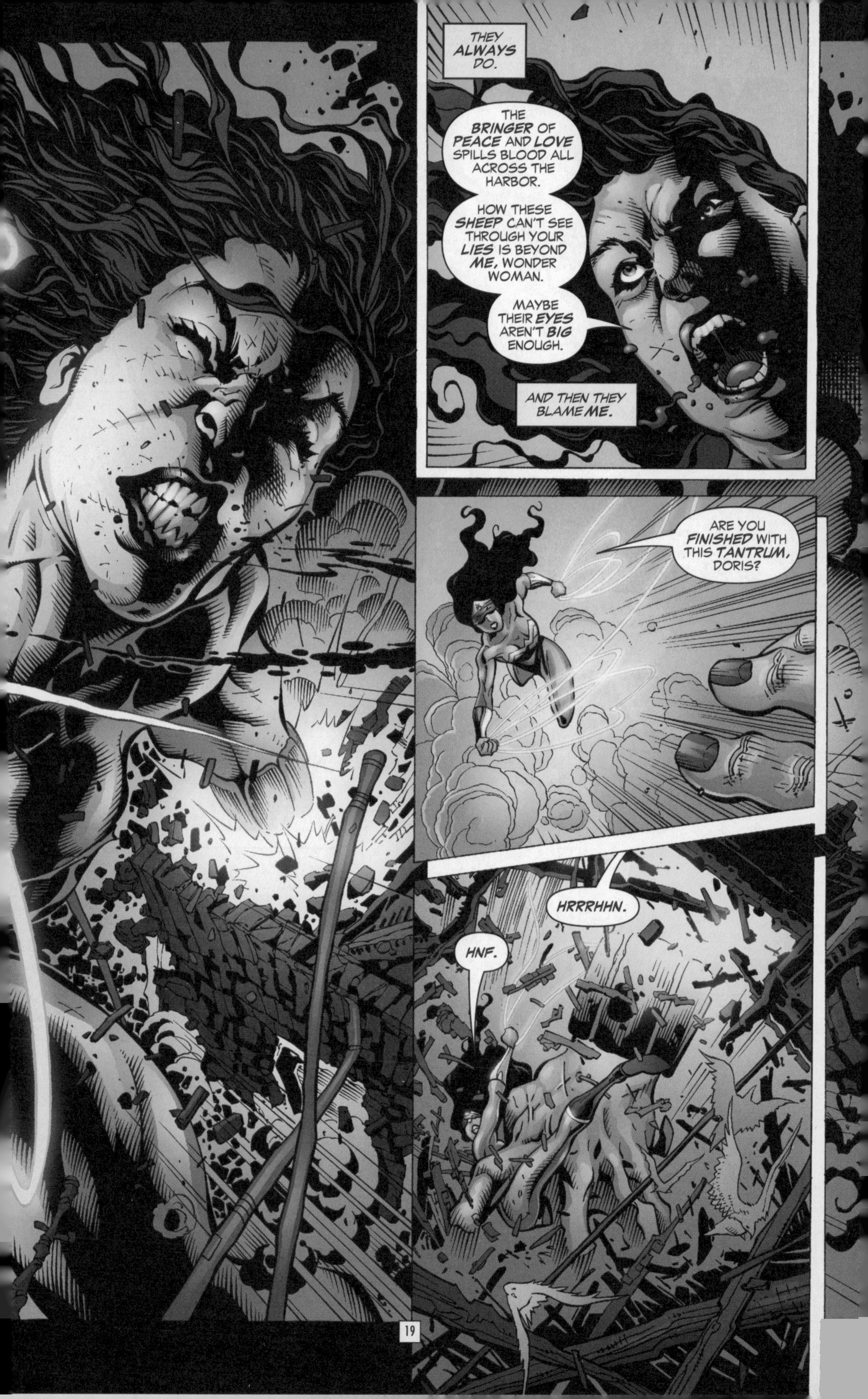
THEY ALWAYS DO.
THE BRINGER OF PEACE AND LOVE SPILLS BLOOD ALL ACROSS THE HARBOR.
HOW THESE SHEEP CAN'T SEE THROUGH YOUR LIES IS BEYOND ME, WONDER WOMAN.
MAYBE THEIR EYES AREN'T BIG ENOUGH.
AND THEN THEY BLAME ME.
ARE YOU FINISHED WITH THIS TANTRUM, DORIS?
HRRRHHN.
HNF.

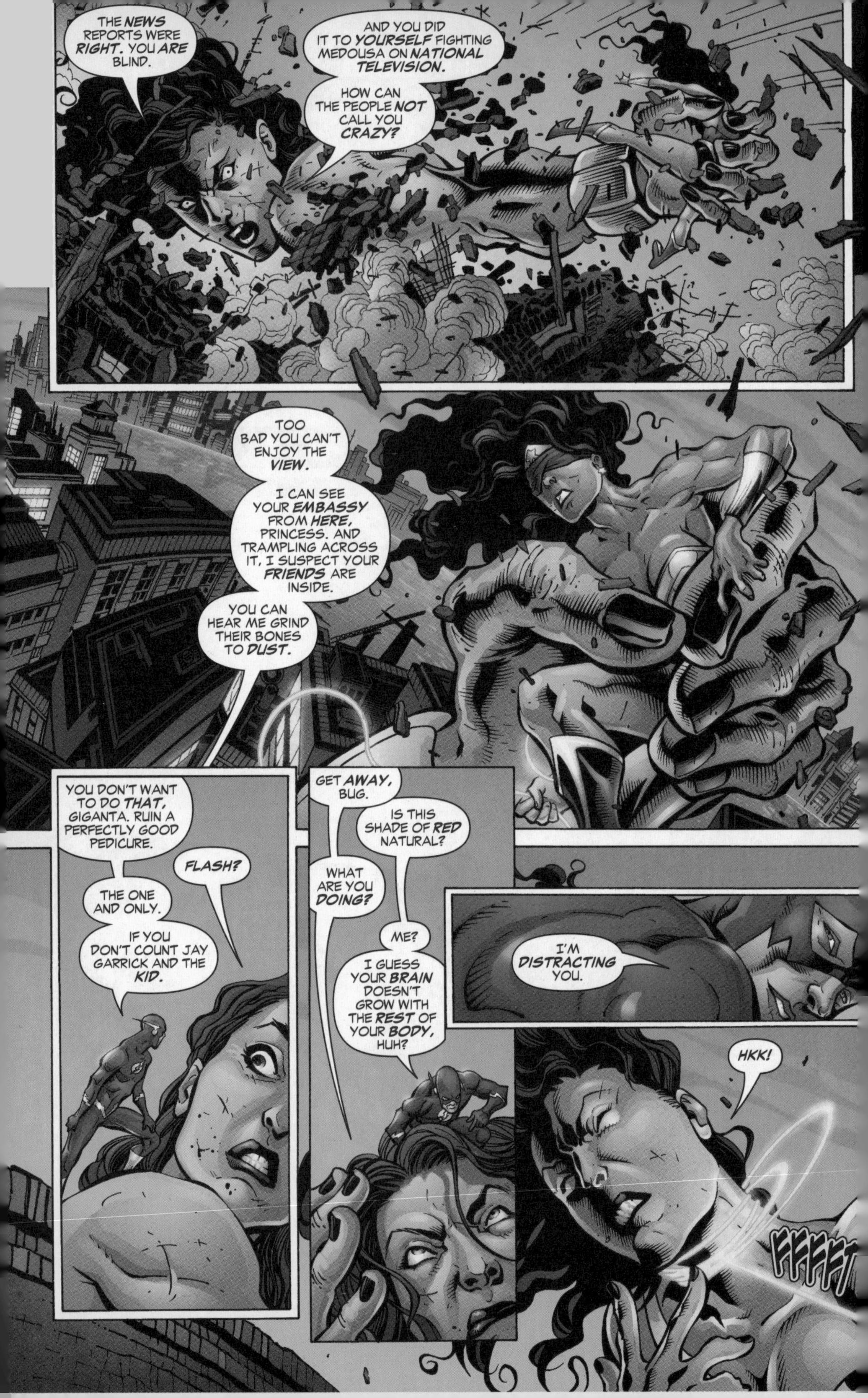
THE NEWS REPORTS WERE RIGHT. YOU ARE BLIND.
AND YOU DID IT TO YOURSELF FIGHTING MEDOUSA ON NATIONAL TELEVISION.
HOW CAN THE PEOPLE NOT CALL YOU CRAZY?
TOO BAD YOU CAN'T ENJOY THE VIEW.
I CAN SEE YOUR EMBASSY FROM HERE, PRINCESS. AND TRAMPLING ACROSS IT, I SUSPECT YOUR FRIENDS ARE INSIDE.
YOU CAN HEAR ME GRIND THEIR BONES TO DUST.
YOU DON'T WANT TO DO THAT, GIGANTA. RUIN A PERFECTLY GOOD PEDICURE.
FLASH?
THE ONE AND ONLY.
IF YOU DON'T COUNT JAY GARRICK AND THE KID.
GET AWAY, BUG.
IS THIS SHADE OF RED NATURAL?
WHAT ARE YOU DOING?
ME?
I GUESS YOUR BRAIN DOESN'T GROW WITH THE REST OF YOUR BODY, HUH?
I'M DISTRACTING YOU.
HKK!

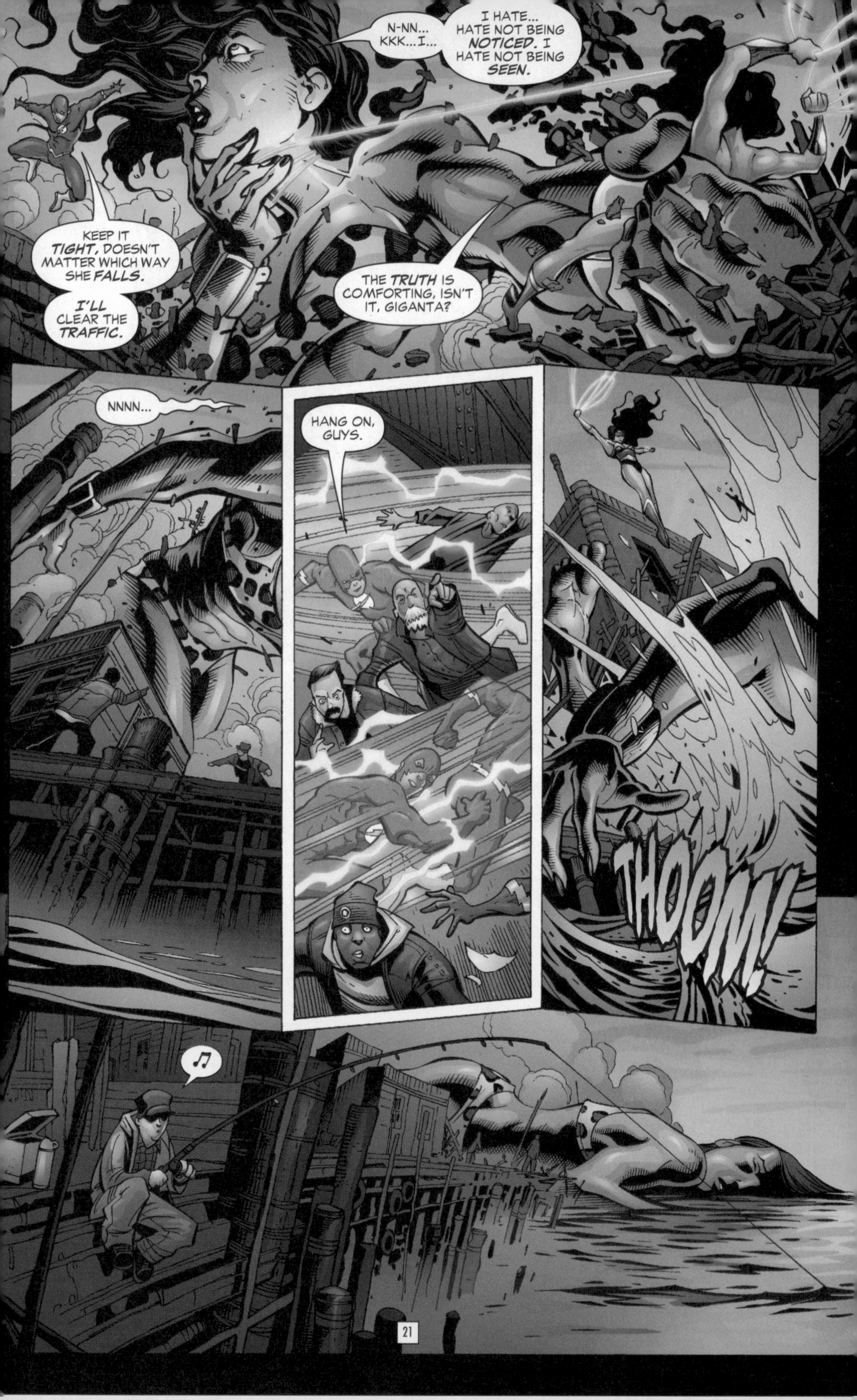
N-NN... KKK...I...
I HATE... HATE NOT BEING NOTICED. I HATE NOT BEING SEEN.
KEEP IT TIGHT, DOESN'T MATTER WHICH WAY SHE FALLS.
I'LL CLEAR THE TRAFFIC.
THE TRUTH IS COMFORTING, ISN'T IT, GIGANTA?
NNNN...
HANG ON, GUYS.
THOOM!
♫

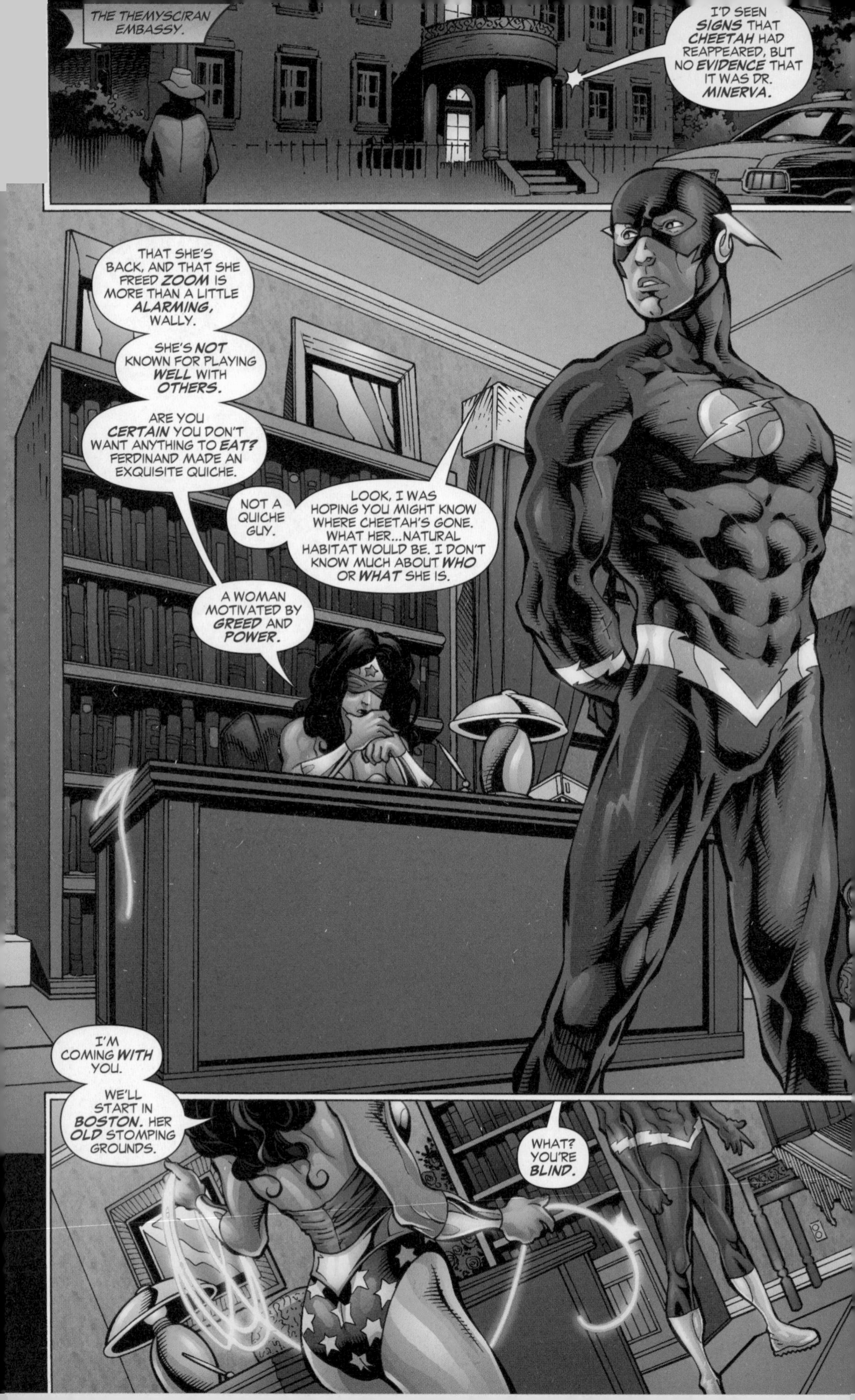
THE THEMYSCIRAN EMBASSY.
I'D SEEN SIGNS THAT CHEETAH HAD REAPPEARED, BUT NO EVIDENCE THAT IT WAS DR. MINERVA.
THAT SHE'S BACK, AND THAT SHE FREED ZOOM IS MORE THAN A LITTLE ALARMING, WALLY.
SHE'S NOT KNOWN FOR PLAYING WELL WITH OTHERS.
ARE YOU CERTAIN YOU DON'T WANT ANYTHING TO EAT? FERDINAND MADE AN EXQUISITE QUICHE.
NOT A QUICHE GUY.
LOOK, I WAS HOPING YOU MIGHT KNOW WHERE CHEETAH'S GONE. WHAT HER...NATURAL HABITAT WOULD BE. I DON'T KNOW MUCH ABOUT WHO OR WHAT SHE IS.
A WOMAN MOTIVATED BY GREED AND POWER.
I'M COMING WITH YOU.
WE'LL START IN BOSTON. HER OLD STOMPING GROUNDS.
WHAT? YOU'RE BLIND.

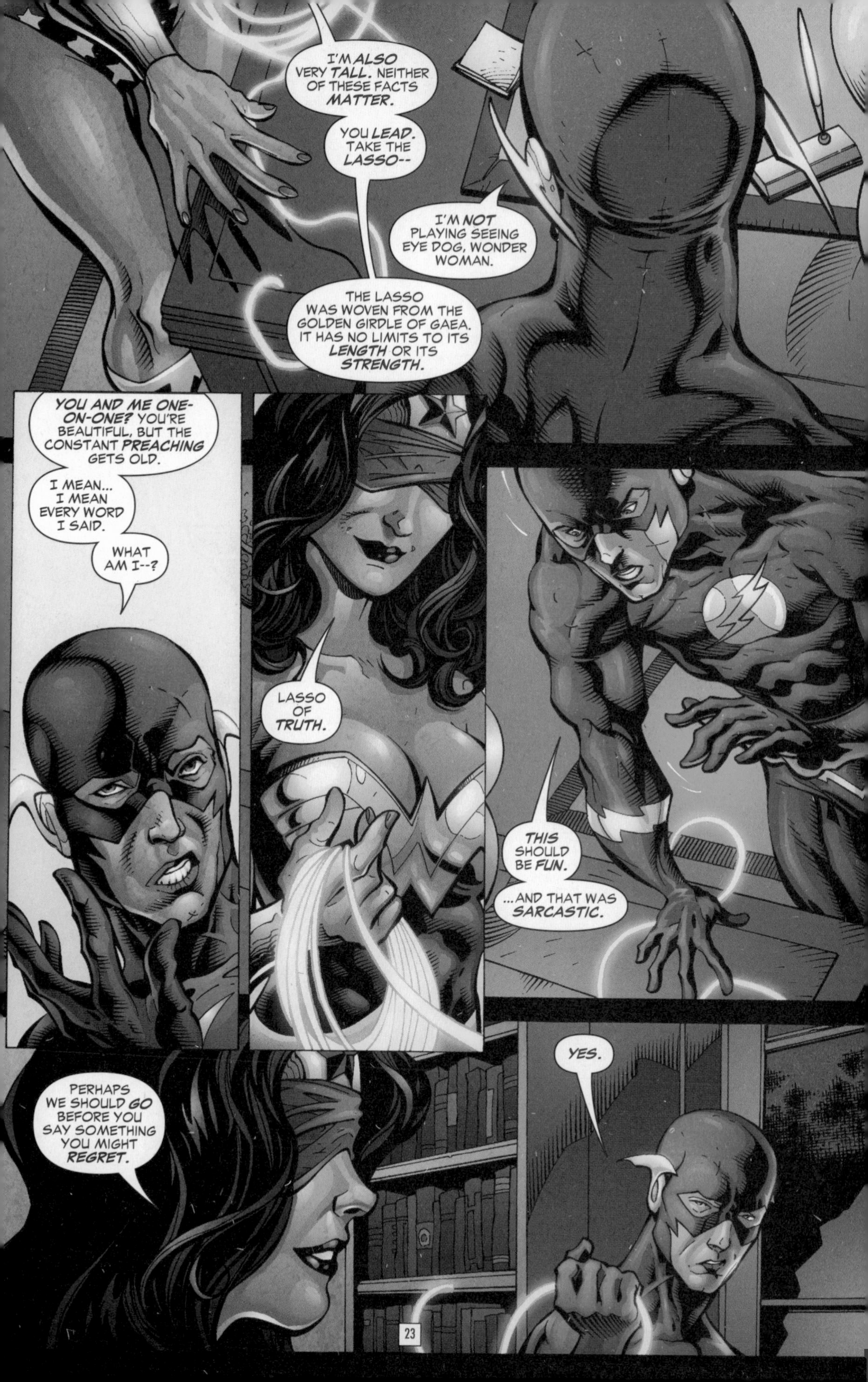
I'M ALSO VERY TALL. NEITHER OF THESE FACTS MATTER.
YOU LEAD. TAKE THE LASSO--
I'M NOT PLAYING SEEING EYE DOG, WONDER WOMAN.
THE LASSO WAS WOVEN FROM THE GOLDEN GIRDLE OF GAEA. IT HAS NO LIMITS TO ITS LENGTH OR ITS STRENGTH.
YOU AND ME ONE-ON-ONE? YOU'RE BEAUTIFUL, BUT THE CONSTANT PREACHING GETS OLD.
I MEAN... I MEAN EVERY WORD I SAID.
WHAT AM I--?
LASSO OF TRUTH.
THIS SHOULD BE FUN.
...AND THAT WAS SARCASTIC.
PERHAPS WE SHOULD GO BEFORE YOU SAY SOMETHING YOU MIGHT REGRET.
YES.

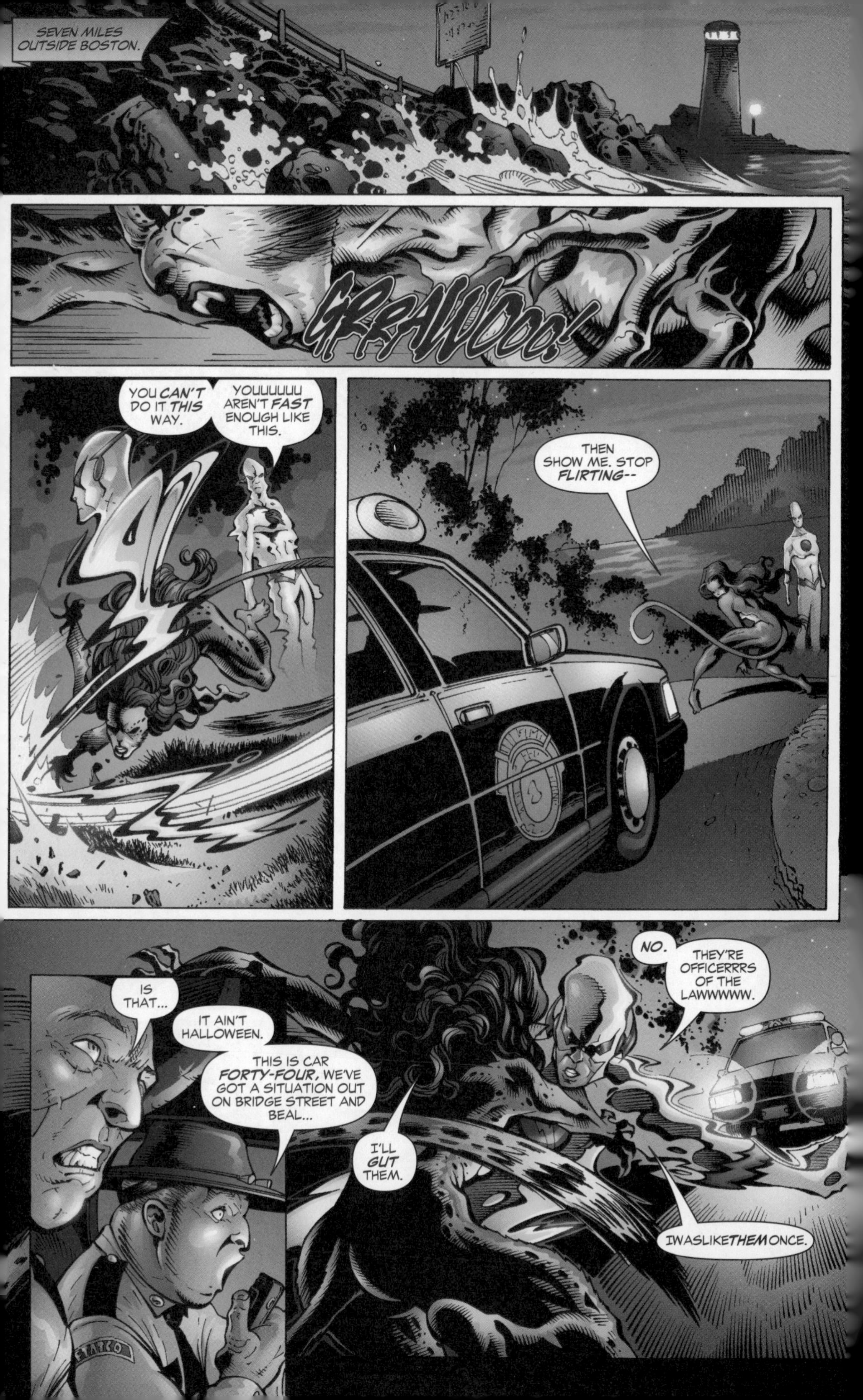
SEVEN MILES OUTSIDE BOSTON.
GRRAWOOO!
YOU CAN'T DO IT THIS WAY.
YOUUUUUUU AREN'T FAST ENOUGH LIKE THIS.
THEN SHOW ME. STOP FLIRTING--
IS THAT...
IT AIN'T HALLOWEEN.
THIS IS CAR FORTY-FOUR, WE'VE GOT A SITUATION OUT ON BRIDGE STREET AND BEAL...
I'LL GUT THEM.
NO.
THEY'RE OFFICERRRS OF THE LAWWWWW.
IWASLIKETHEMONCE.

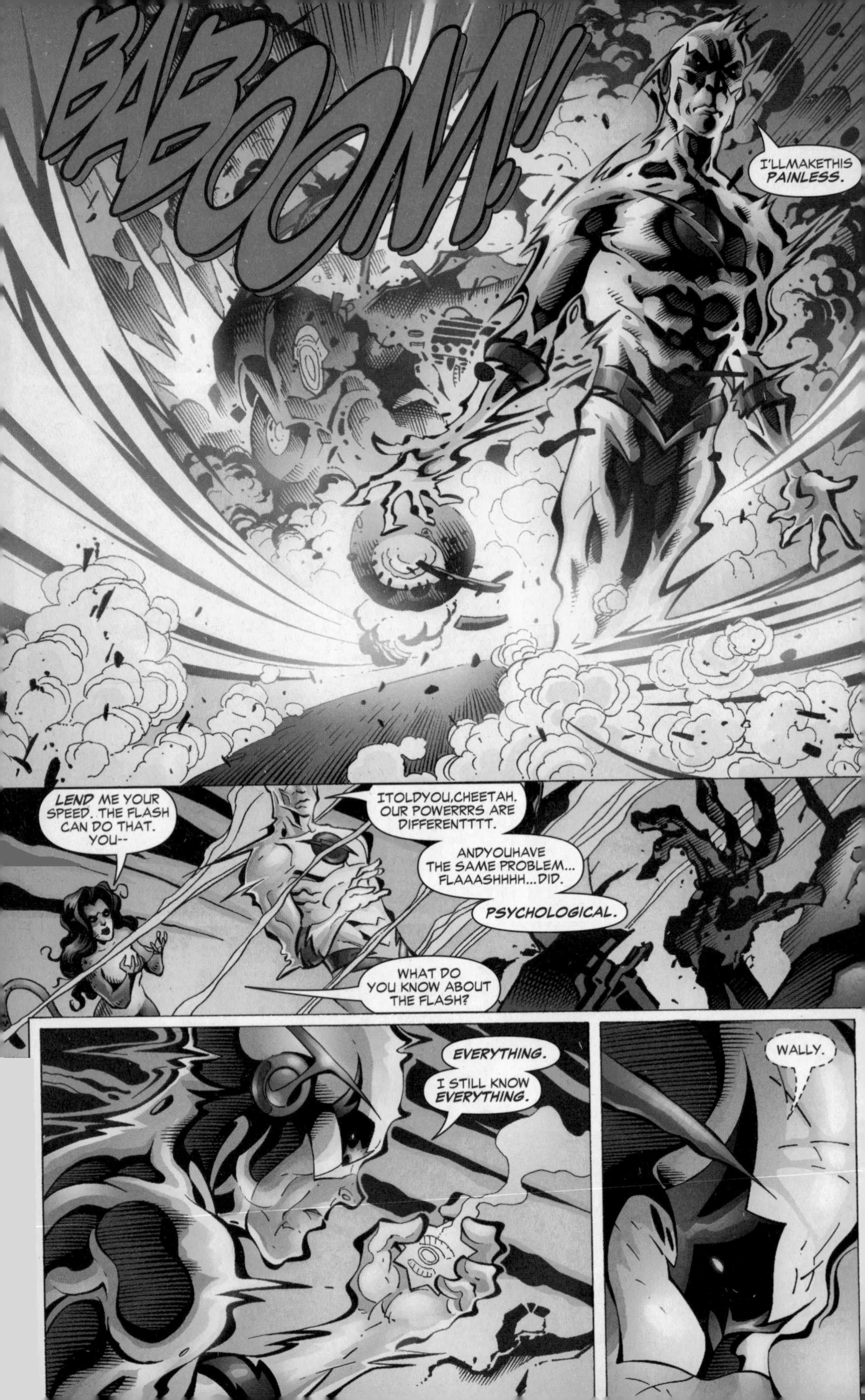
BABOOM!
I'LLMAKETHIS PAINLESS.
LEND ME YOUR SPEED. THE FLASH CAN DO THAT. YOU--
ITOLDYOU,CHEETAH. OUR POWERRRS ARE DIFFERENTTTT.
ANDYOUHAVE THE SAME PROBLEM... FLAAASHHHH...DID.
PSYCHOLOGICAL.
WHAT DO YOU KNOW ABOUT THE FLASH?
EVERYTHING.
I STILL KNOW EVERYTHING.
WALLY.

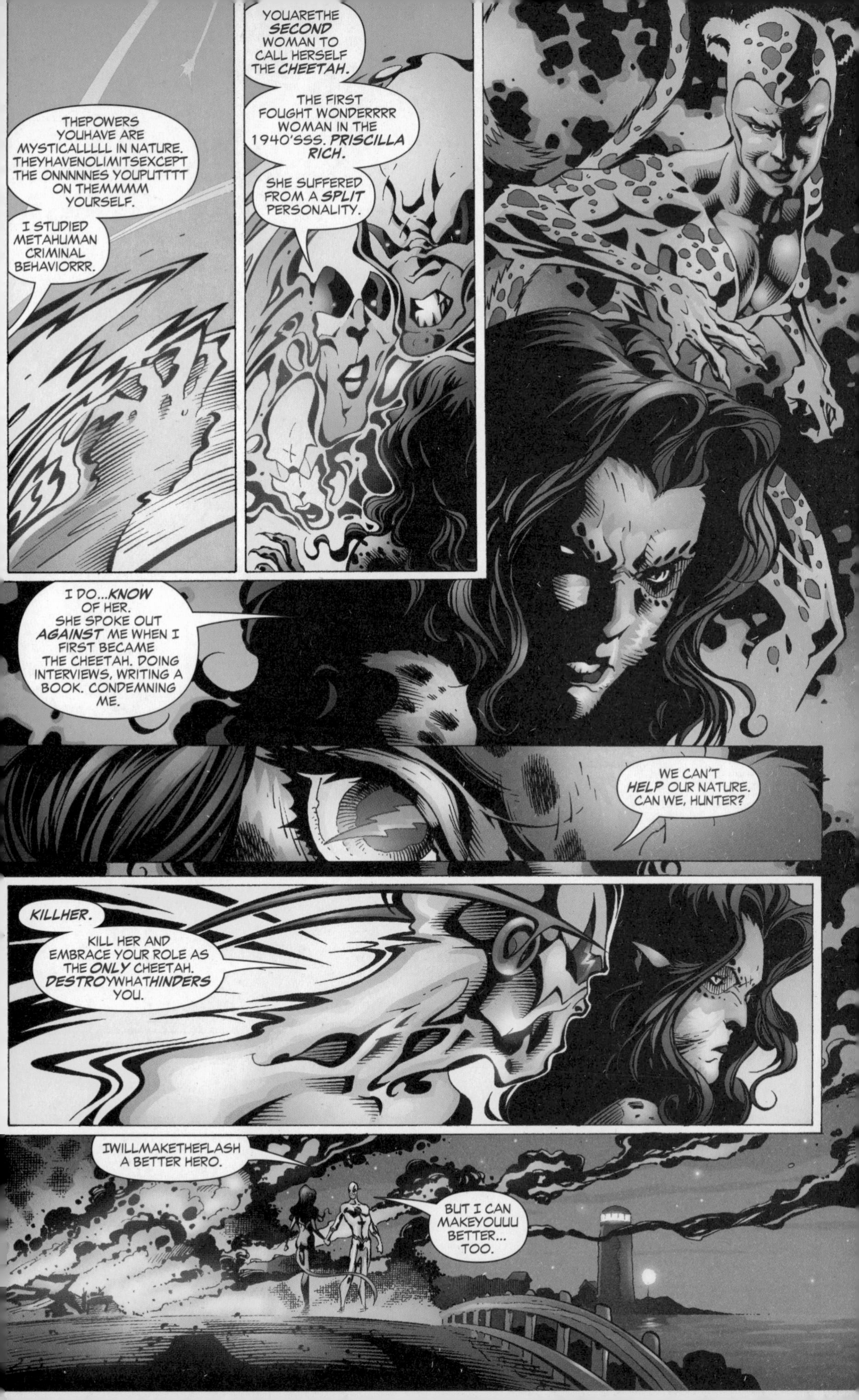
THEPOWERS YOUHAVE ARE MYSTICALLLLL IN NATURE. THEYHAVENOLIMITSEXCEPT THE ONNNNNES YOUPUTTTT ON THEMMMM YOURSELF.
I STUDIED METAHUMAN CRIMINAL BEHAVIORRR.
YOUARETHE SECOND WOMAN TO CALL HERSELF THE CHEETAH.
THE FIRST FOUGHT WONDERRRR WOMAN IN THE 1940'SSS. PRISCILLA RICH.
SHE SUFFERED FROM A SPLIT PERSONALITY.
I DO...KNOW OF HER. SHE SPOKE OUT AGAINST ME WHEN I FIRST BECAME THE CHEETAH. DOING INTERVIEWS, WRITING A BOOK. CONDEMNING ME.
WE CAN'T HELP OUR NATURE. CAN WE, HUNTER?
KILLHER.
KILL HER AND EMBRACE YOUR ROLE AS THE ONLY CHEETAH. DESTROYWHATHINDERS YOU.
IWILLMAKETHEFLASH A BETTER HERO.
BUT I CAN MAKEYOUUU BETTER... TOO.

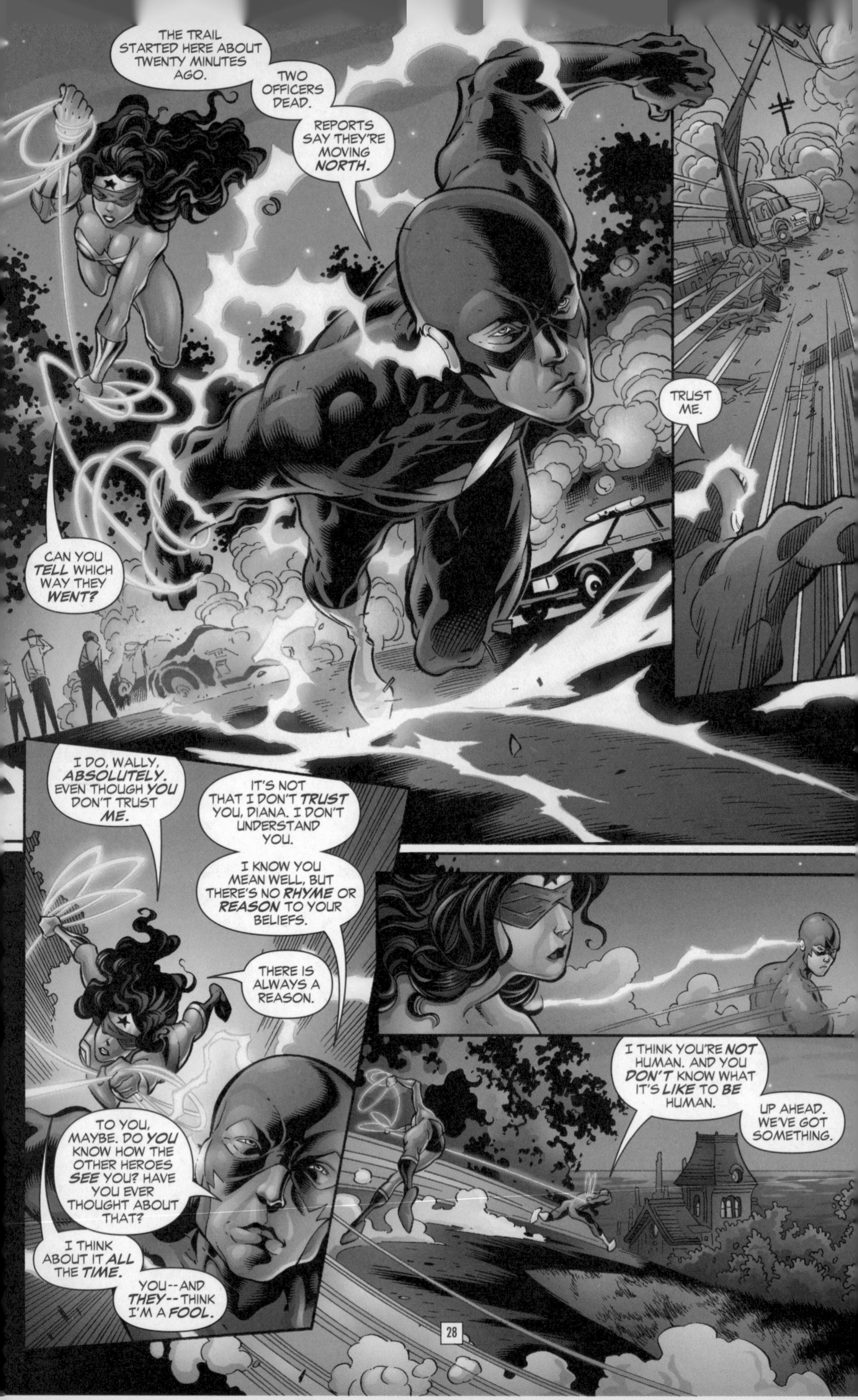

THE TRAIL STARTED HERE ABOUT TWENTY MINUTES AGO.
TWO OFFICERS DEAD.
REPORTS SAY THEY'RE MOVING NORTH.
CAN YOU TELL WHICH WAY THEY WENT?
TRUST ME.
I DO, WALLY, ABSOLUTELY. EVEN THOUGH YOU DON'T TRUST ME.
IT'S NOT THAT I DON'T TRUST YOU, DIANA. I DON'T UNDERSTAND YOU.
I KNOW YOU MEAN WELL, BUT THERE'S NO RHYME OR REASON TO YOUR BELIEFS.
THERE IS ALWAYS A REASON.
TO YOU, MAYBE. DO YOU KNOW HOW THE OTHER HEROES SEE YOU? HAVE YOU EVER THOUGHT ABOUT THAT?
I THINK ABOUT IT ALL THE TIME.
YOU--AND THEY--THINK I'M A FOOL.
I THINK YOU'RE NOT HUMAN. AND YOU DON'T KNOW WHAT IT'S LIKE TO BE HUMAN.
UP AHEAD. WE'VE GOT SOMETHING.

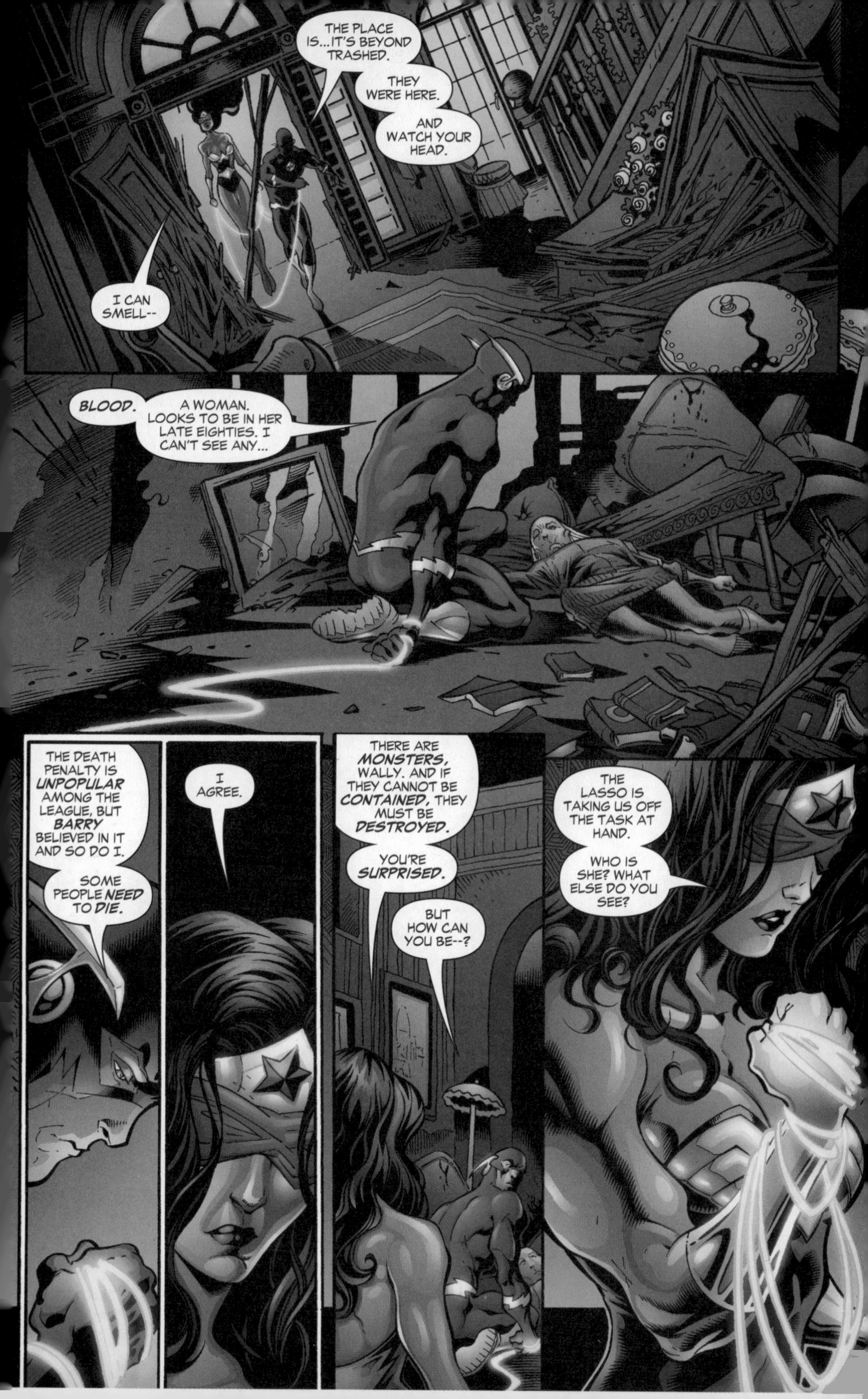
THE PLACE IS...IT'S BEYOND TRASHED.
THEY WERE HERE.
AND WATCH YOUR HEAD.
I CAN SMELL--
BLOOD.
A WOMAN. LOOKS TO BE IN HER LATE EIGHTIES. I CAN'T SEE ANY...
THE DEATH PENALTY IS UNPOPULAR AMONG THE LEAGUE, BUT BARRY BELIEVED IN IT AND SO DO I.
SOME PEOPLE NEED TO DIE.
I AGREE.
THERE ARE MONSTERS, WALLY. AND IF THEY CANNOT BE CONTAINED, THEY MUST BE DESTROYED.
YOU'RE SURPRISED.
BUT HOW CAN YOU BE--?
THE LASSO IS TAKING US OFF THE TASK AT HAND.
WHO IS SHE? WHAT ELSE DO YOU SEE?

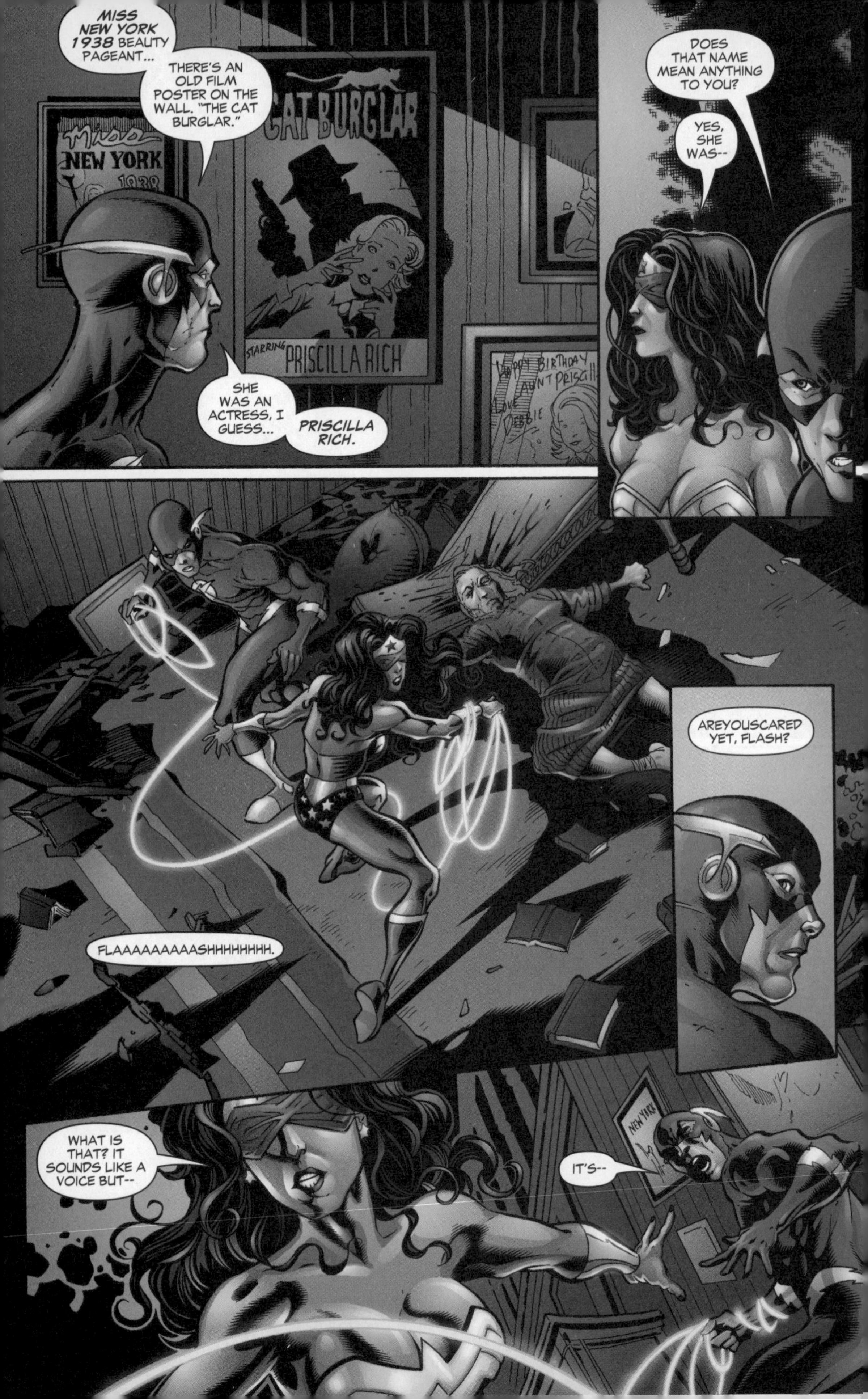
MISS NEW YORK 1938 BEAUTY PAGEANT...
THERE'S AN OLD FILM POSTER ON THE WALL. "THE CAT BURGLAR."
MISS NEW YORK 1938
CAT BURGLAR
STARRING PRISCILLA RICH
HAPPY BIRTHDAY AUNT PRISCILLA LOVE DEBBIE
SHE WAS AN ACTRESS, I GUESS...
PRISCILLA RICH.
DOES THAT NAME MEAN ANYTHING TO YOU?
YES, SHE WAS--
FLAAAAAAAAASHHHHHHHH.
AREYOUSCARED YET, FLASH?
WHAT IS THAT? IT SOUNDS LIKE A VOICE BUT--
IT'S--
NEW YORK

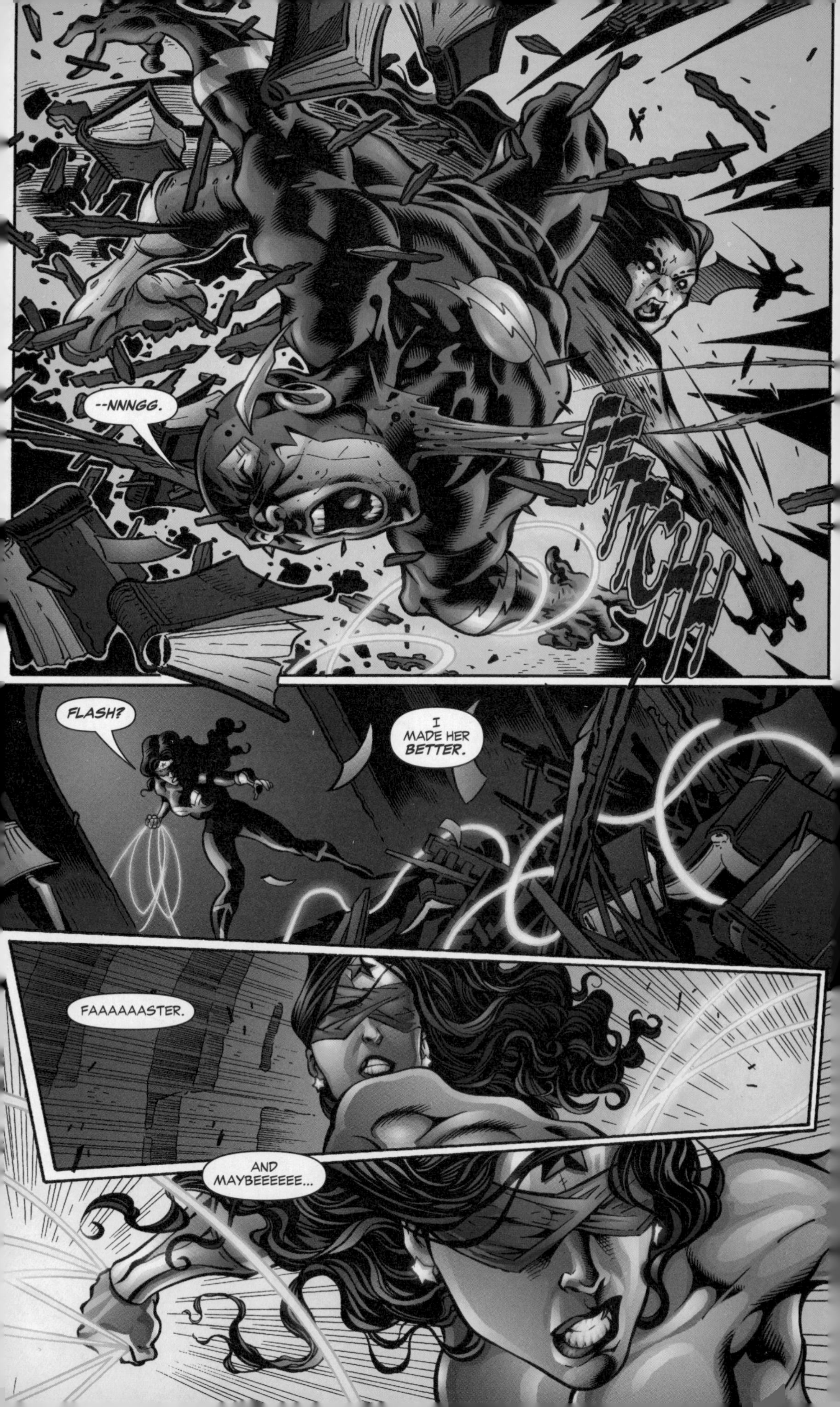
--NNNGG.
FFTCHH
FLASH?
I MADE HER BETTER.
FAAAAAASTER.
AND MAYBEEEEEE...

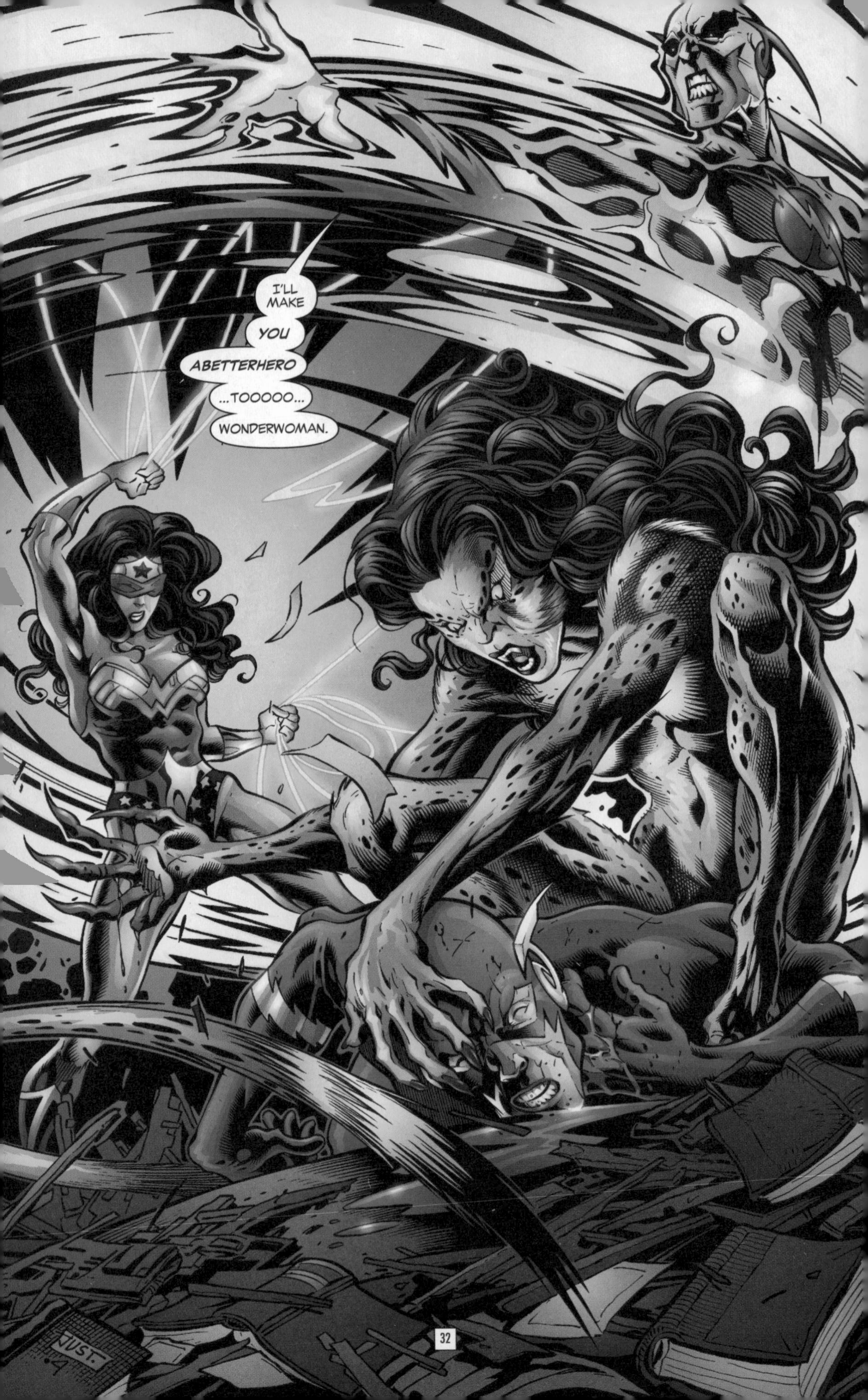
I'LL MAKE
YOU
ABETTERHERO
...TOOOOO...
WONDERWOMAN.
JUST. '04

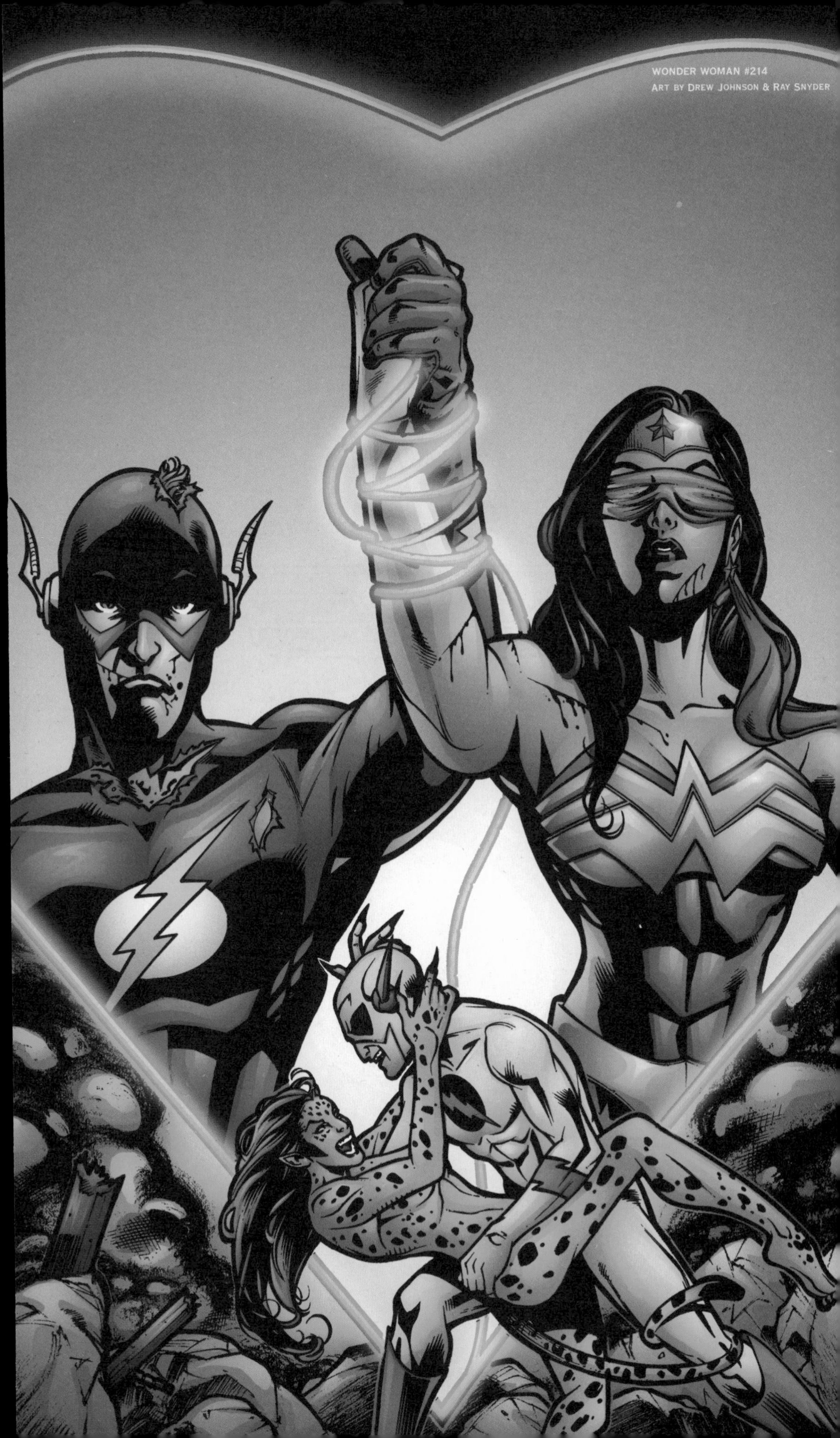
WONDER WOMAN #214
ART BY DREW JOHNSON & RAY SNYDER

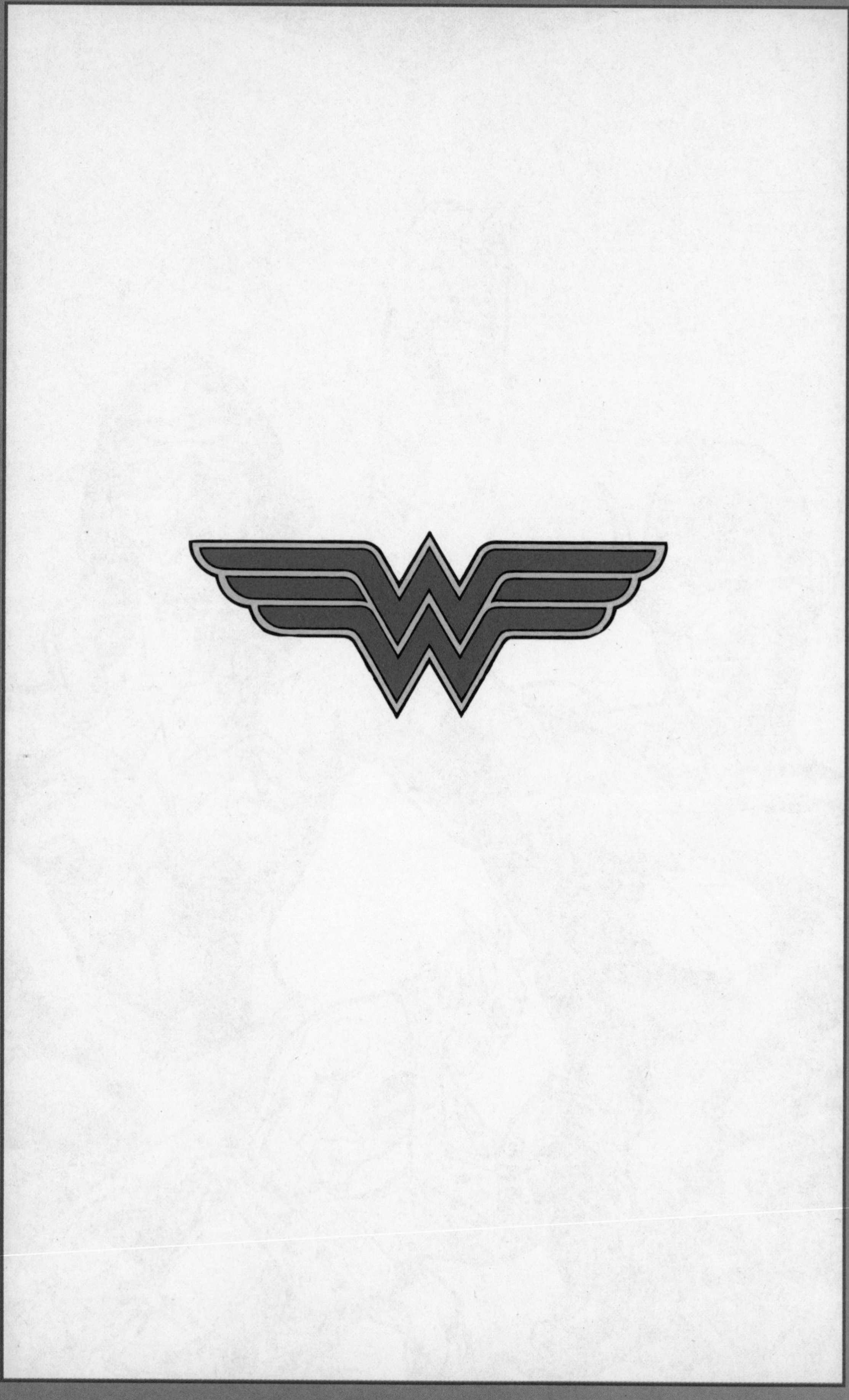

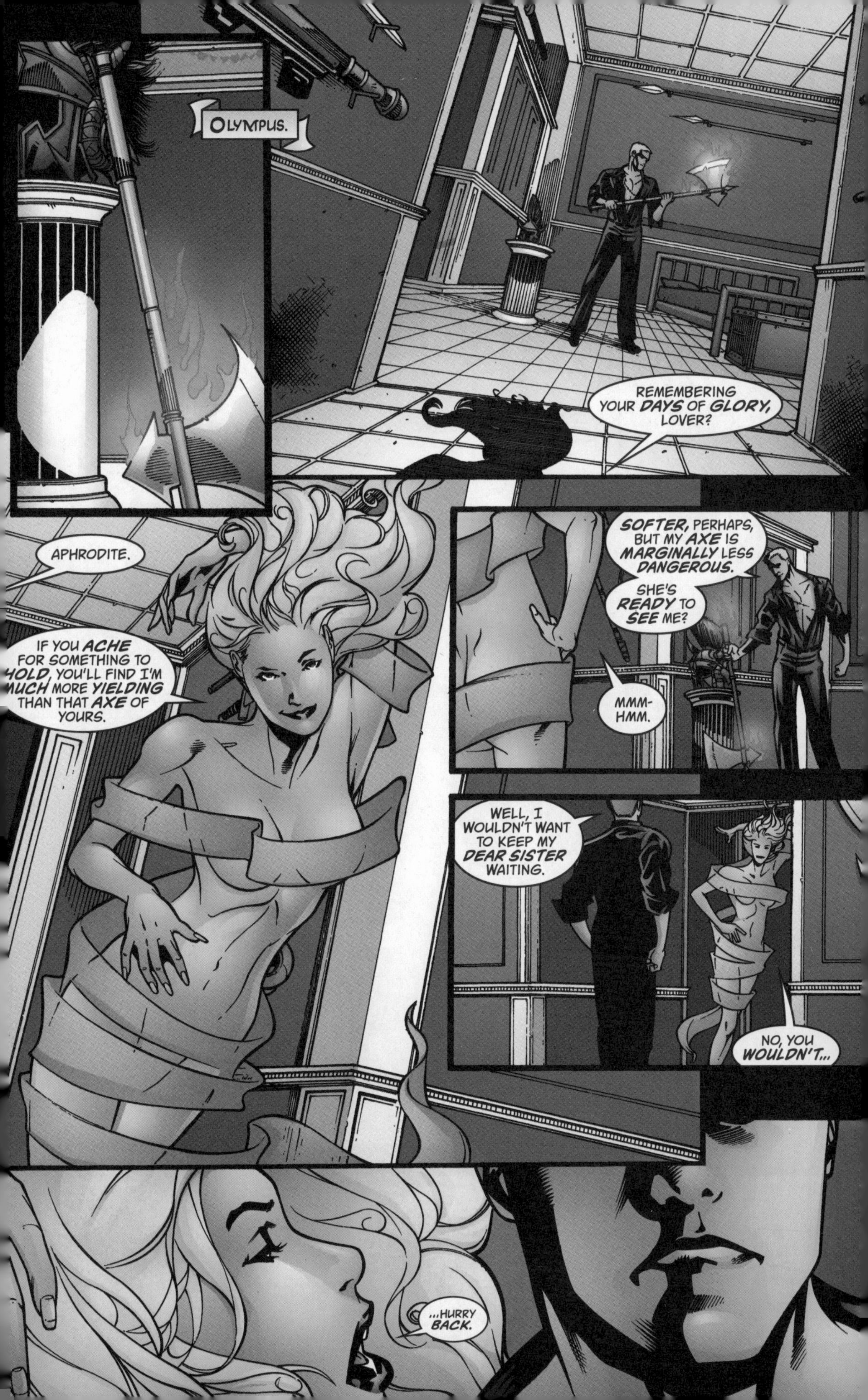
OLYMPUS.
REMEMBERING YOUR DAYS OF GLORY, LOVER?
APHRODITE.
IF YOU ACHE FOR SOMETHING TO HOLD, YOU'LL FIND I'M MUCH MORE YIELDING THAN THAT AXE OF YOURS.
SOFTER, PERHAPS, BUT MY AXE IS MARGINALLY LESS DANGEROUS.
SHE'S READY TO SEE ME?
MMM-HMM.
WELL, I WOULDN'T WANT TO KEEP MY DEAR SISTER WAITING.
NO, YOU WOULDN'T...
...HURRY BACK.

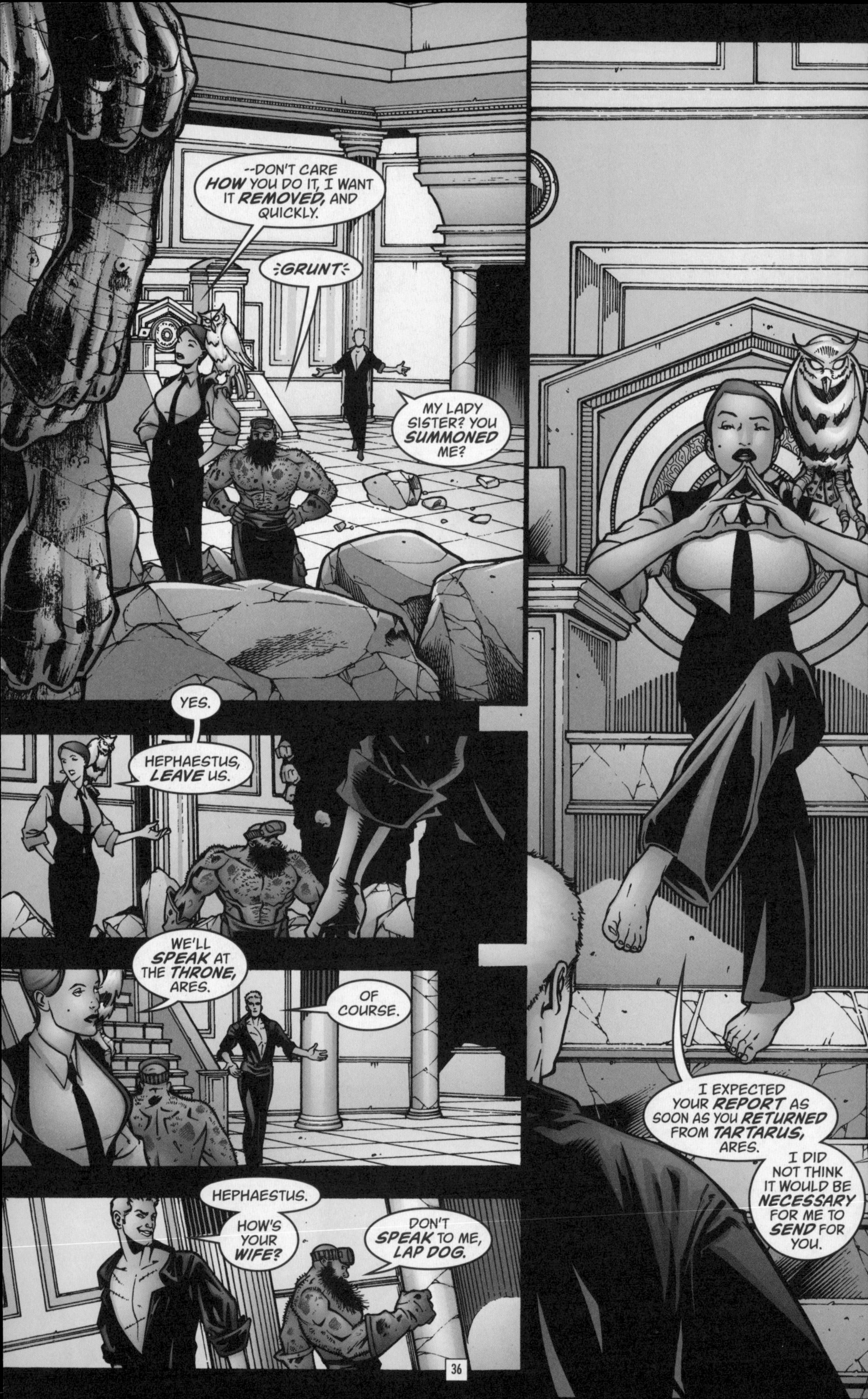
--DON'T CARE HOW YOU DO IT, I WANT IT REMOVED, AND QUICKLY.
GRUNT
MY LADY SISTER? YOU SUMMONED ME?
YES.
HEPHAESTUS, LEAVE US.
WE'LL SPEAK AT THE THRONE, ARES.
OF COURSE.
HEPHAESTUS.
HOW'S YOUR WIFE?
DON'T SPEAK TO ME, LAP DOG.
I EXPECTED YOUR REPORT AS SOON AS YOU RETURNED FROM TARTARUS, ARES.
I DID NOT THINK IT WOULD BE NECESSARY FOR ME TO SEND FOR YOU.

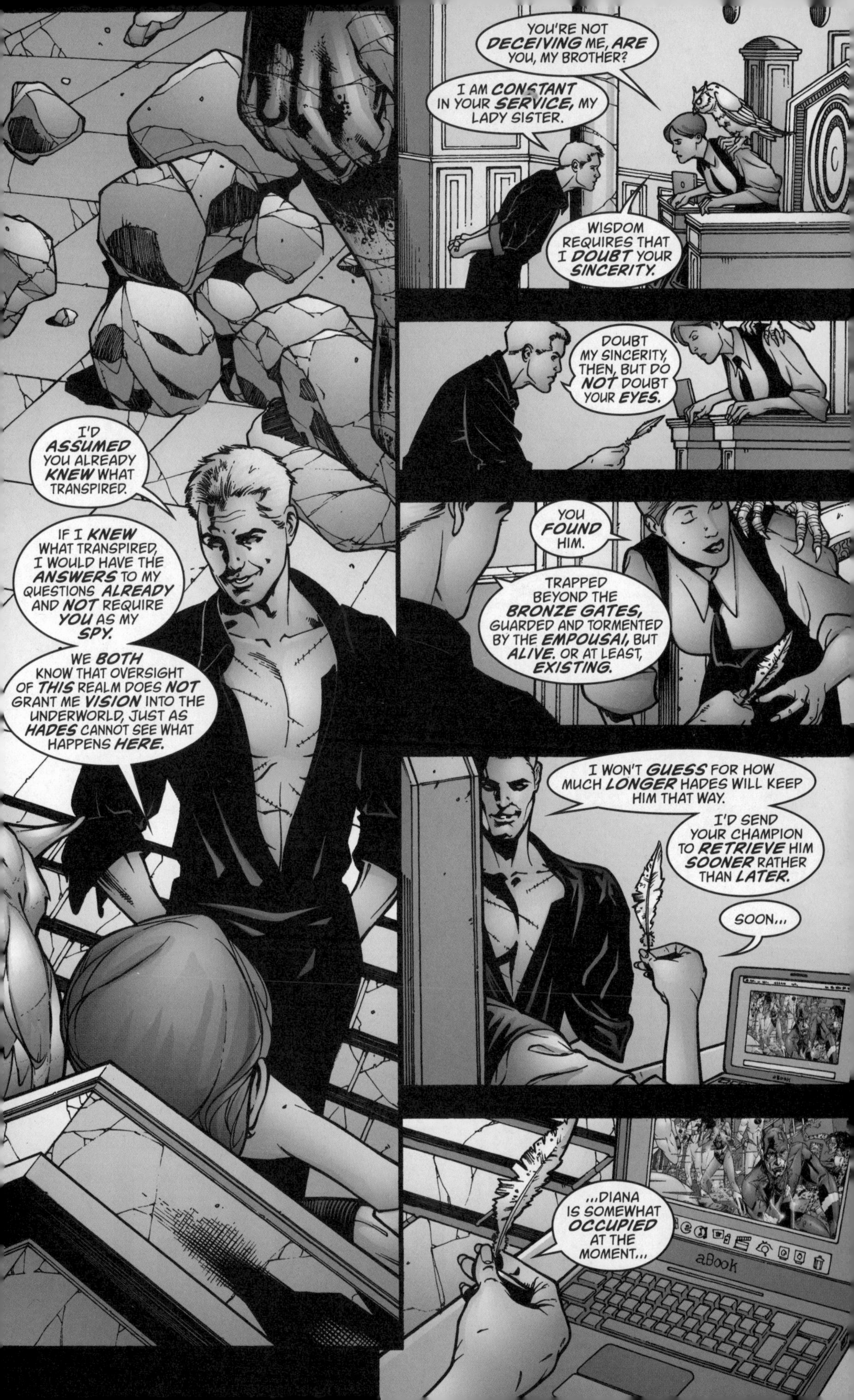

YOU'RE NOT DECEIVING ME, ARE YOU, MY BROTHER?
I AM CONSTANT IN YOUR SERVICE, MY LADY SISTER.
WISDOM REQUIRES THAT I DOUBT YOUR SINCERITY.
DOUBT MY SINCERITY, THEN, BUT DO NOT DOUBT YOUR EYES.
YOU FOUND HIM.
TRAPPED BEYOND THE BRONZE GATES, GUARDED AND TORMENTED BY THE EMPOUSAI, BUT ALIVE. OR AT LEAST, EXISTING.
I WON'T GUESS FOR HOW MUCH LONGER HADES WILL KEEP HIM THAT WAY.
I'D SEND YOUR CHAMPION TO RETRIEVE HIM SOONER RATHER THAN LATER.
SOON...
...DIANA IS SOMEWHAT OCCUPIED AT THE MOMENT...
aBook
I'D ASSUMED YOU ALREADY KNEW WHAT TRANSPIRED.
IF I KNEW WHAT TRANSPIRED, I WOULD HAVE THE ANSWERS TO MY QUESTIONS ALREADY AND NOT REQUIRE YOU AS MY SPY.
WE BOTH KNOW THAT OVERSIGHT OF THIS REALM DOES NOT GRANT ME VISION INTO THE UNDERWORLD, JUST AS HADES CANNOT SEE WHAT HAPPENS HERE.

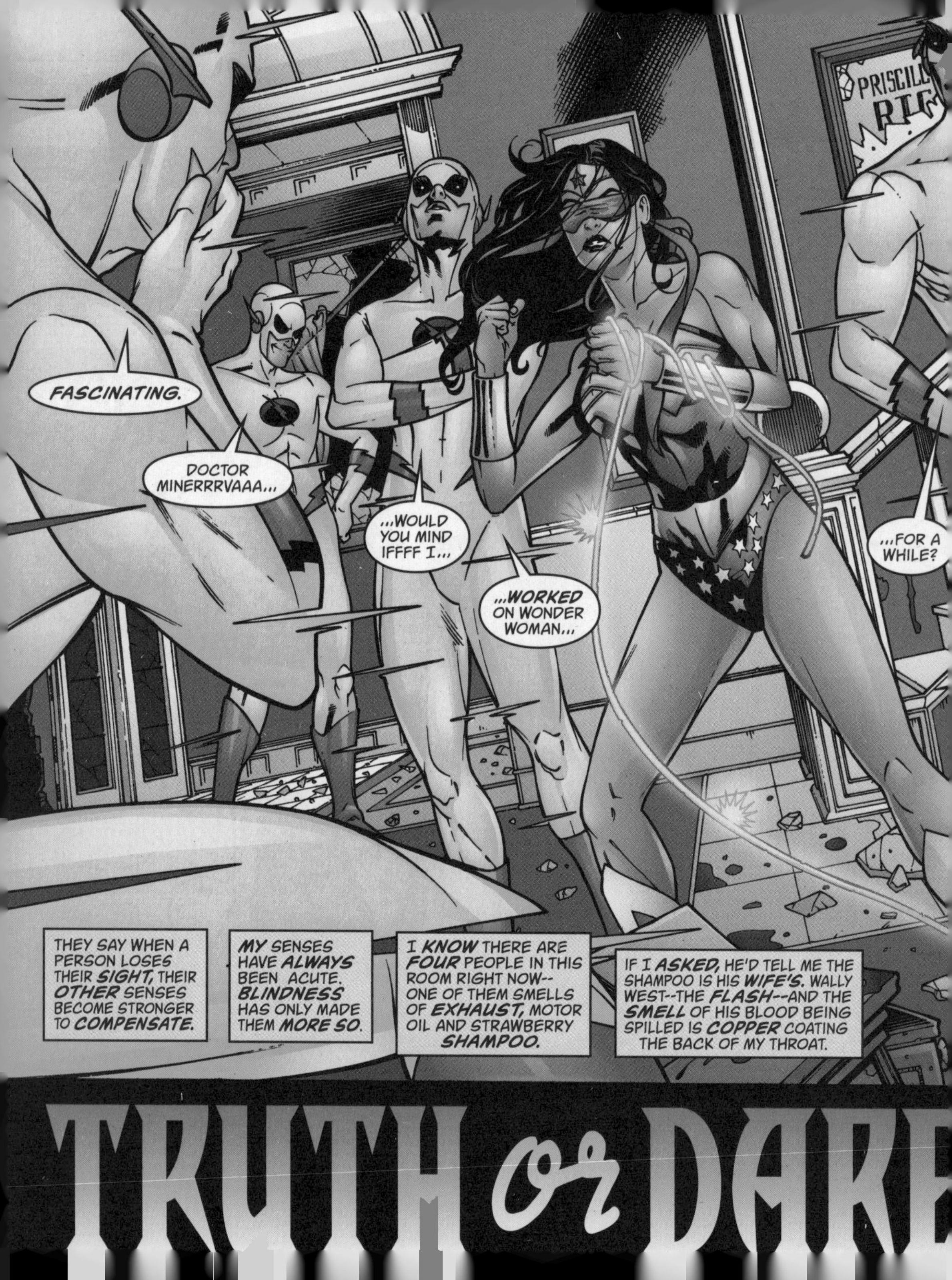
PRISCILL
FASCINATING.
DOCTOR MINERRRVAAA...
...WOULD YOU MIND IFFFF I...
...WORKED ON WONDER WOMAN...
...FOR A WHILE?
THEY SAY WHEN A PERSON LOSES THEIR SIGHT, THEIR OTHER SENSES BECOME STRONGER TO COMPENSATE.
MY SENSES HAVE ALWAYS BEEN ACUTE. BLINDNESS HAS ONLY MADE THEM MORE SO.
I KNOW THERE ARE FOUR PEOPLE IN THIS ROOM RIGHT NOW--ONE OF THEM SMELLS OF EXHAUST, MOTOR OIL AND STRAWBERRY SHAMPOO.
IF I ASKED, HE'D TELL ME THE SHAMPOO IS HIS WIFE'S. WALLY WEST--THE FLASH--AND THE SMELL OF HIS BLOOD BEING SPILLED IS COPPER COATING THE BACK OF MY THROAT.
TRUTH or DARE

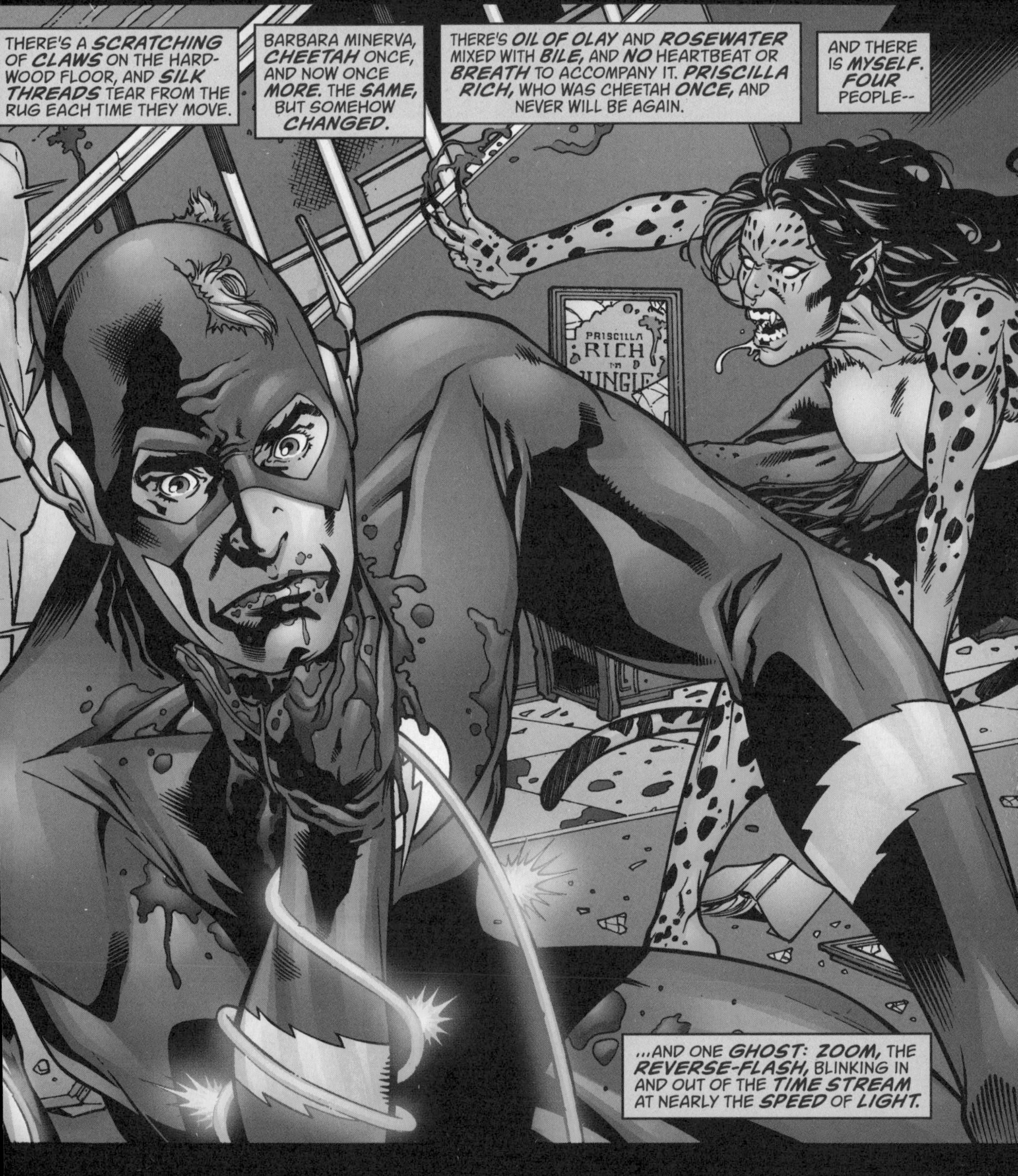
THERE'S A SCRATCHING OF CLAWS ON THE HARDWOOD FLOOR, AND SILK THREADS TEAR FROM THE RUG EACH TIME THEY MOVE.
BARBARA MINERVA, CHEETAH ONCE, AND NOW ONCE MORE. THE SAME, BUT SOMEHOW CHANGED.
THERE'S OIL OF OLAY AND ROSEWATER MIXED WITH BILE, AND NO HEARTBEAT OR BREATH TO ACCOMPANY IT. PRISCILLA RICH, WHO WAS CHEETAH ONCE, AND NEVER WILL BE AGAIN.
AND THERE IS MYSELF. FOUR PEOPLE--
PRISCILLA RICH
...AND ONE GHOST: ZOOM, THE REVERSE-FLASH, BLINKING IN AND OUT OF THE TIME STREAM AT NEARLY THE SPEED OF LIGHT.

·PART TWO·

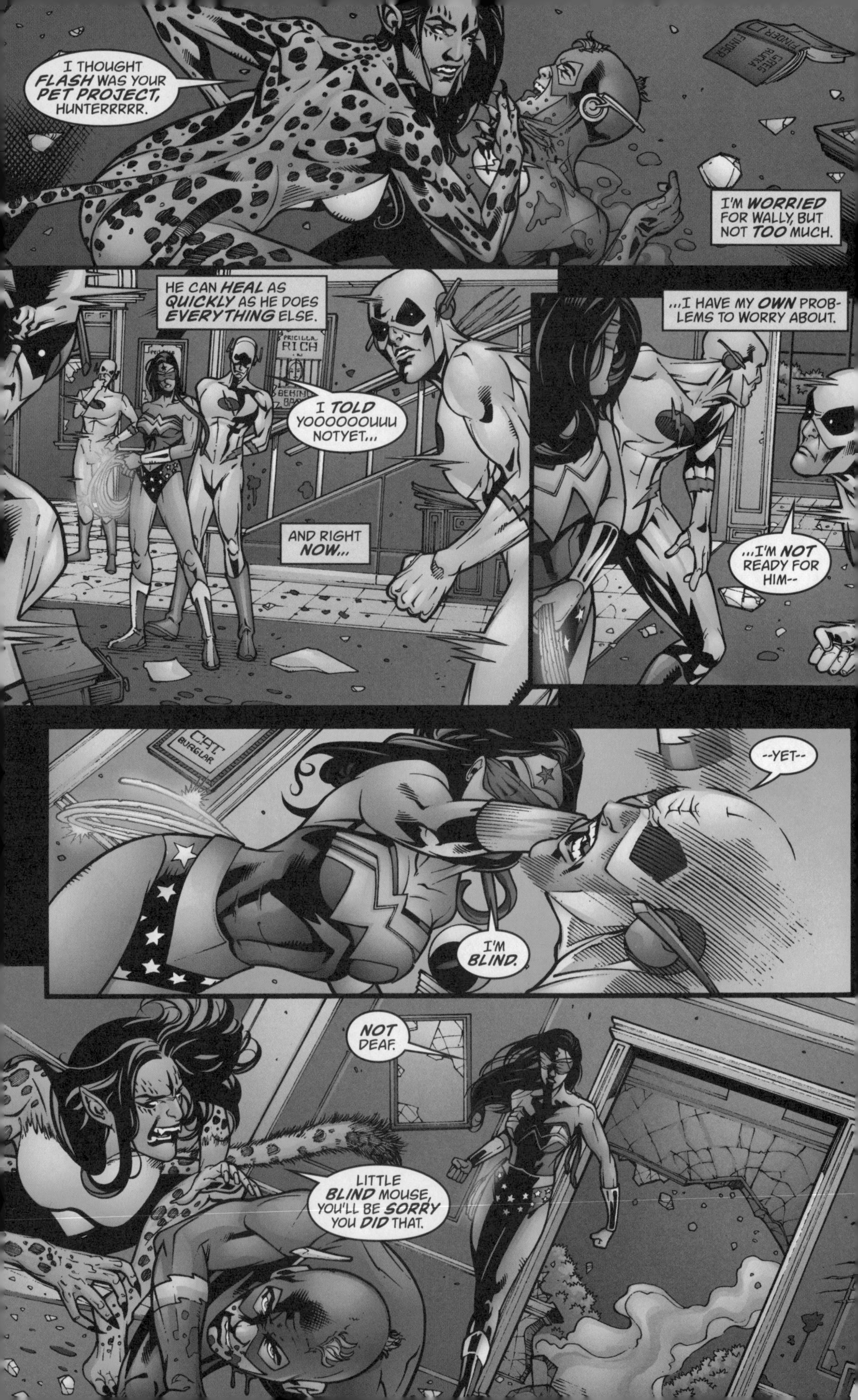
I THOUGHT FLASH WAS YOUR PET PROJECT, HUNTERRRRR.
FINDER
GREG RUCKA
I'M WORRIED FOR WALLY, BUT NOT TOO MUCH.
HE CAN HEAL AS QUICKLY AS HE DOES EVERYTHING ELSE.
PRICILLA RICH
I TOLD YOOOOOOUUU NOTYET...
AND RIGHT NOW...
...I HAVE MY OWN PROBLEMS TO WORRY ABOUT.
...I'M NOT READY FOR HIM--
CAT BURGLAR
--YET--
I'M BLIND.
NOT DEAF.
LITTLE BLIND MOUSE, YOU'LL BE SORRY YOU DID THAT.

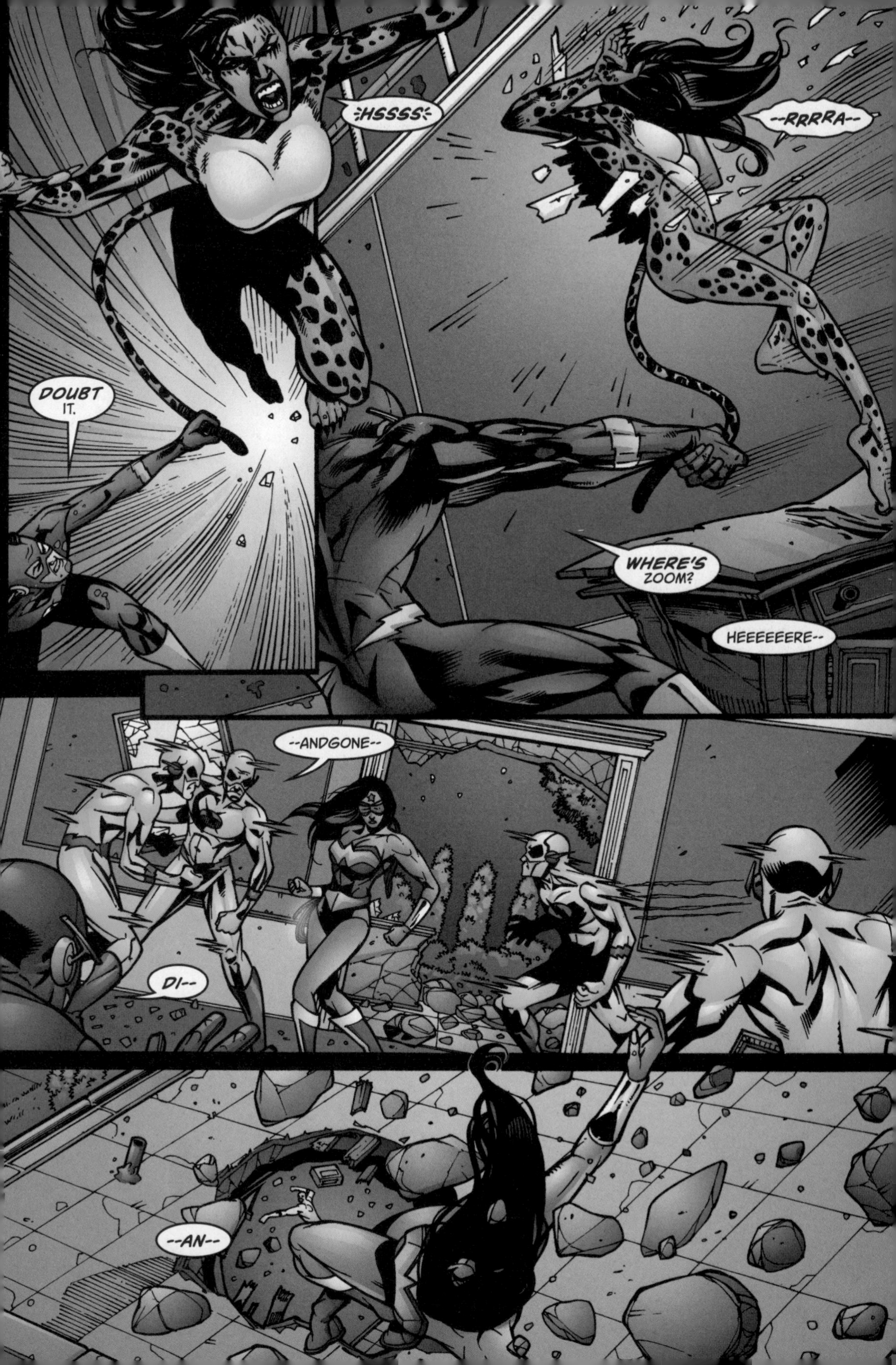
HSSSS
--RRRRA--
DOUBT IT.
WHERE'S ZOOM?
HEEEEEERE--
--ANDGONE--
DI--
--AN--

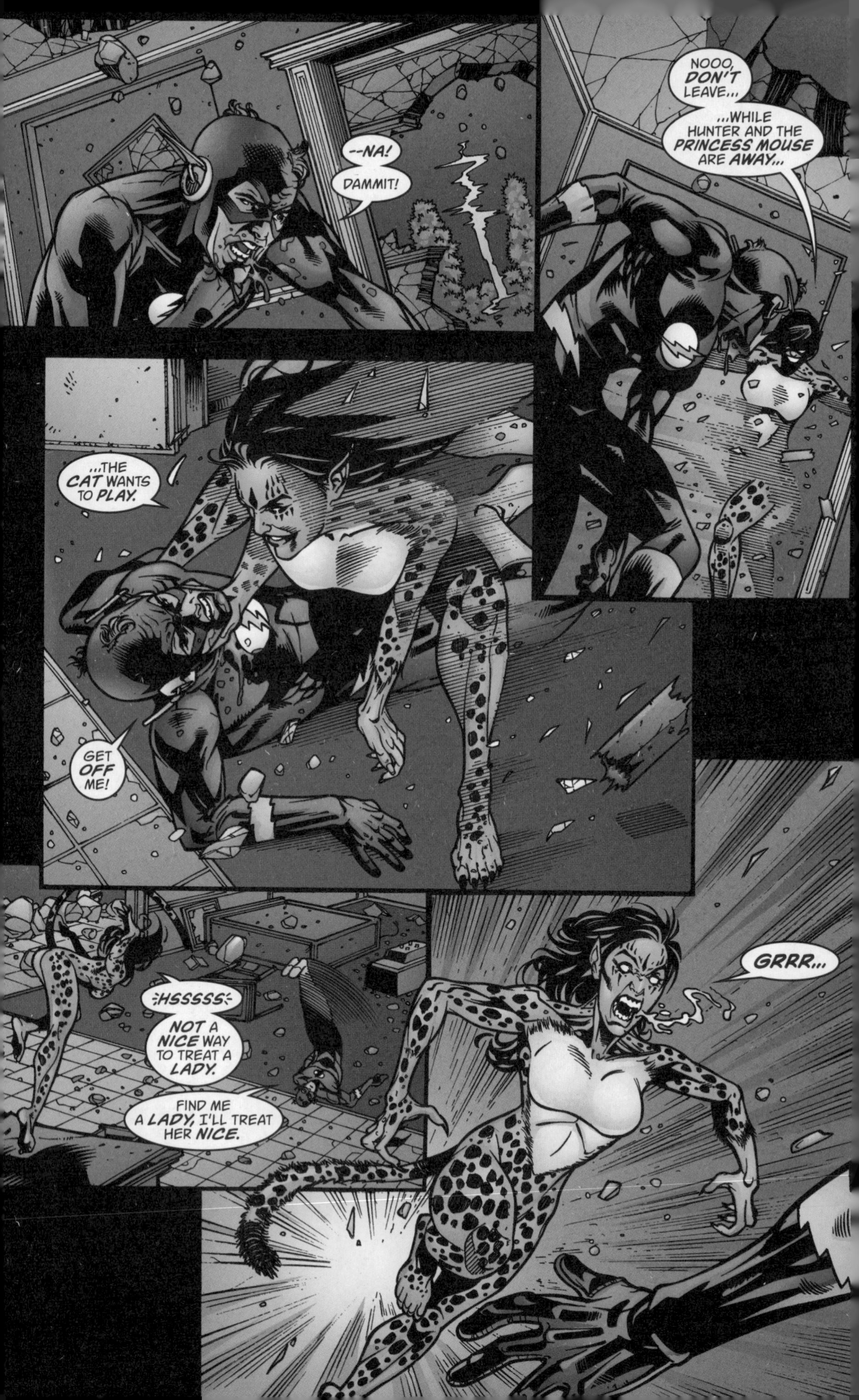
--NA!
DAMMIT!
NOOO, DON'T LEAVE...
...WHILE HUNTER AND THE PRINCESS MOUSE ARE AWAY...
...THE CAT WANTS TO PLAY.
GET OFF ME!
HSSSSS
NOT A NICE WAY TO TREAT A LADY.
FIND ME A LADY, I'LL TREAT HER NICE.
GRRR...

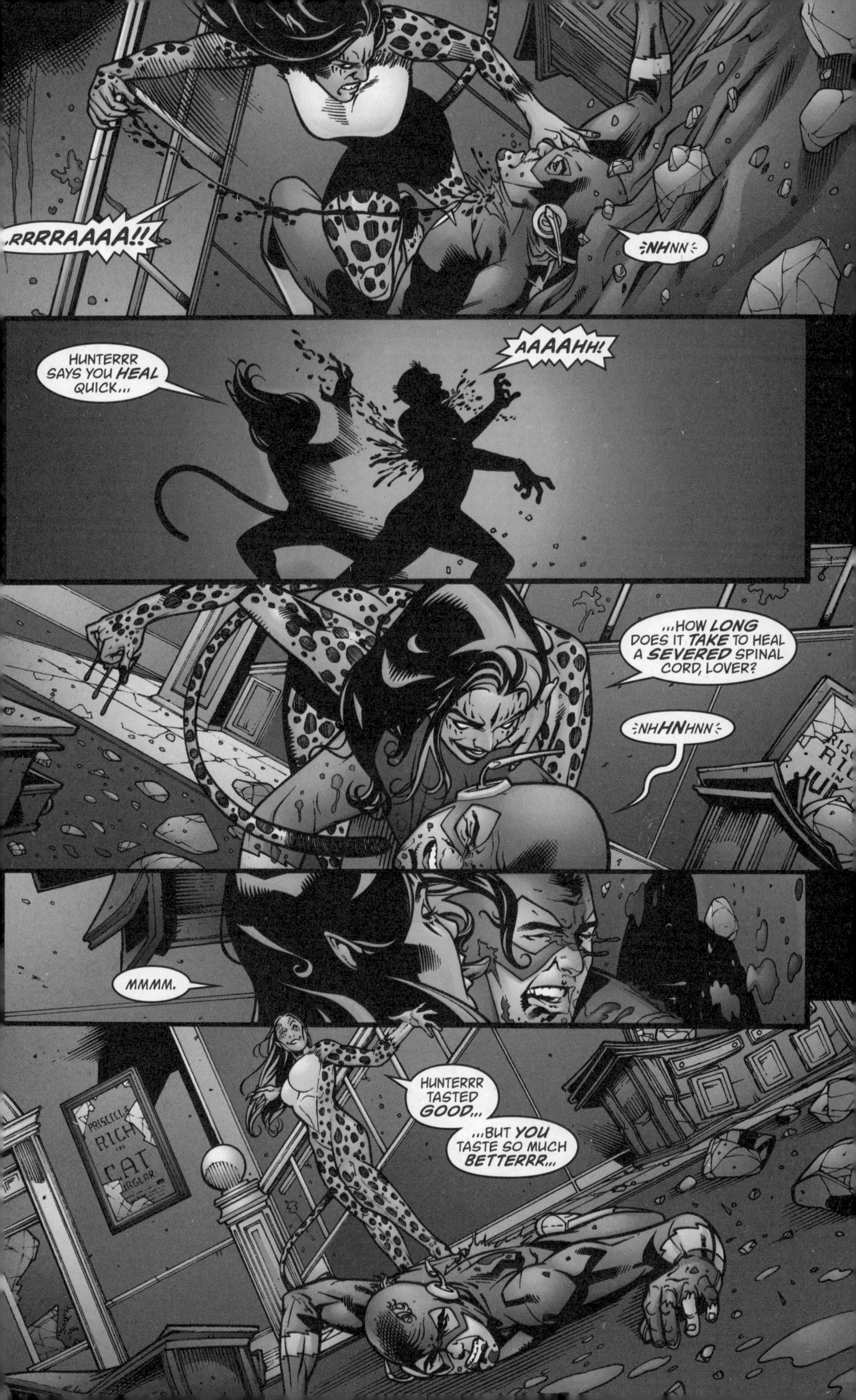
RRRRAAAA!!
NHNN
HUNTERRR SAYS YOU HEAL QUICK...
AAAAHH!
...HOW LONG DOES IT TAKE TO HEAL A SEVERED SPINAL CORD, LOVER?
NHHNHNN
MMMM.
PRISCILLA RICH IN CAT
HUNTERRR TASTED GOOD...
...BUT YOU TASTE SO MUCH BETTERRR...

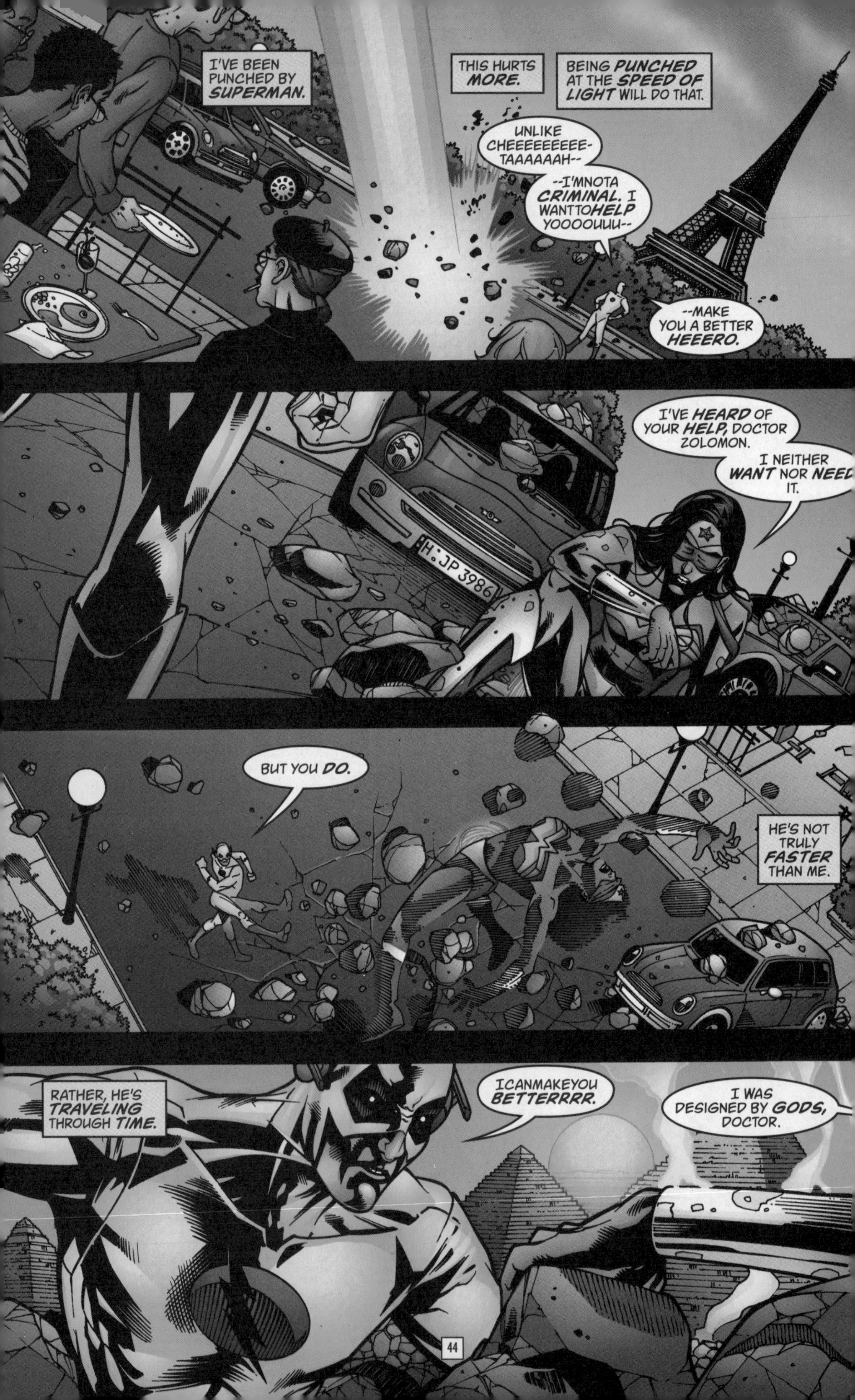
I'VE BEEN PUNCHED BY SUPERMAN.
THIS HURTS MORE.
BEING PUNCHED AT THE SPEED OF LIGHT WILL DO THAT.
UNLIKE CHEEEEEEEEE-TAAAAAAH--
--I'MNOTA CRIMINAL. I WANTTOHELP YOOOOUUU--
--MAKE YOU A BETTER HEEERO.
I'VE HEARD OF YOUR HELP, DOCTOR ZOLOMON.
I NEITHER WANT NOR NEED IT.
H.JP 3986
BUT YOU DO.
HE'S NOT TRULY FASTER THAN ME.
RATHER, HE'S TRAVELING THROUGH TIME.
ICANMAKEYOU BETTERRRR.
I WAS DESIGNED BY GODS, DOCTOR.

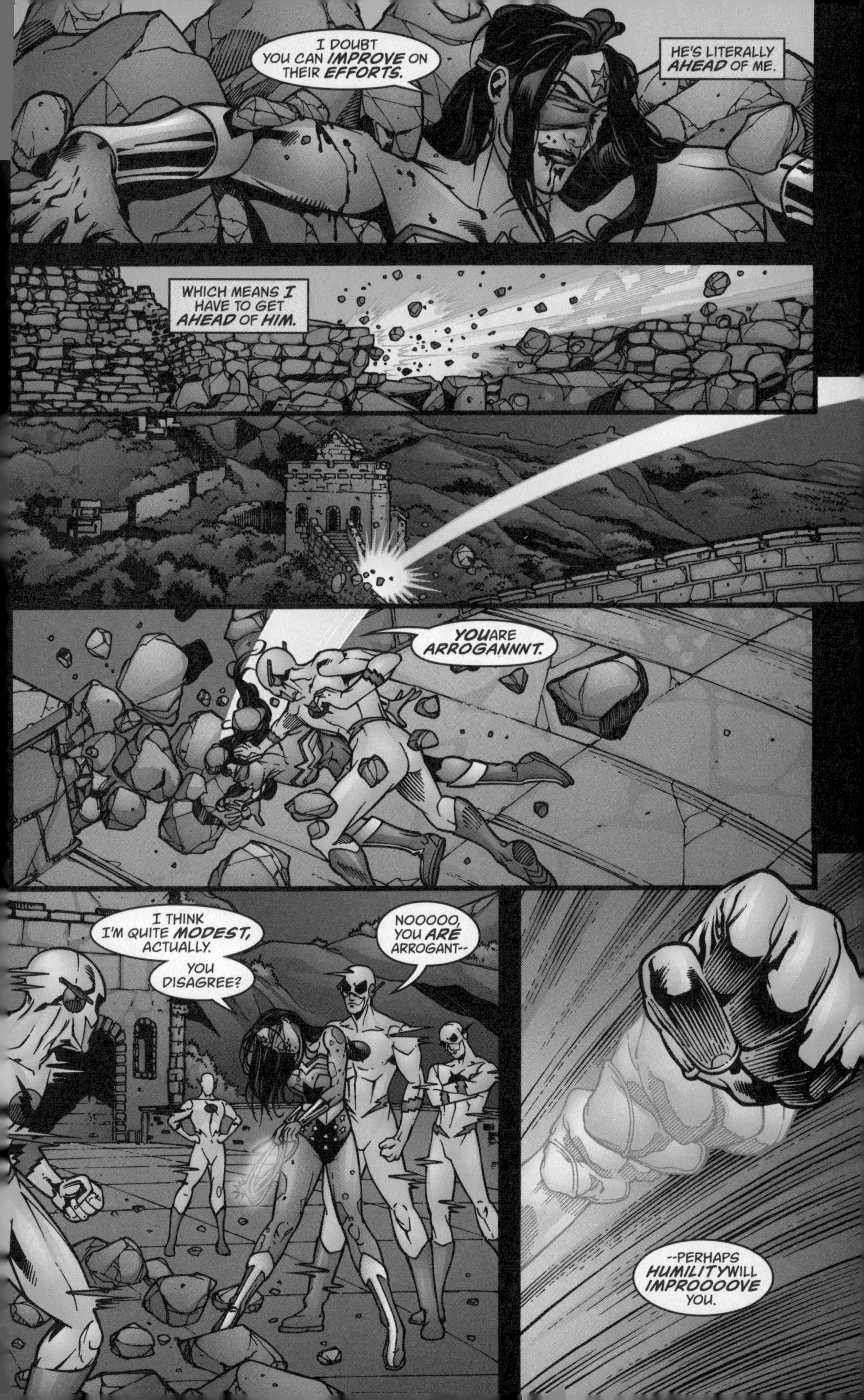
I DOUBT YOU CAN IMPROVE ON THEIR EFFORTS.
HE'S LITERALLY AHEAD OF ME.
WHICH MEANS I HAVE TO GET AHEAD OF HIM.
YOU ARE ARROGANNNT.
I THINK I'M QUITE MODEST, ACTUALLY.
YOU DISAGREE?
NOOOOO, YOU ARE ARROGANT--
--PERHAPS HUMILITY WILL IMPROOOOVE YOU.

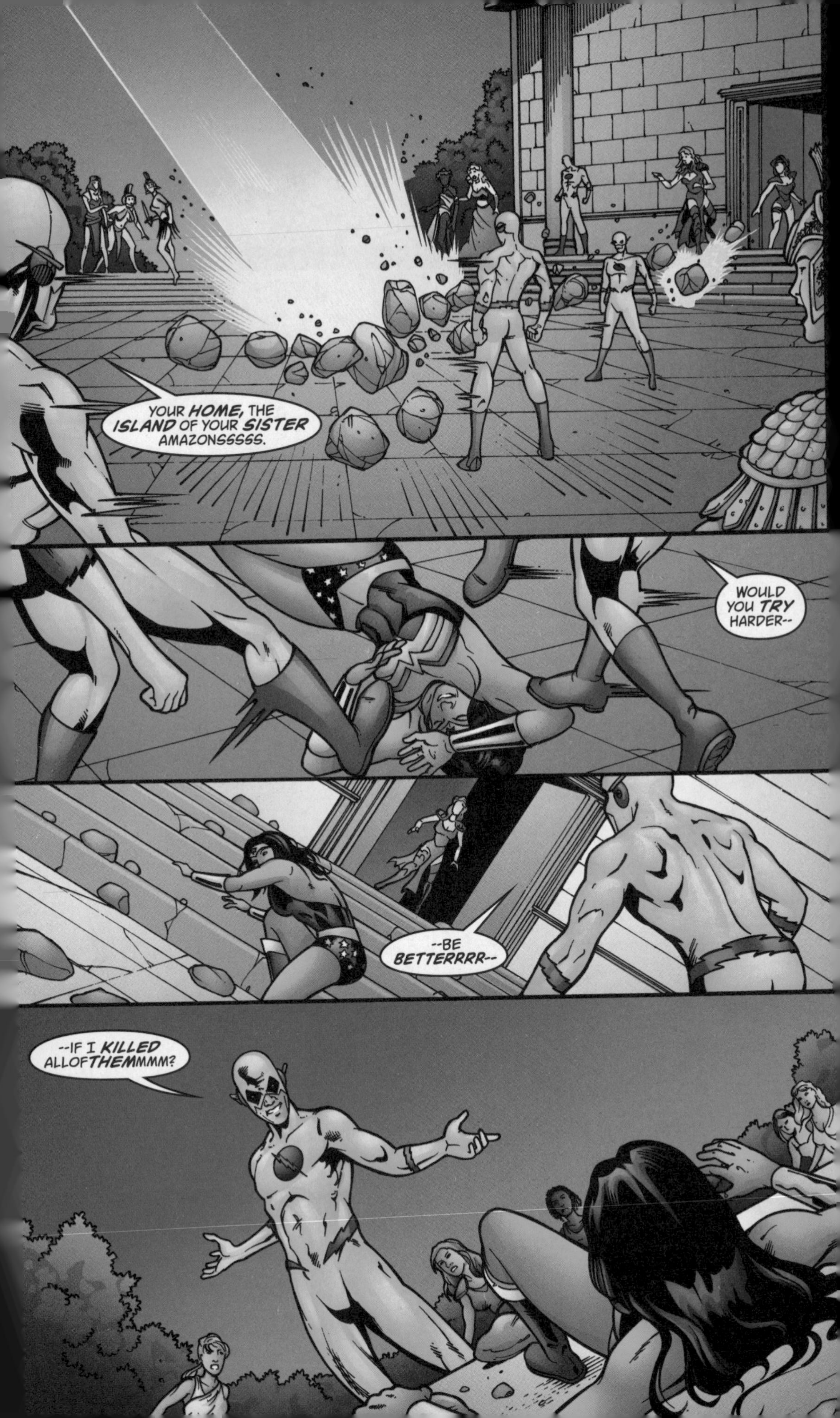
YOUR HOME, THE ISLAND OF YOUR SISTER AMAZONSSSSS.
WOULD YOU TRY HARDER--
--BE BETTERRRR--
--IF I KILLED ALLOFTHEMMMM?

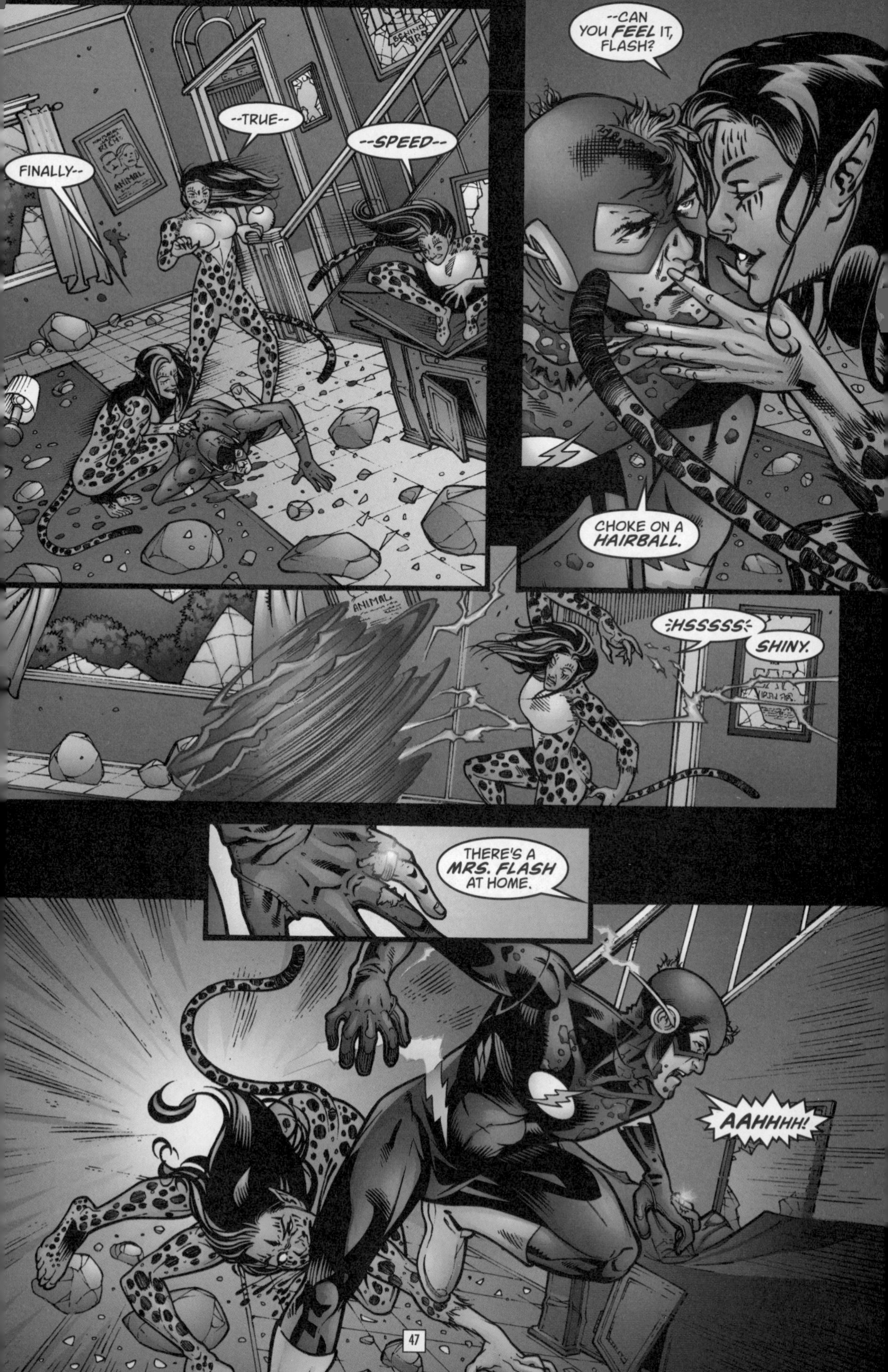
FINALLY--
--TRUE--
--SPEED--
--CAN YOU FEEL IT, FLASH?
CHOKE ON A HAIRBALL.
HSSSSS
SHINY.
THERE'S A MRS. FLASH AT HOME.
AAHHHH!

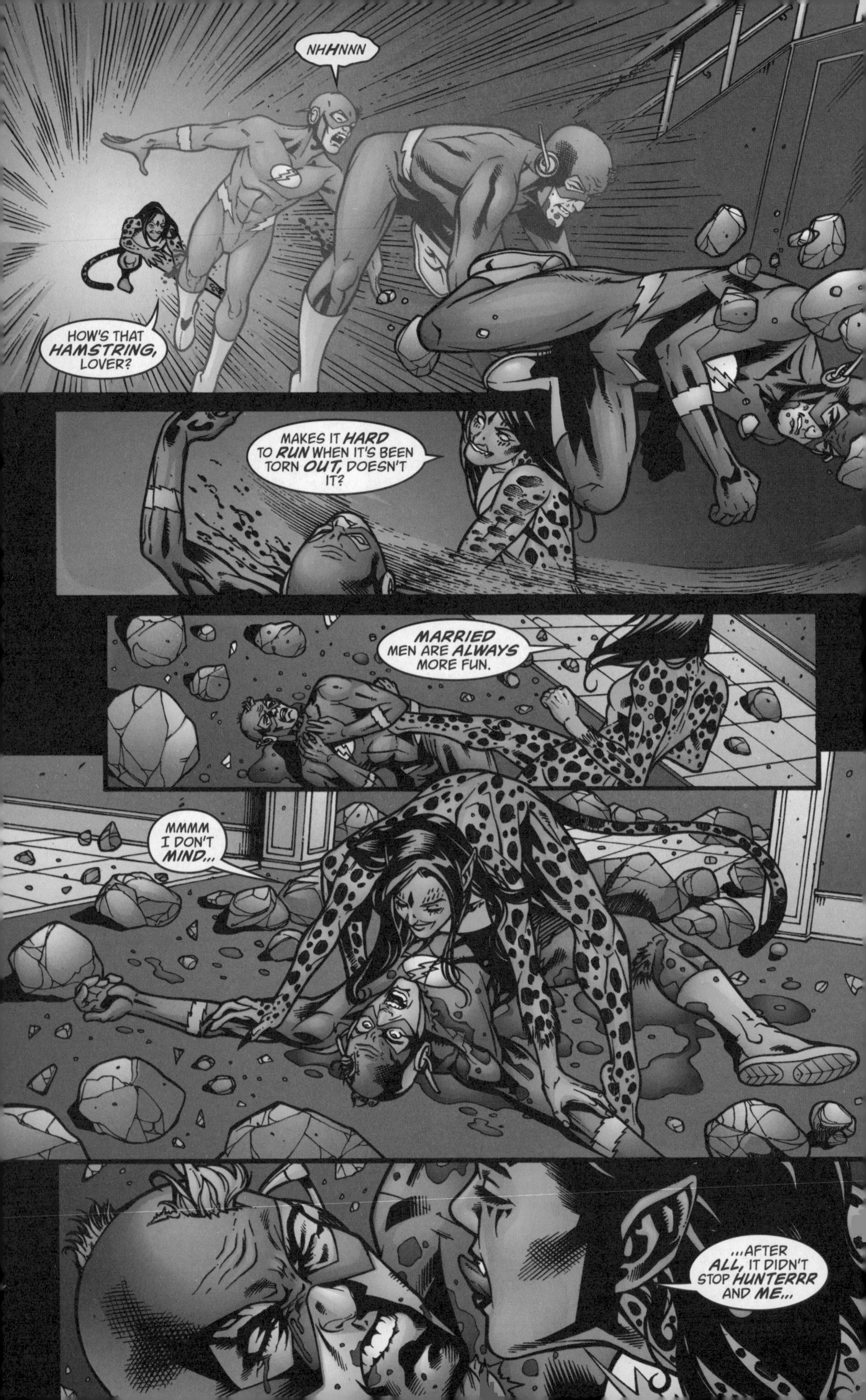
NHHNNN
HOW'S THAT HAMSTRING, LOVER?
MAKES IT HARD TO RUN WHEN IT'S BEEN TORN OUT, DOESN'T IT?
MARRIED MEN ARE ALWAYS MORE FUN.
MMMM I DON'T MIND...
...AFTER ALL, IT DIDN'T STOP HUNTERRR AND ME...

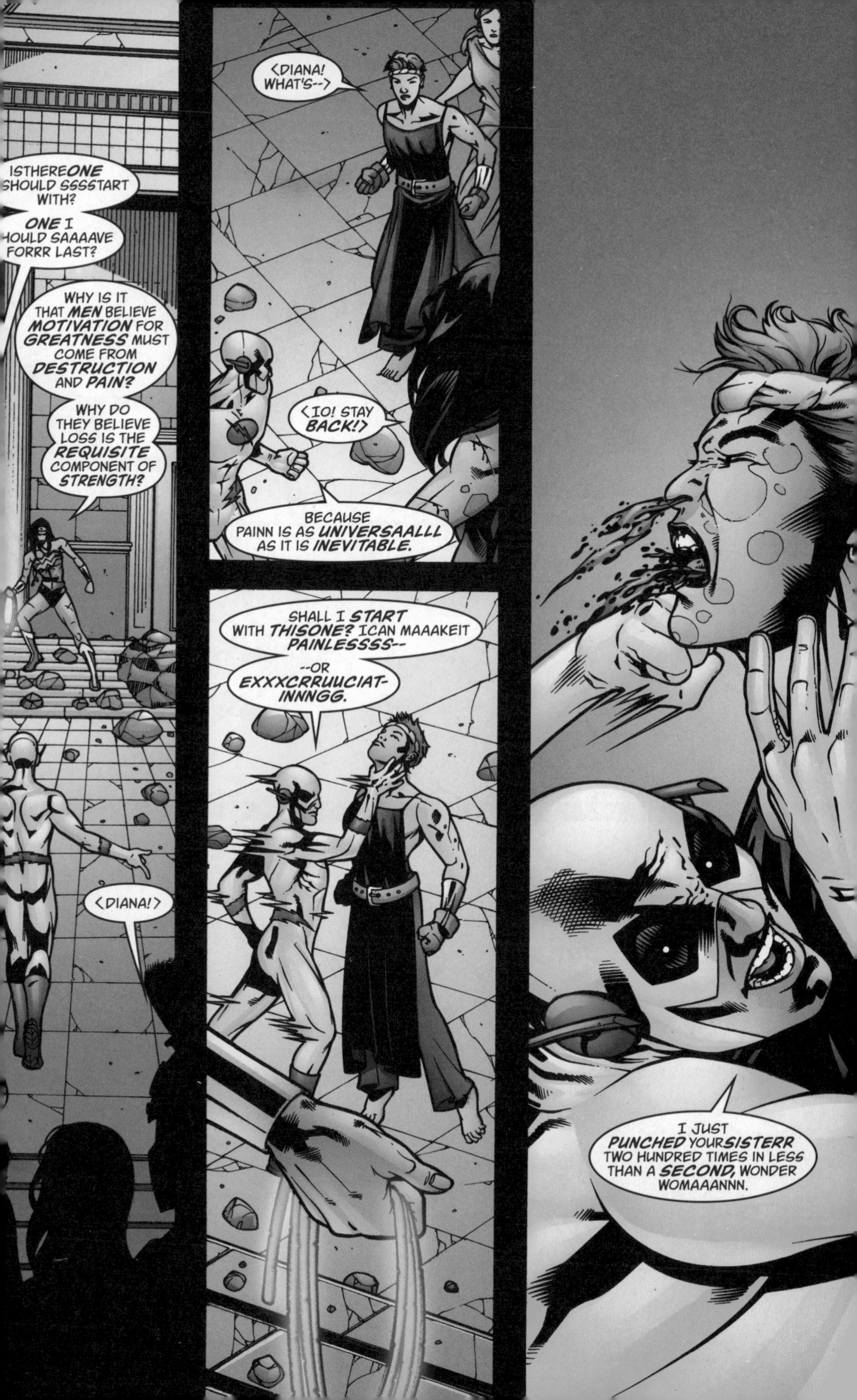
ISTHEREONE
SHOULD SSSSTART
WITH?
ONE I
HOULD SAAAAVE
FORRR LAST?
WHY IS IT THAT MEN BELIEVE MOTIVATION FOR GREATNESS MUST COME FROM DESTRUCTION AND PAIN?
WHY DO THEY BELIEVE LOSS IS THE REQUISITE COMPONENT OF STRENGTH?
<DIANA!>
<DIANA! WHAT'S-->
<IO! STAY BACK!>
BECAUSE PAINN IS AS UNIVERSAALLL AS IT IS INEVITABLE.
SHALL I START WITH THISONE? ICAN MAAAKEIT PAINLESSSS--
--OR EXXXCRRUUCIAT-INNNGG.
I JUST PUNCHED YOURSISTERR TWO HUNDRED TIMES IN LESS THAN A SECOND, WONDER WOMAAANNN.

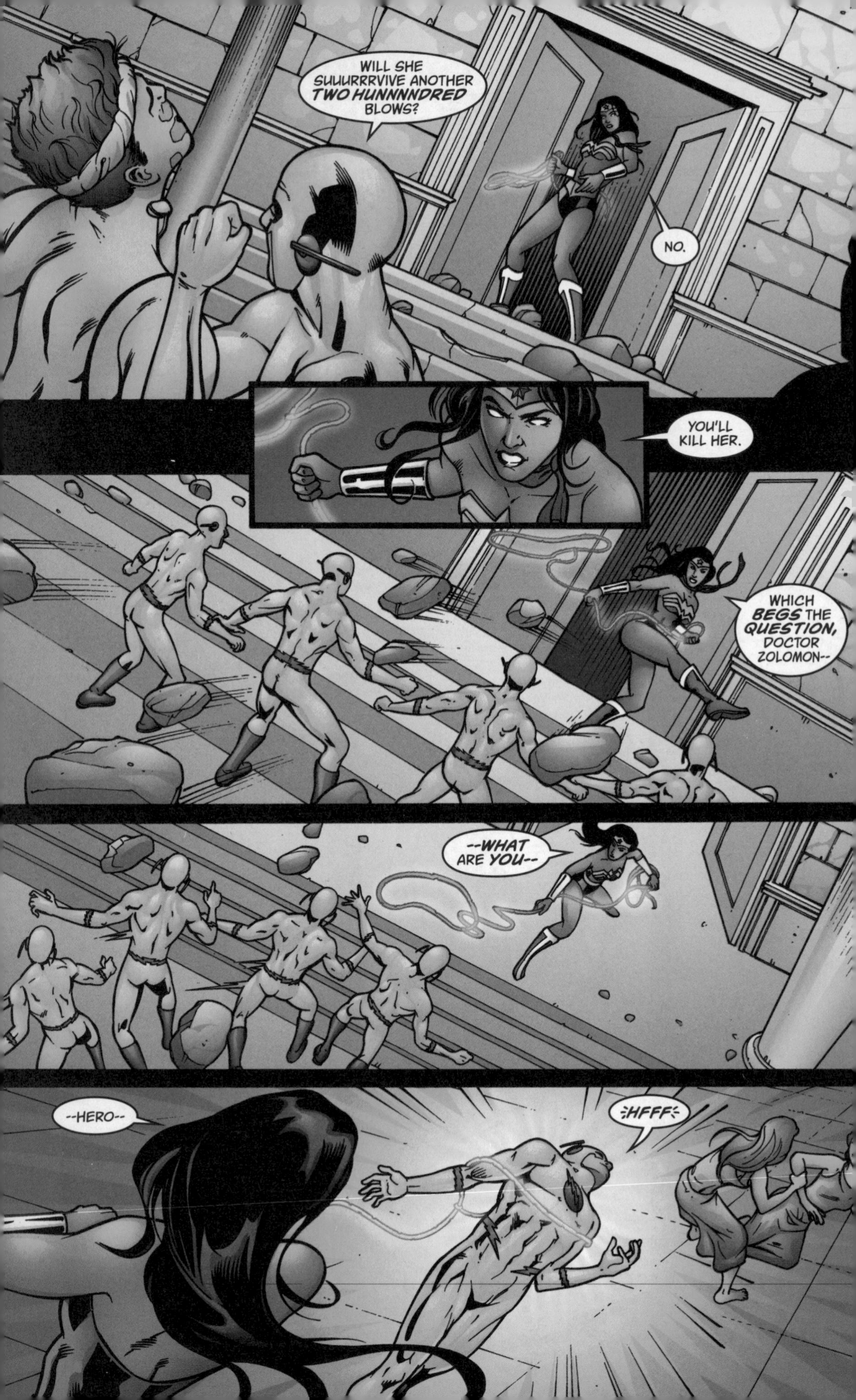
WILL SHE SUUURRRVIVE ANOTHER TWO HUNNNNDRED BLOWS?
NO.
YOU'LL KILL HER.
WHICH BEGS THE QUESTION, DOCTOR ZOLOMON--
--WHAT ARE YOU--
--HERO--
HFFF

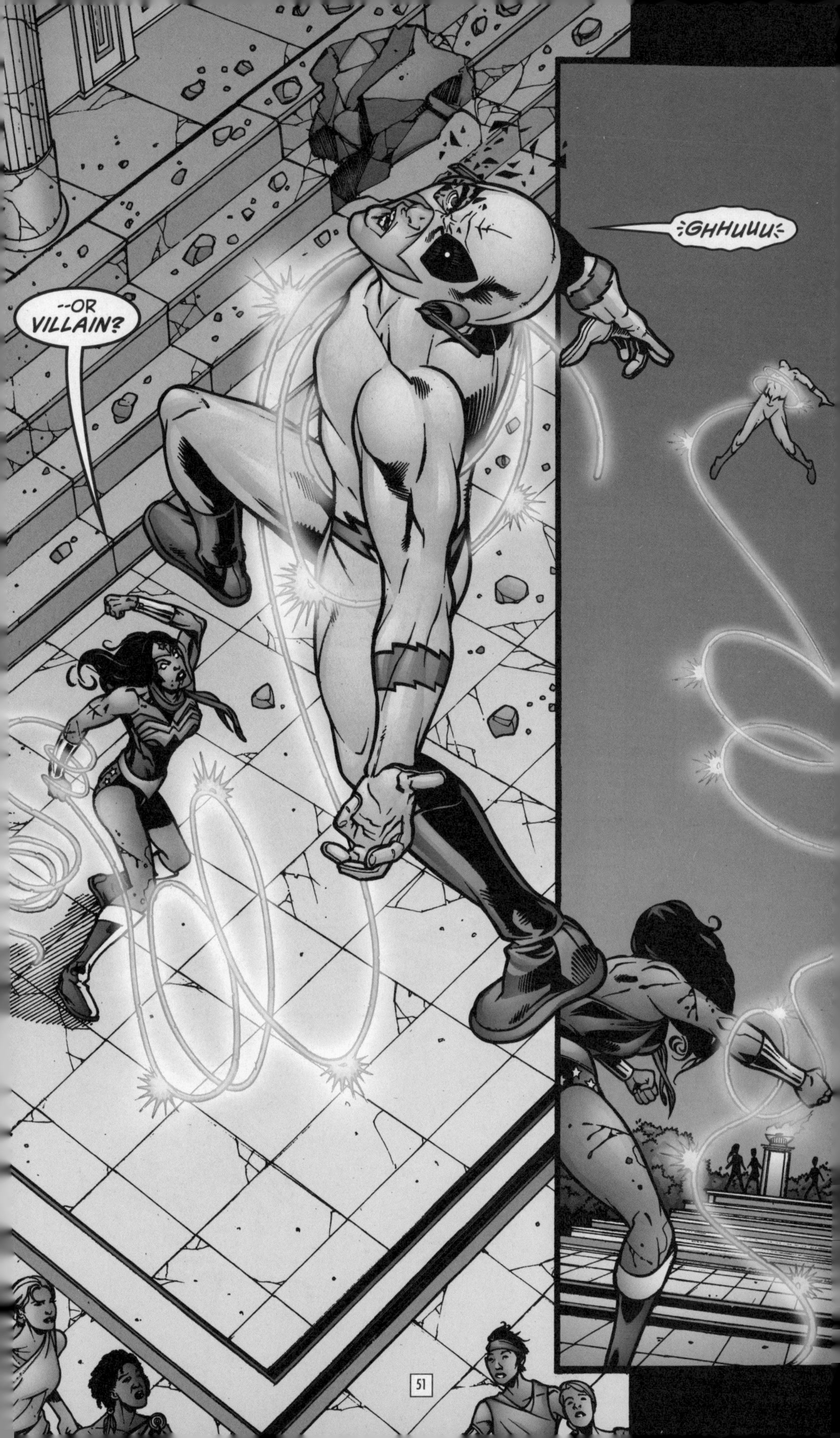
--OR VILLAIN?
GHHUUU

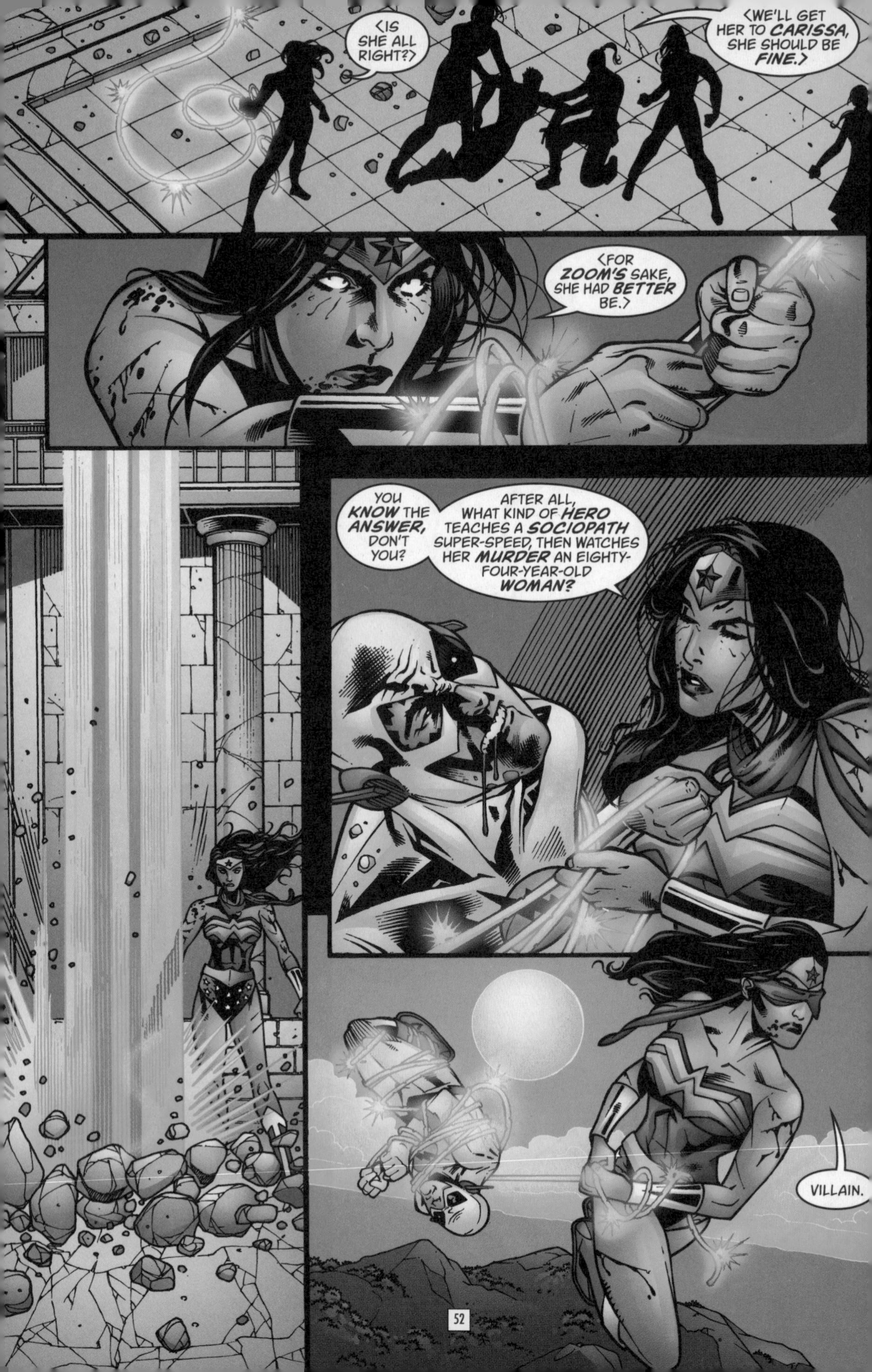

<IS SHE ALL RIGHT?>
<WE'LL GET HER TO CARISSA, SHE SHOULD BE FINE.>
<FOR ZOOM'S SAKE, SHE HAD BETTER BE.>
YOU KNOW THE ANSWER, DON'T YOU?
AFTER ALL, WHAT KIND OF HERO TEACHES A SOCIOPATH SUPER-SPEED, THEN WATCHES HER MURDER AN EIGHTY-FOUR-YEAR-OLD WOMAN?
VILLAIN.

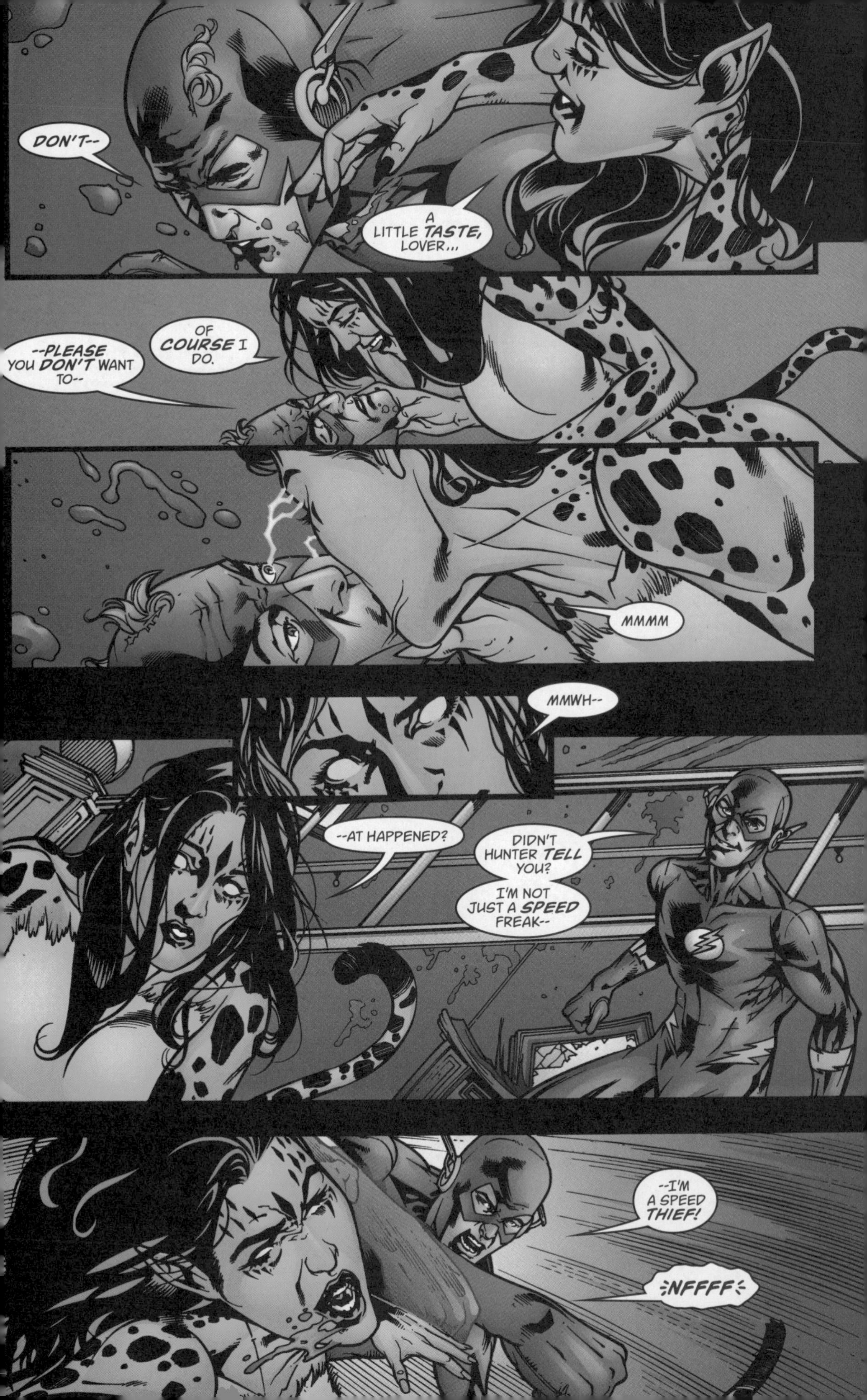
DON'T--
A LITTLE TASTE, LOVER...
--PLEASE YOU DON'T WANT TO--
OF COURSE I DO.
MMMM
MMWH--
--AT HAPPENED?
DIDN'T HUNTER TELL YOU?
I'M NOT JUST A SPEED FREAK--
--I'M A SPEED THIEF!
NFFFF

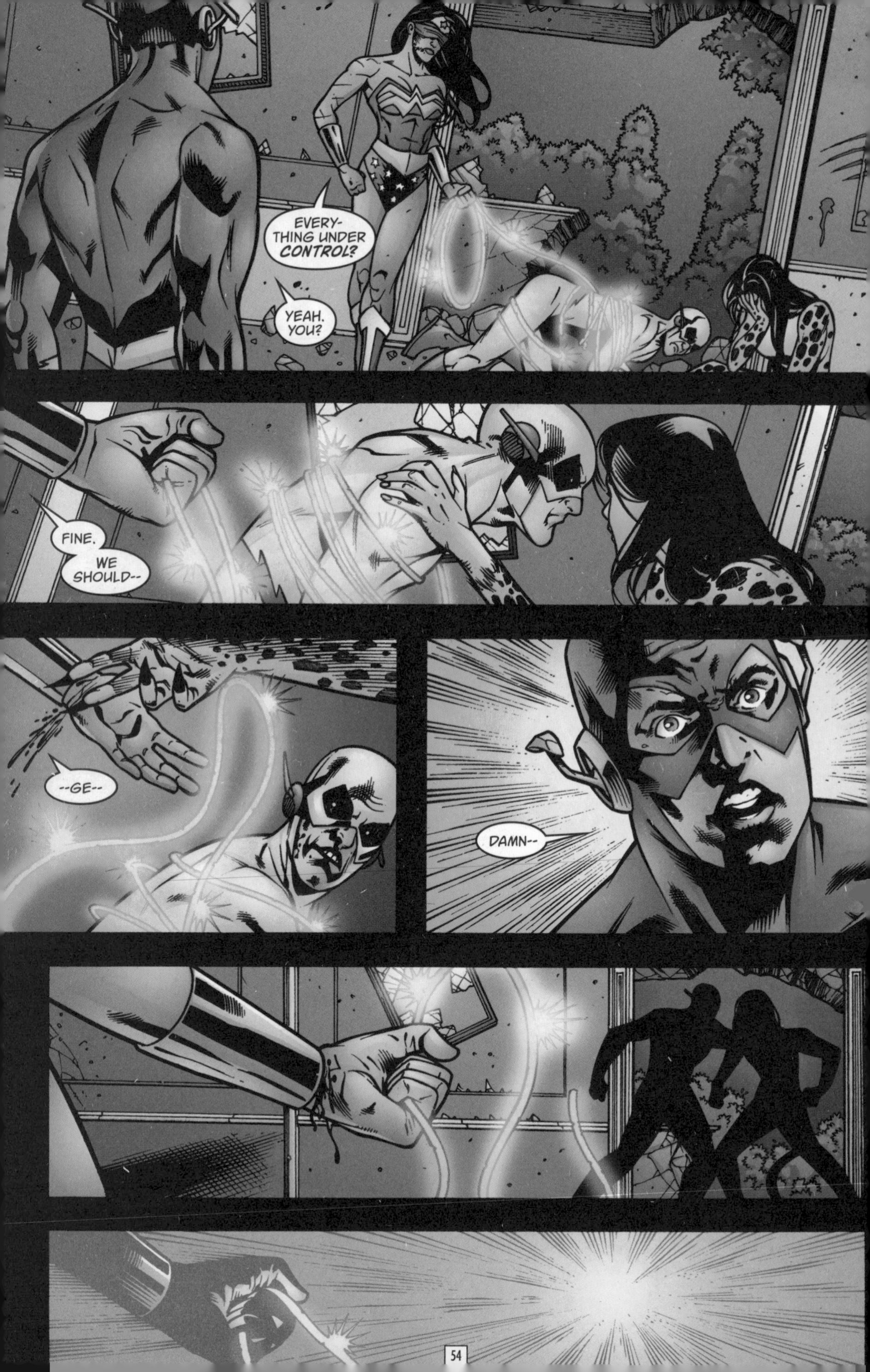
EVERY-THING UNDER CONTROL?
YEAH. YOU?
FINE. WE SHOULD--
--GE--
DAMN--

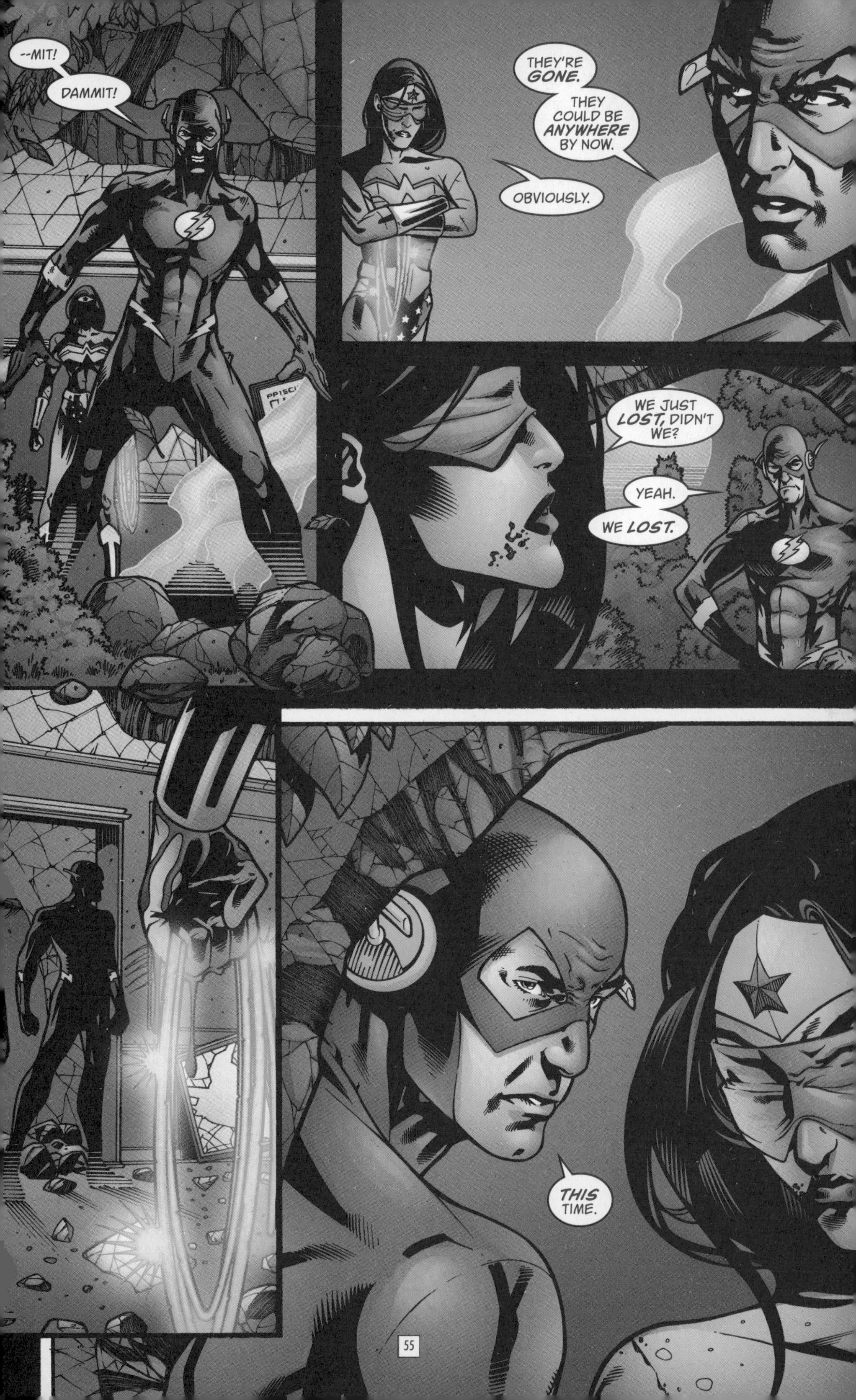
--MIT!
DAMMIT!
THEY'RE GONE.
THEY COULD BE ANYWHERE BY NOW.
OBVIOUSLY.
WE JUST LOST, DIDN'T WE?
YEAH.
WE LOST.
THIS TIME.

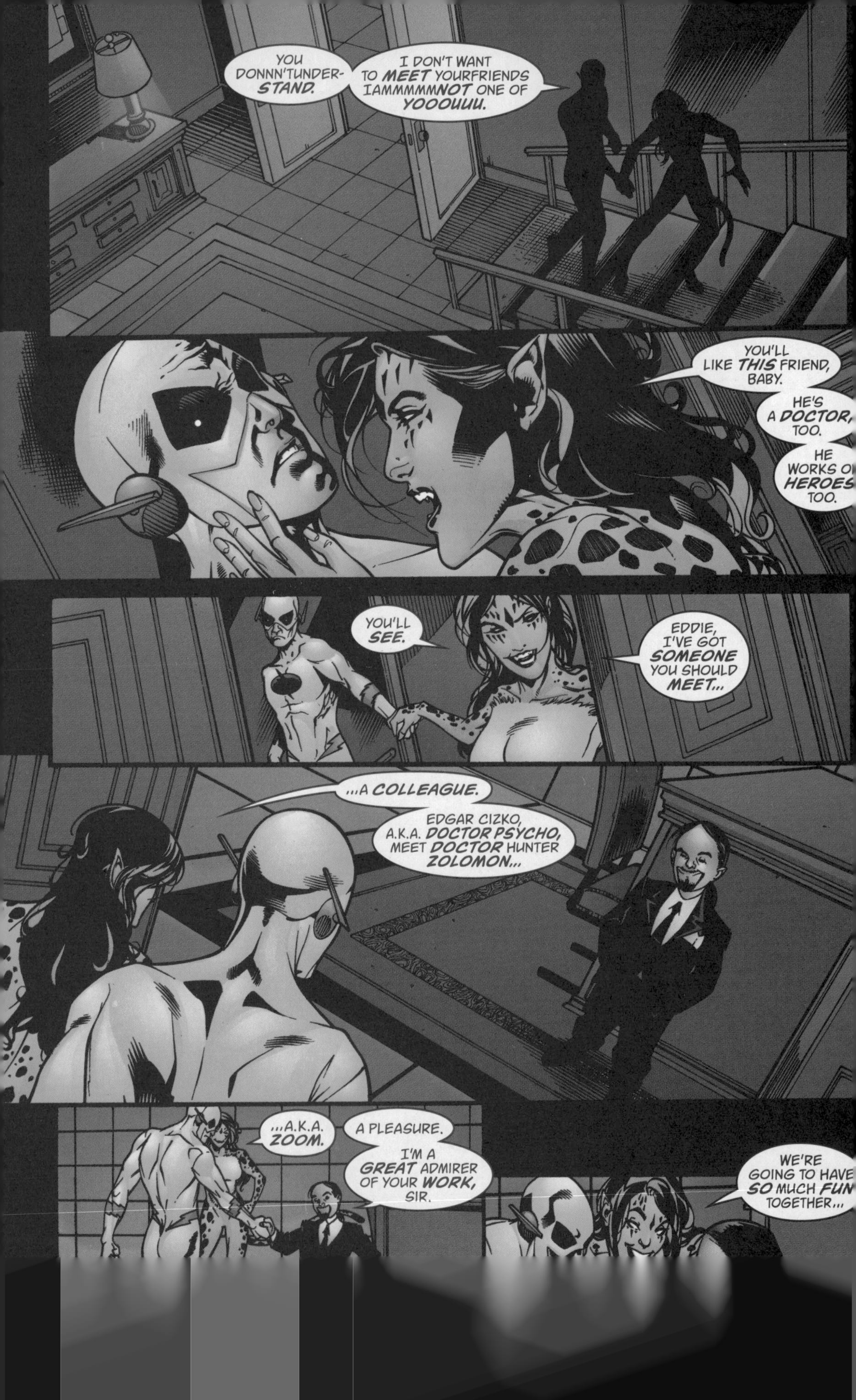
YOU DONNN'TUNDER-STAND.
I DON'T WANT TO MEET YOURFRIENDS IAMMMMMNOT ONE OF YOOOUUU.
YOU'LL LIKE THIS FRIEND, BABY.
HE'S A DOCTOR, TOO.
HE WORKS O HEROES TOO.
YOU'LL SEE.
EDDIE, I'VE GOT SOMEONE YOU SHOULD MEET...
...A COLLEAGUE.
EDGAR CIZKO, A.K.A. DOCTOR PSYCHO, MEET DOCTOR HUNTER ZOLOMON...
...A.K.A. ZOOM.
A PLEASURE.
I'M A GREAT ADMIRER OF YOUR WORK, SIR.
WE'RE GOING TO HAVE SO MUCH FUN TOGETHER...

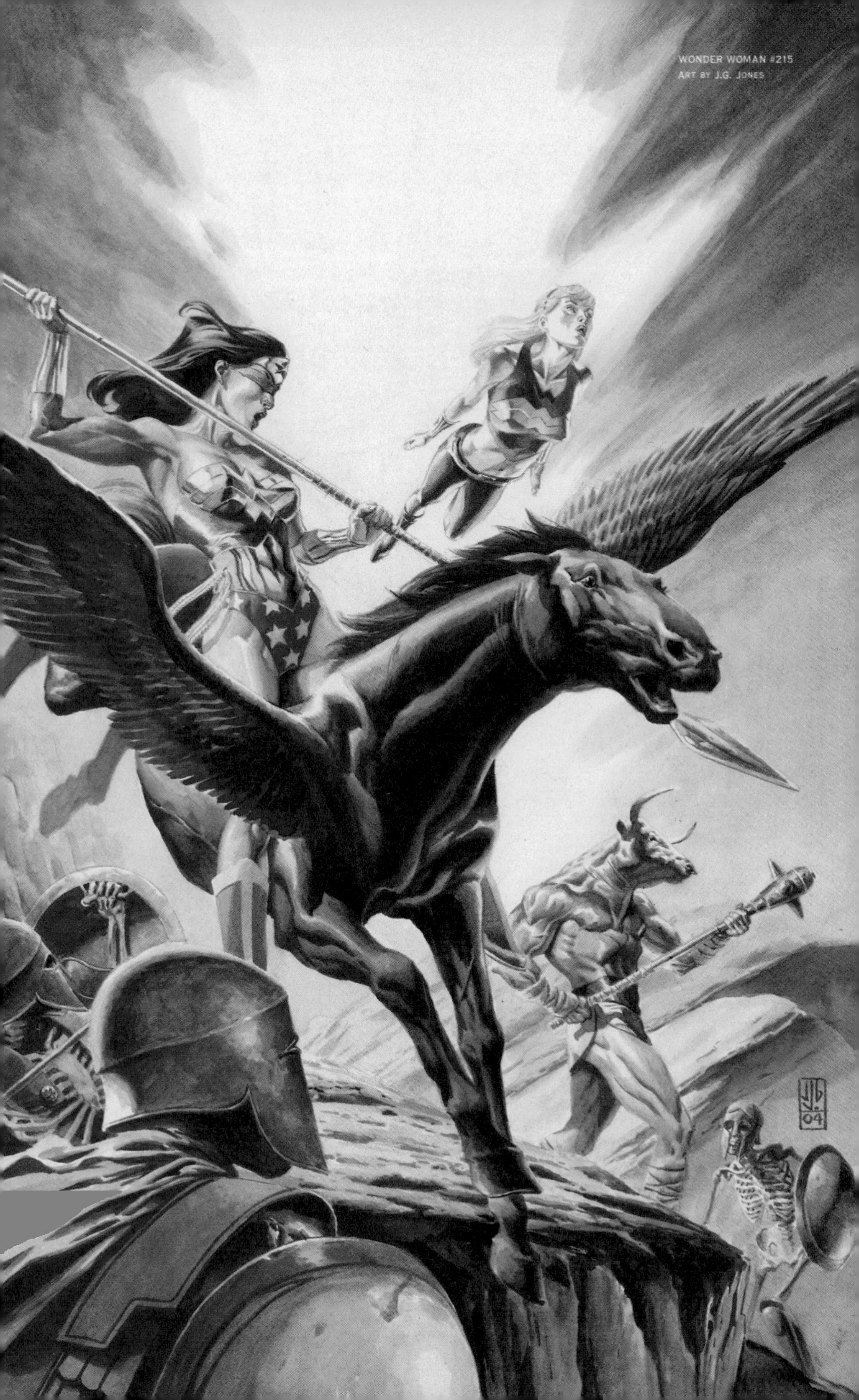

WONDER WOMAN #215
ART BY J.G. JONES

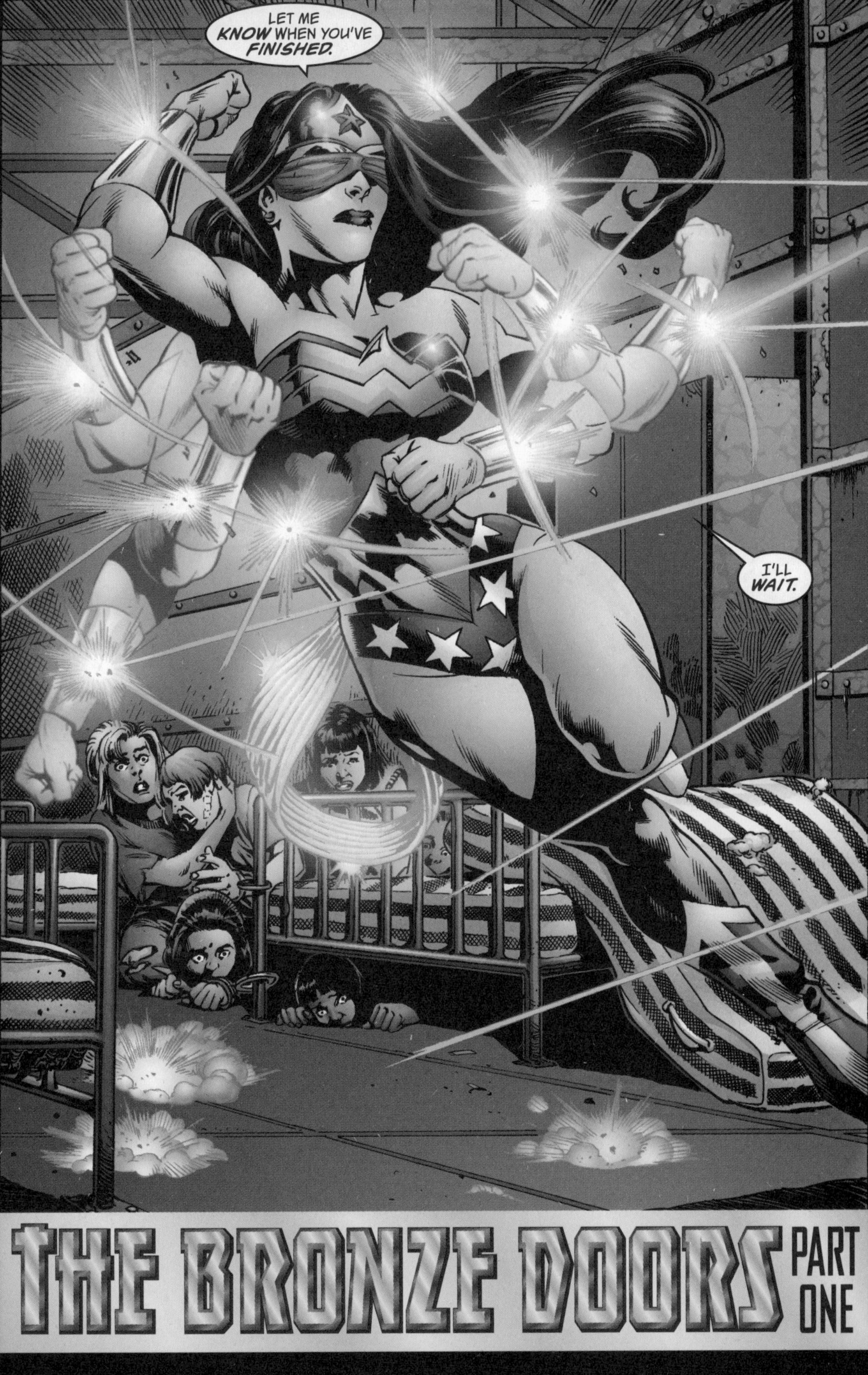
LET ME KNOW WHEN YOU'VE FINISHED.
I'LL WAIT.
THE BRONZE DOORS PART ONE

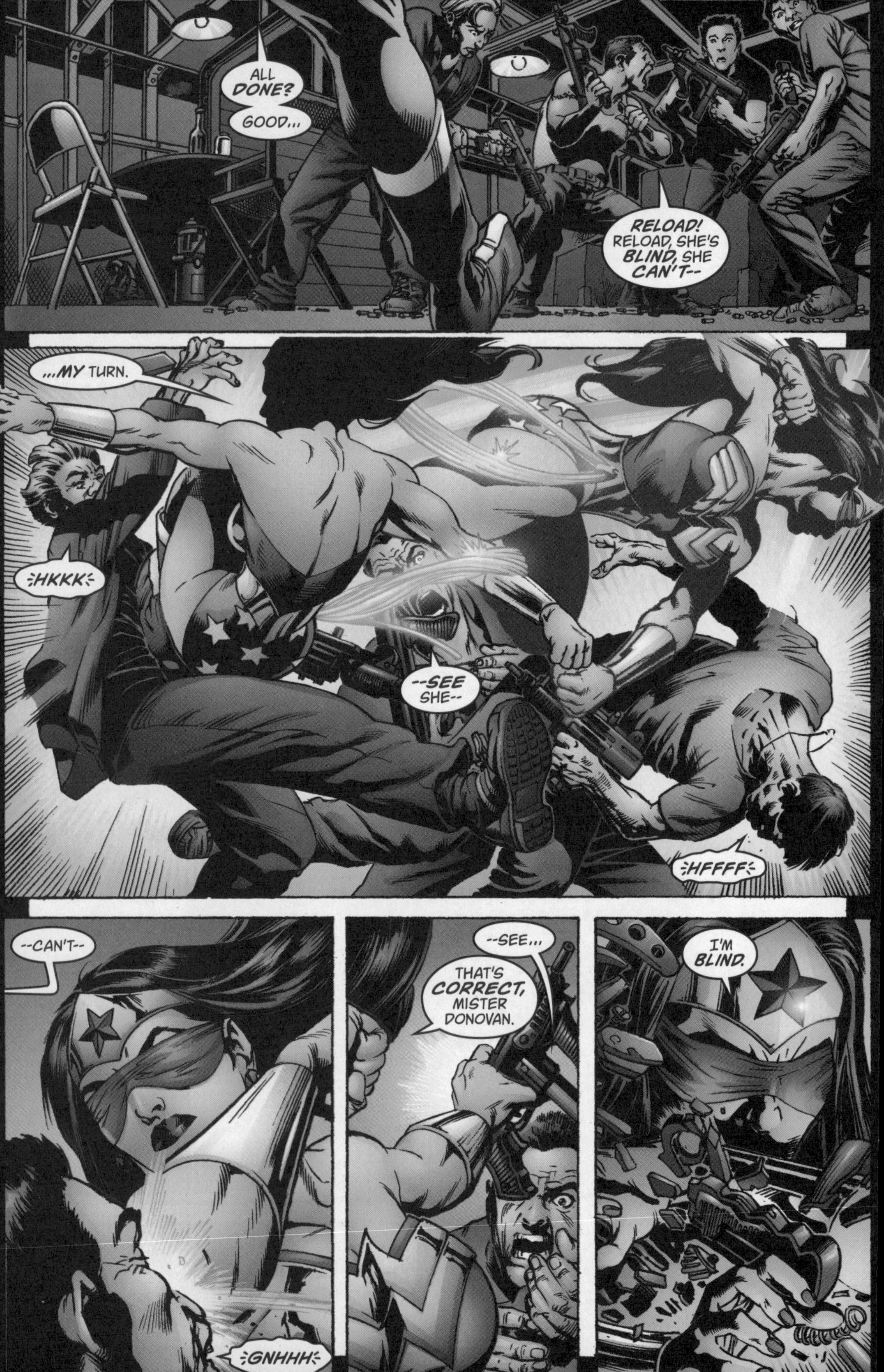
ALL DONE?
GOOD...
RELOAD! RELOAD, SHE'S BLIND, SHE CAN'T--
...MY TURN.
HKKK
--SEE SHE--
HFFFF
--CAN'T--
GNHHH
--SEE...
THAT'S CORRECT, MISTER DONOVAN.
I'M BLIND.

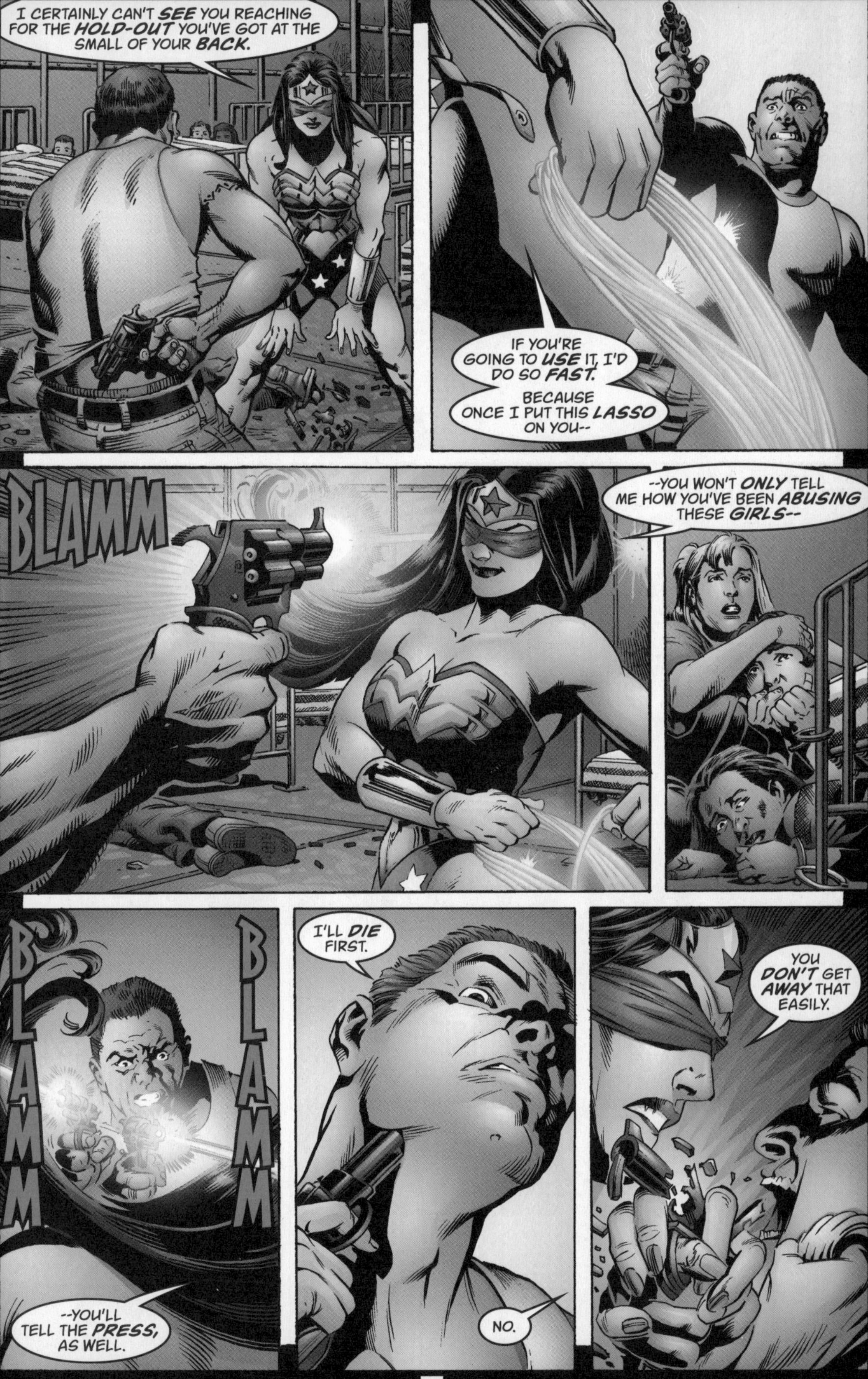
I CERTAINLY CAN'T SEE YOU REACHING FOR THE HOLD-OUT YOU'VE GOT AT THE SMALL OF YOUR BACK.
IF YOU'RE GOING TO USE IT, I'D DO SO FAST.
BECAUSE ONCE I PUT THIS LASSO ON YOU--
BLAMM
--YOU WON'T ONLY TELL ME HOW YOU'VE BEEN ABUSING THESE GIRLS--
BLAMM
BLAMM
--YOU'LL TELL THE PRESS, AS WELL.
I'LL DIE FIRST.
NO.
YOU DON'T GET AWAY THAT EASILY.

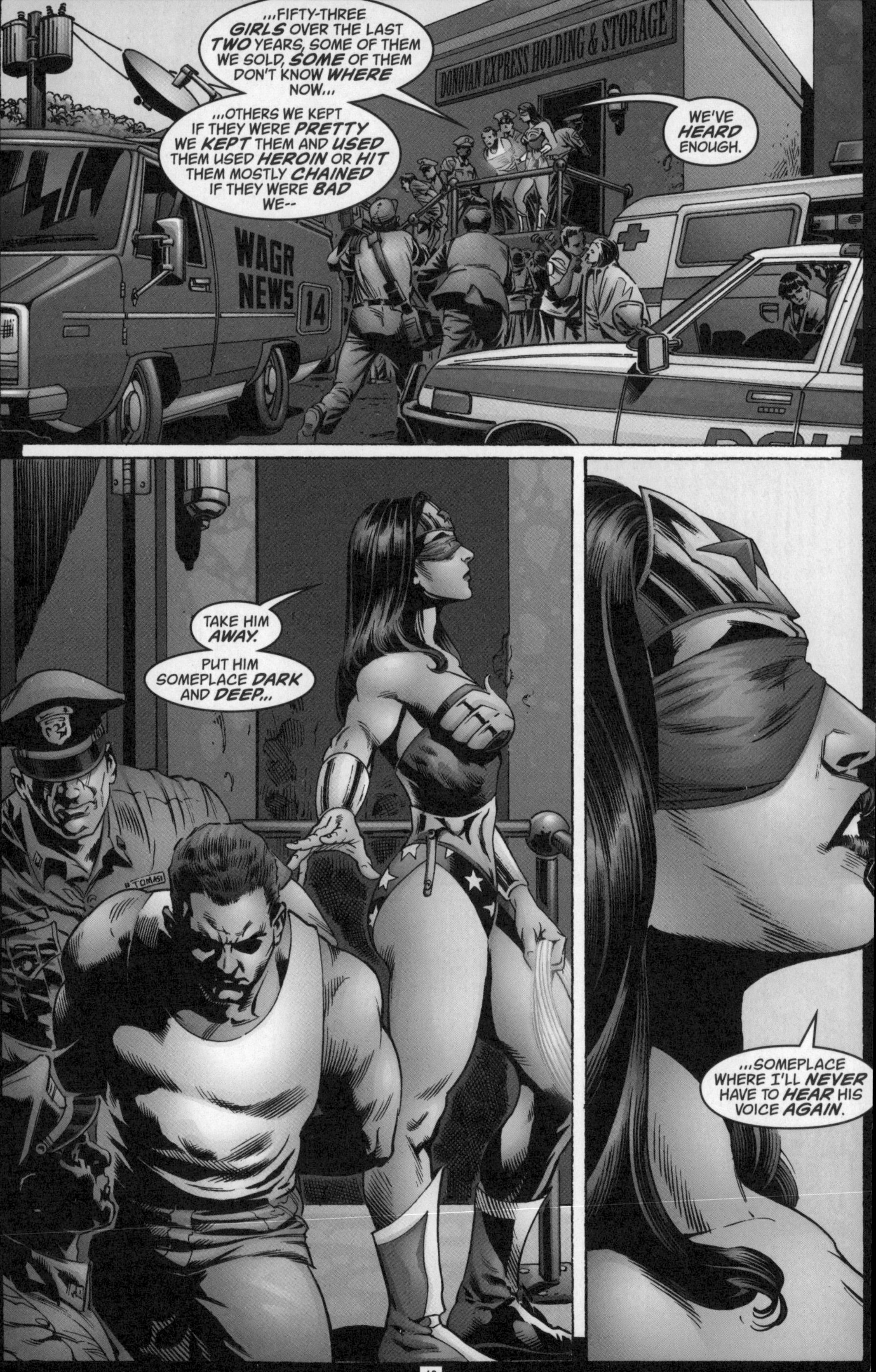
DONOVAN EXPRESS HOLDING & STORAGE
...FIFTY-THREE GIRLS OVER THE LAST TWO YEARS, SOME OF THEM WE SOLD, SOME OF THEM DON'T KNOW WHERE NOW...
...OTHERS WE KEPT IF THEY WERE PRETTY WE KEPT THEM AND USED THEM USED HEROIN OR HIT THEM MOSTLY CHAINED IF THEY WERE BAD WE--
WE'VE HEARD ENOUGH.
WAGR NEWS
14
TAKE HIM AWAY.
PUT HIM SOMEPLACE DARK AND DEEP...
TOMASI
...SOMEPLACE WHERE I'LL NEVER HAVE TO HEAR HIS VOICE AGAIN.

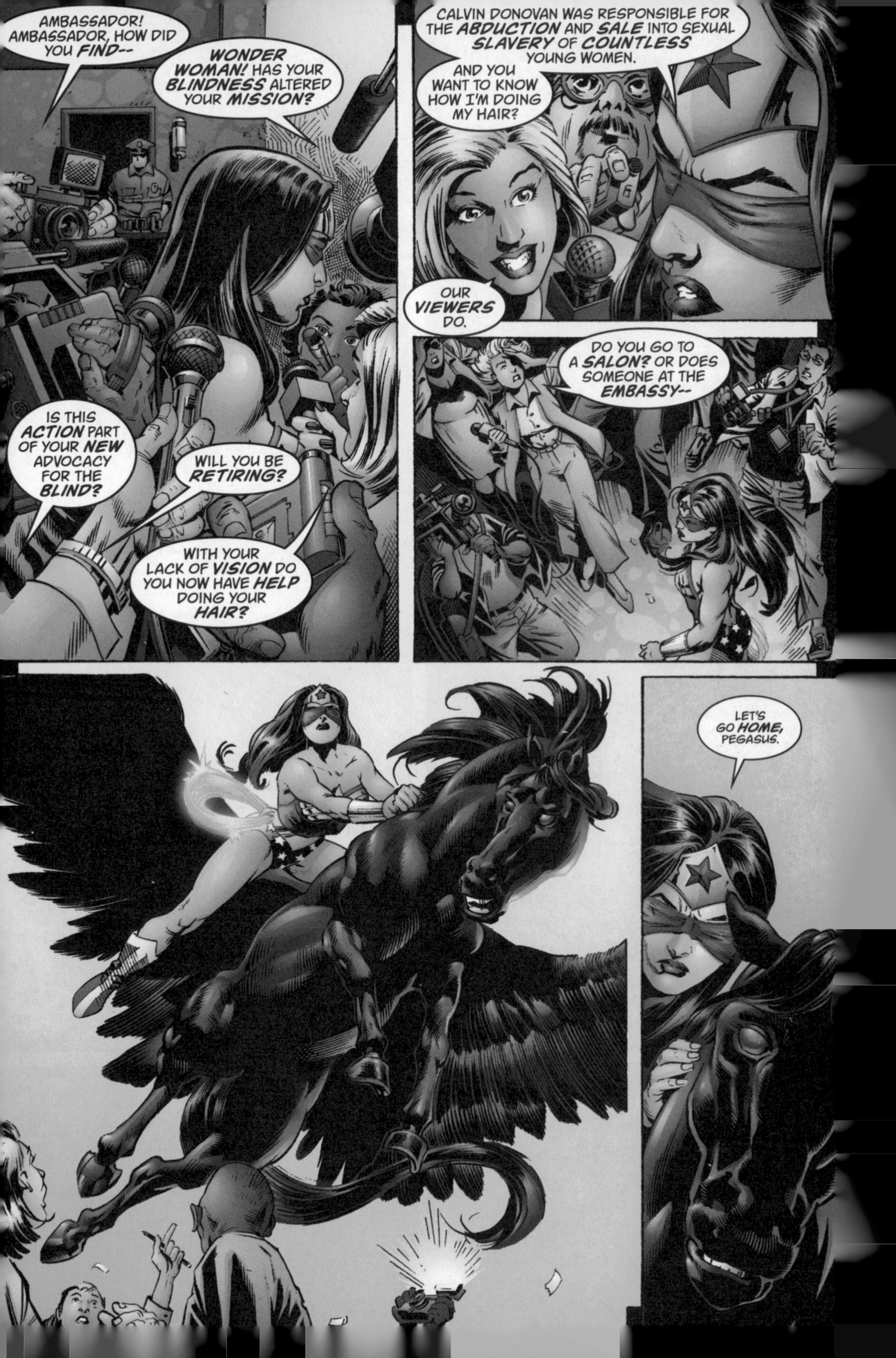
AMBASSADOR! AMBASSADOR, HOW DID YOU FIND--
WONDER WOMAN! HAS YOUR BLINDNESS ALTERED YOUR MISSION?
IS THIS ACTION PART OF YOUR NEW ADVOCACY FOR THE BLIND?
WILL YOU BE RETIRING?
WITH YOUR LACK OF VISION DO YOU NOW HAVE HELP DOING YOUR HAIR?
CALVIN DONOVAN WAS RESPONSIBLE FOR THE ABDUCTION AND SALE INTO SEXUAL SLAVERY OF COUNTLESS YOUNG WOMEN.
AND YOU WANT TO KNOW HOW I'M DOING MY HAIR?
OUR VIEWERS DO.
DO YOU GO TO A SALON? OR DOES SOMEONE AT THE EMBASSY--
LET'S GO HOME, PEGASUS.

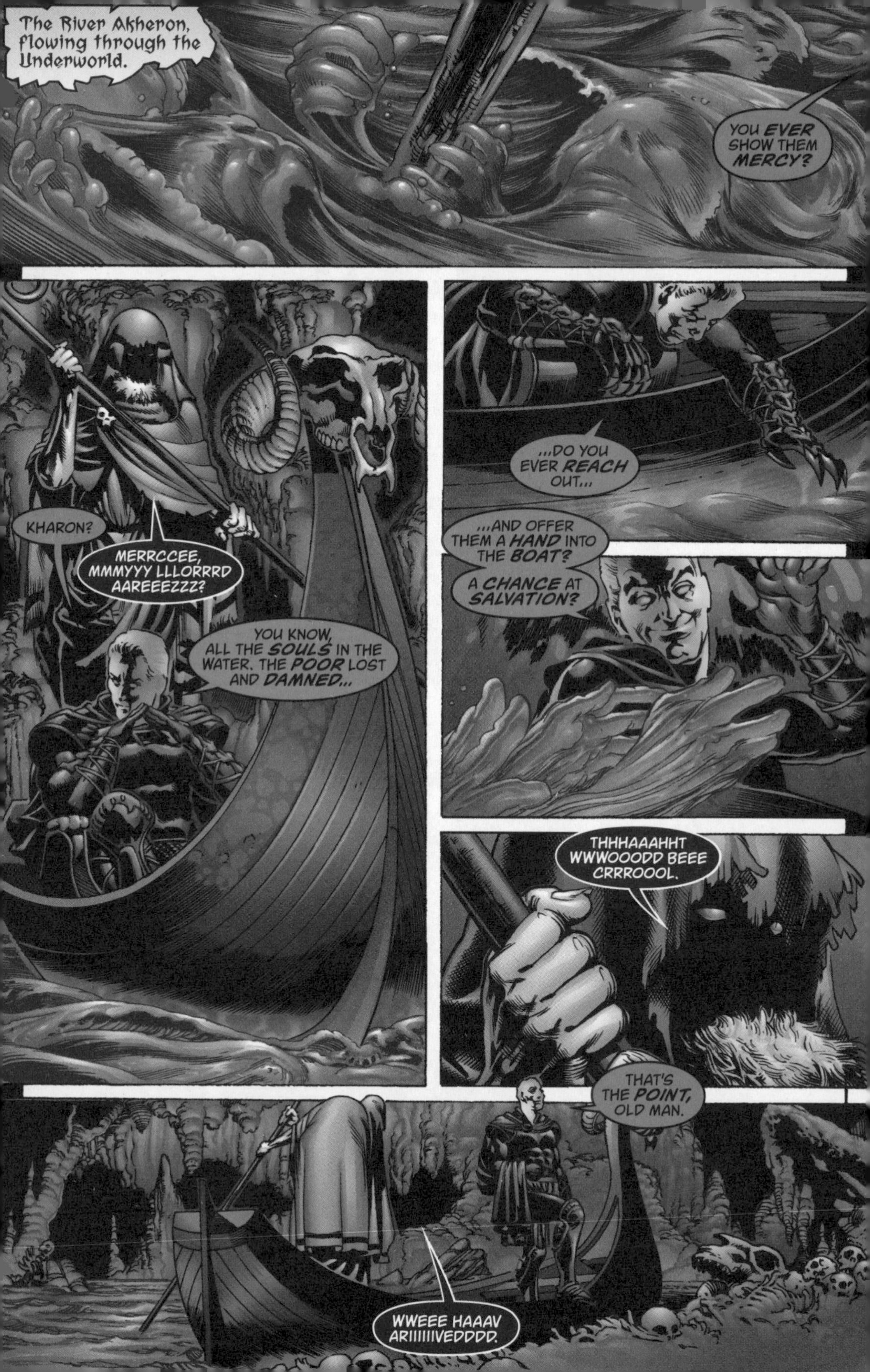
The River Akheron, flowing through the Underworld.
YOU EVER SHOW THEM MERCY?
KHARON?
MERRCCEE, MMMYYY LLLORRRD AAREEEZZZ?
YOU KNOW, ALL THE SOULS IN THE WATER. THE POOR LOST AND DAMNED...
...DO YOU EVER REACH OUT...
...AND OFFER THEM A HAND INTO THE BOAT?
A CHANCE AT SALVATION?
THHHAAAHHT WWWOOODD BEEE CRRROOOL.
THAT'S THE POINT, OLD MAN.
WWEEE HAAAV ARIIIIIIVEDDDD.

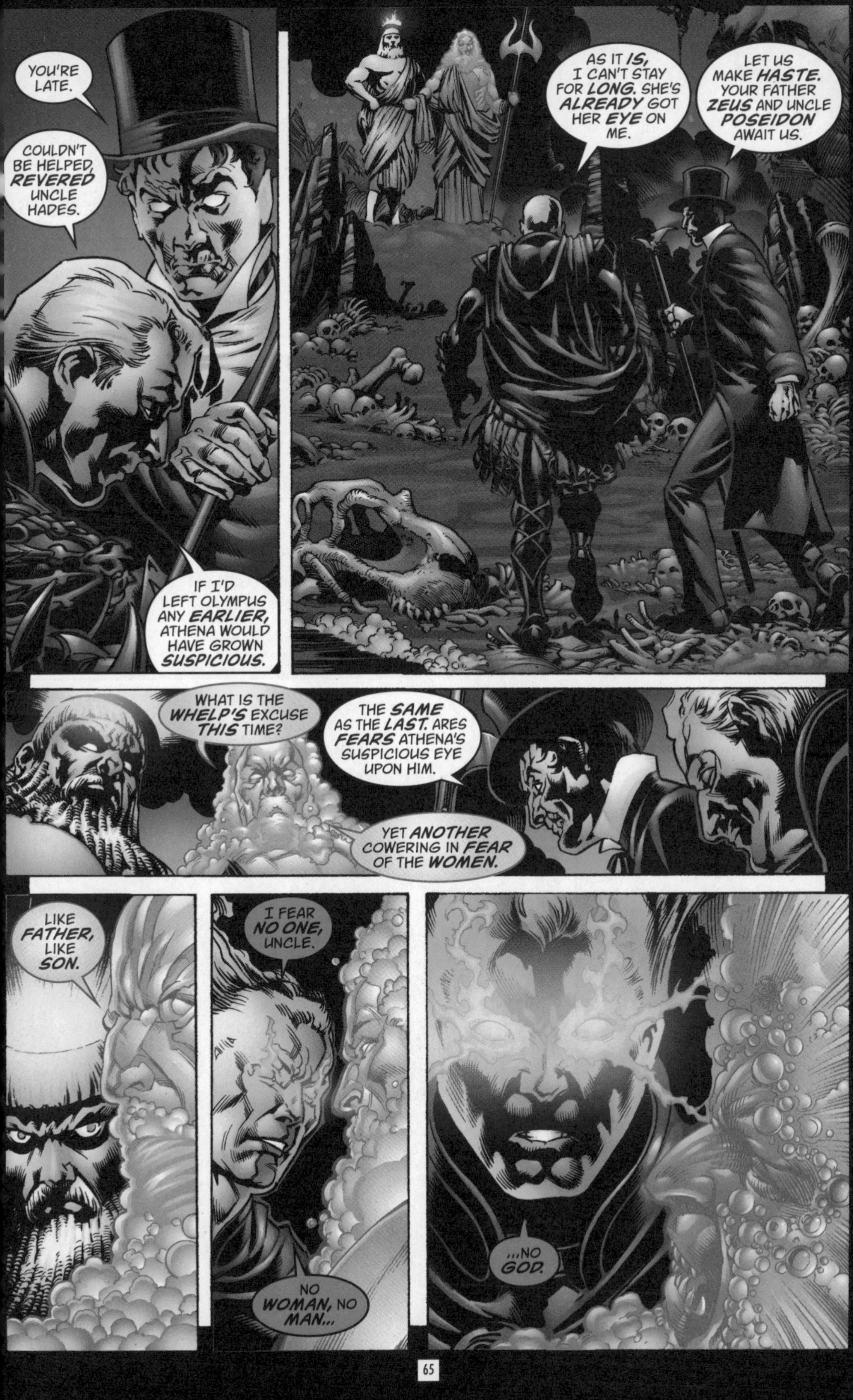

YOU'RE LATE.
COULDN'T BE HELPED, REVERED UNCLE HADES.
IF I'D LEFT OLYMPUS ANY EARLIER, ATHENA WOULD HAVE GROWN SUSPICIOUS.
AS IT IS, I CAN'T STAY FOR LONG. SHE'S ALREADY GOT HER EYE ON ME.
LET US MAKE HASTE. YOUR FATHER ZEUS AND UNCLE POSEIDON AWAIT US.
WHAT IS THE WHELP'S EXCUSE THIS TIME?
THE SAME AS THE LAST. ARES FEARS ATHENA'S SUSPICIOUS EYE UPON HIM.
YET ANOTHER COWERING IN FEAR OF THE WOMEN.
LIKE FATHER, LIKE SON.
I FEAR NO ONE, UNCLE.
NO WOMAN, NO MAN...
...NO GOD.

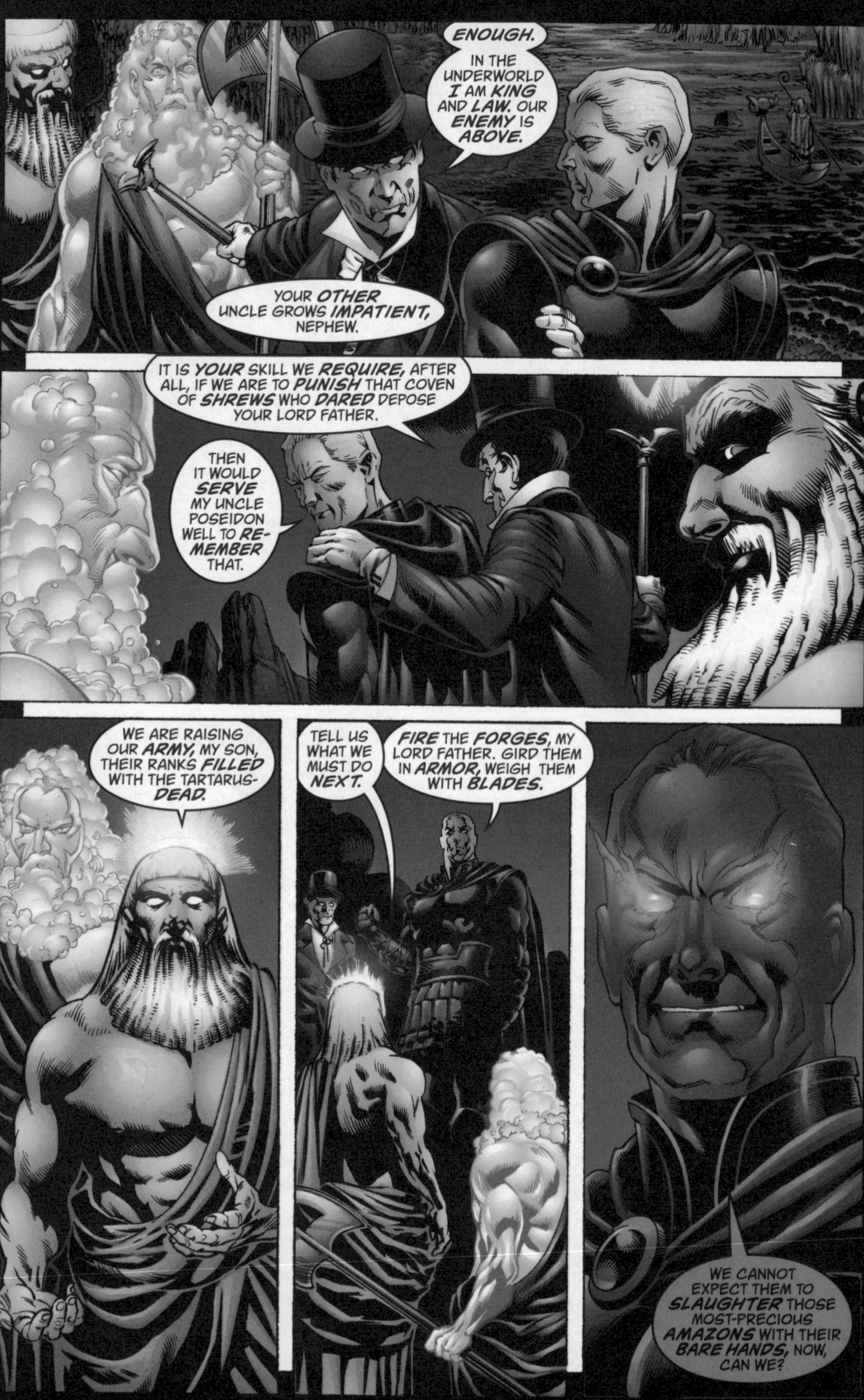
ENOUGH.
IN THE UNDERWORLD I AM KING AND LAW. OUR ENEMY IS ABOVE.
YOUR OTHER UNCLE GROWS IMPATIENT, NEPHEW.
IT IS YOUR SKILL WE REQUIRE, AFTER ALL, IF WE ARE TO PUNISH THAT COVEN OF SHREWS WHO DARED DEPOSE YOUR LORD FATHER.
THEN IT WOULD SERVE MY UNCLE POSEIDON WELL TO REMEMBER THAT.
WE ARE RAISING OUR ARMY, MY SON, THEIR RANKS FILLED WITH THE TARTARUS-DEAD.
TELL US WHAT WE MUST DO NEXT.
FIRE THE FORGES, MY LORD FATHER. GIRD THEM IN ARMOR, WEIGH THEM WITH BLADES.
WE CANNOT EXPECT THEM TO SLAUGHTER THOSE MOST-PRECIOUS AMAZONS WITH THEIR BARE HANDS, NOW, CAN WE?

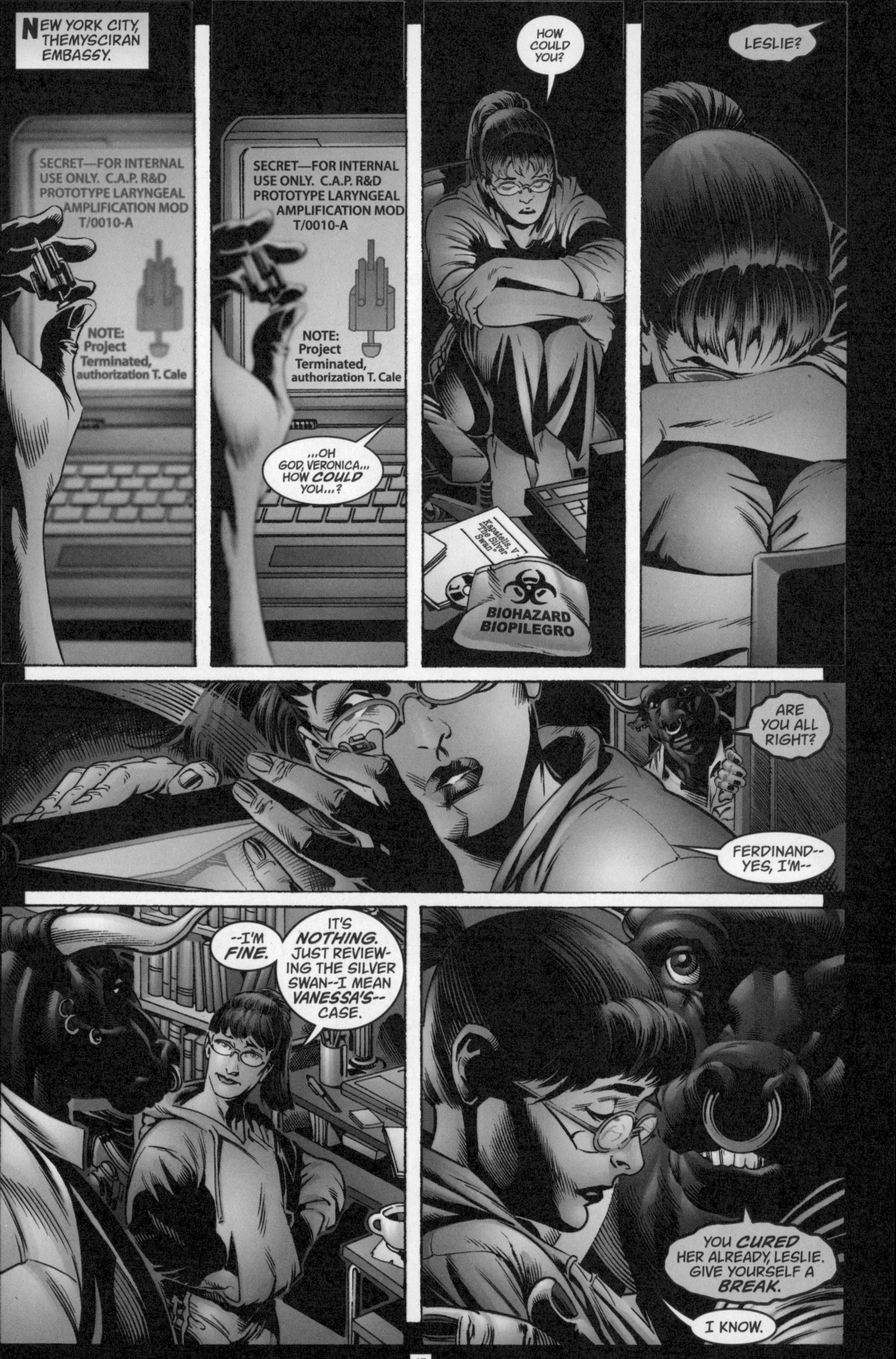
NEW YORK CITY, THEMYSCIRAN EMBASSY.
SECRET—FOR INTERNAL USE ONLY. C.A.P. R&D PROTOTYPE LARYNGEAL AMPLIFICATION MOD T/0010-A
NOTE: Project Terminated, authorization T. Cale
SECRET—FOR INTERNAL USE ONLY. C.A.P. R&D PROTOTYPE LARYNGEAL AMPLIFICATION MOD T/0010-A
NOTE: Project Terminated, authorization T. Cale
...OH GOD, VERONICA... HOW COULD YOU...?
HOW COULD YOU?
Kapatelis, V.
"The Silver Swan"
BIOHAZARD BIOPILEGRO
LESLIE?
ARE YOU ALL RIGHT?
FERDINAND-- YES, I'M--
--I'M FINE.
IT'S NOTHING. JUST REVIEWING THE SILVER SWAN--I MEAN VANESSA'S-- CASE.
YOU CURED HER ALREADY, LESLIE. GIVE YOURSELF A BREAK.
I KNOW.

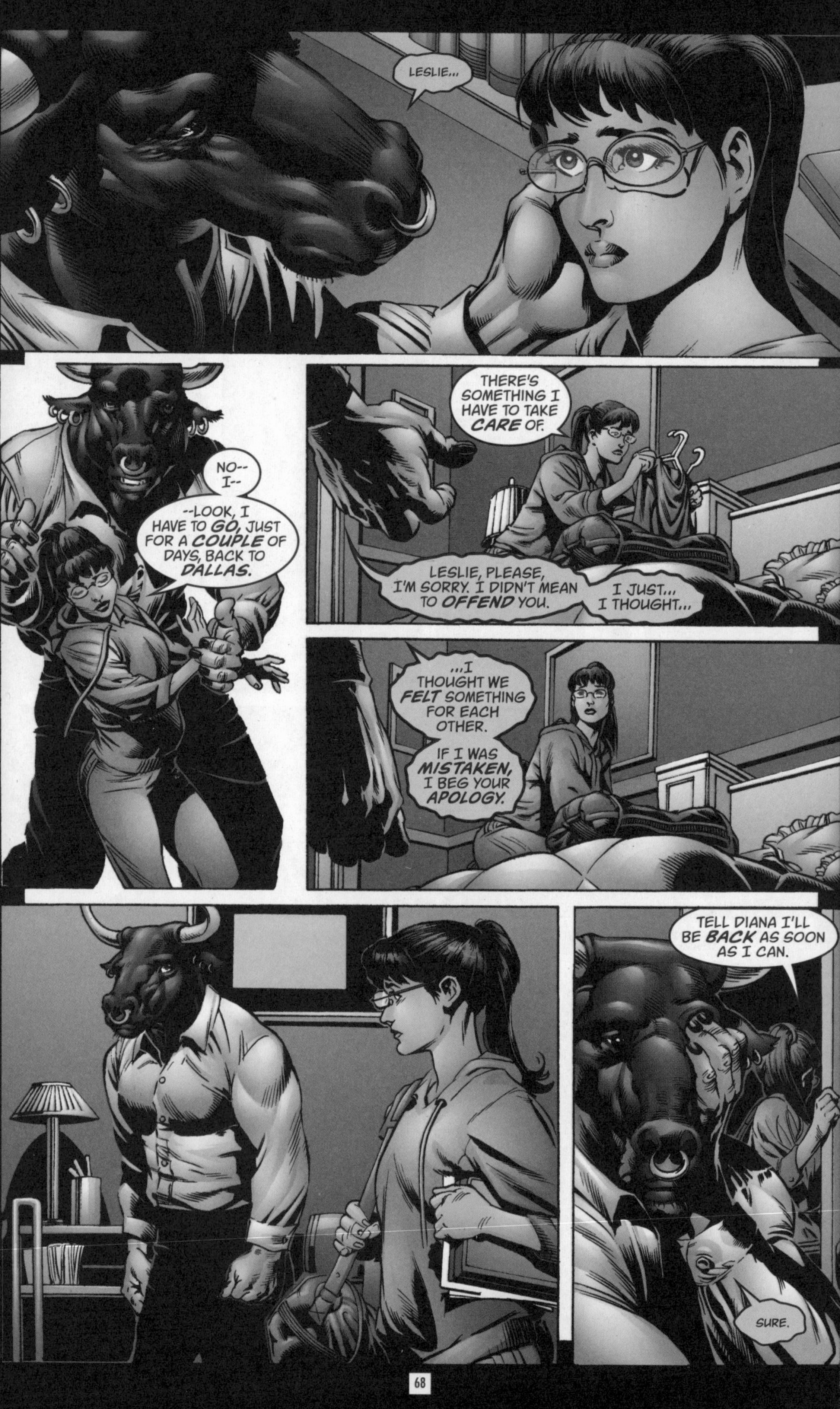

LESLIE...
NO-- I--
--LOOK, I HAVE TO GO, JUST FOR A COUPLE OF DAYS, BACK TO DALLAS.
THERE'S SOMETHING I HAVE TO TAKE CARE OF.
LESLIE, PLEASE, I'M SORRY. I DIDN'T MEAN TO OFFEND YOU.
I JUST... I THOUGHT...
...I THOUGHT WE FELT SOMETHING FOR EACH OTHER.
IF I WAS MISTAKEN, I BEG YOUR APOLOGY.
TELL DIANA I'LL BE BACK AS SOON AS I CAN.
SURE.

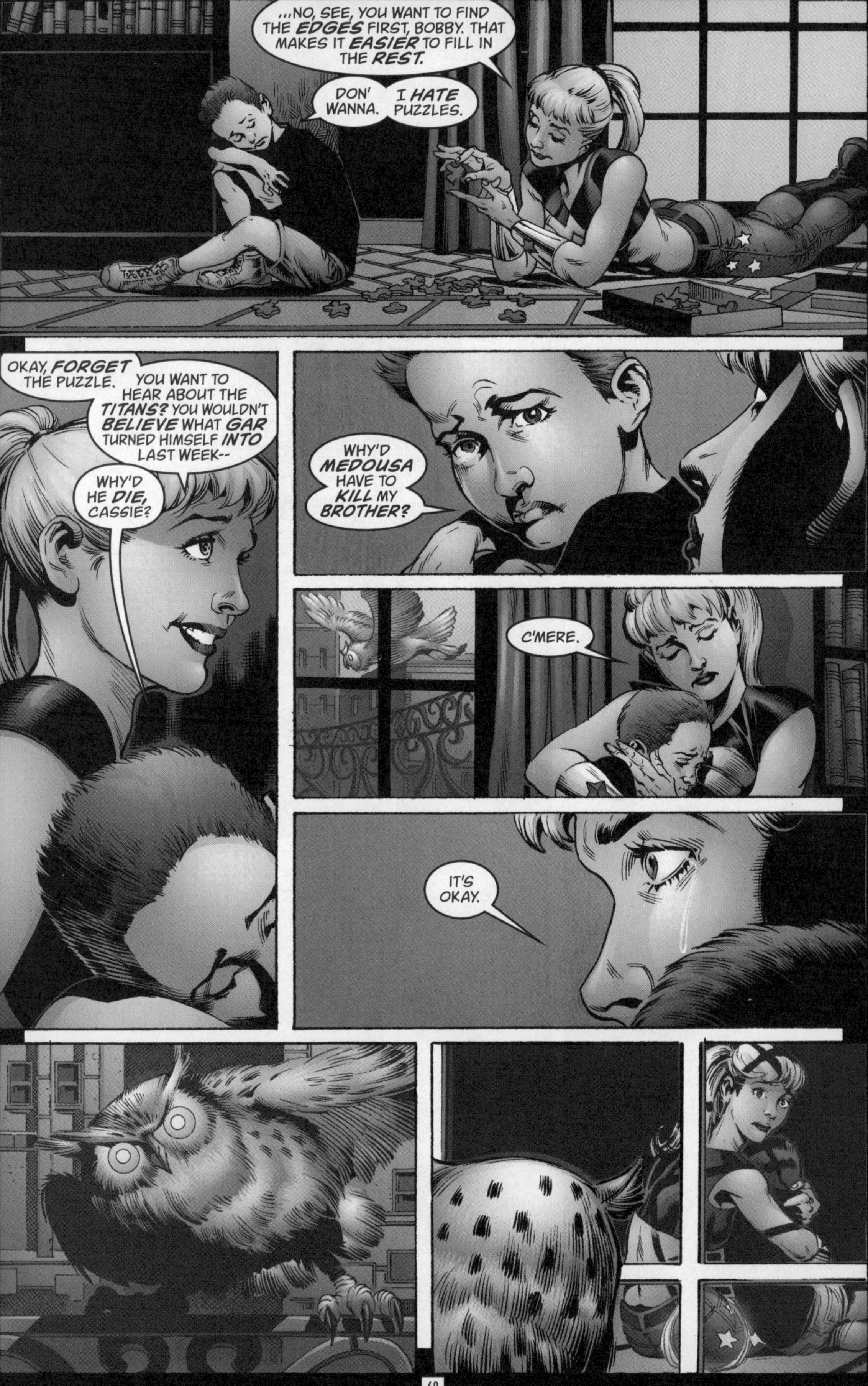
...NO, SEE, YOU WANT TO FIND THE EDGES FIRST, BOBBY. THAT MAKES IT EASIER TO FILL IN THE REST.
DON' WANNA.
I HATE PUZZLES.
OKAY, FORGET THE PUZZLE.
YOU WANT TO HEAR ABOUT THE TITANS? YOU WOULDN'T BELIEVE WHAT GAR TURNED HIMSELF INTO LAST WEEK--
WHY'D HE DIE, CASSIE?
WHY'D MEDOUSA HAVE TO KILL MY BROTHER?
C'MERE.
IT'S OKAY.

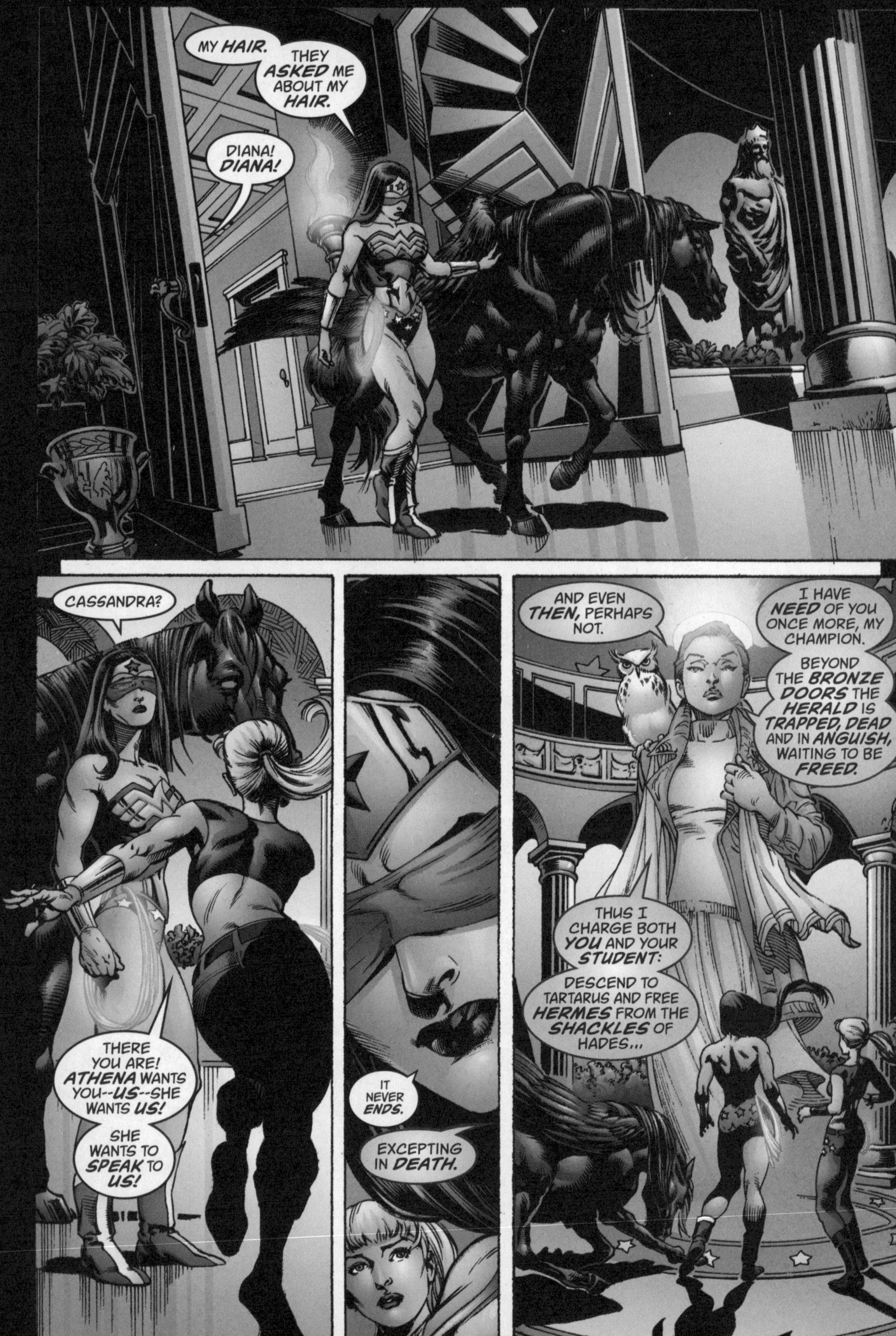

MY HAIR.
THEY ASKED ME ABOUT MY HAIR.
DIANA! DIANA!
CASSANDRA?
THERE YOU ARE! ATHENA WANTS YOU--US--SHE WANTS US!
SHE WANTS TO SPEAK TO US!
IT NEVER ENDS.
EXCEPTING IN DEATH.
AND EVEN THEN, PERHAPS NOT.
I HAVE NEED OF YOU ONCE MORE, MY CHAMPION.
BEYOND THE BRONZE DOORS THE HERALD IS TRAPPED, DEAD AND IN ANGUISH, WAITING TO BE FREED.
THUS I CHARGE BOTH YOU AND YOUR STUDENT:
DESCEND TO TARTARUS AND FREE HERMES FROM THE SHACKLES OF HADES...

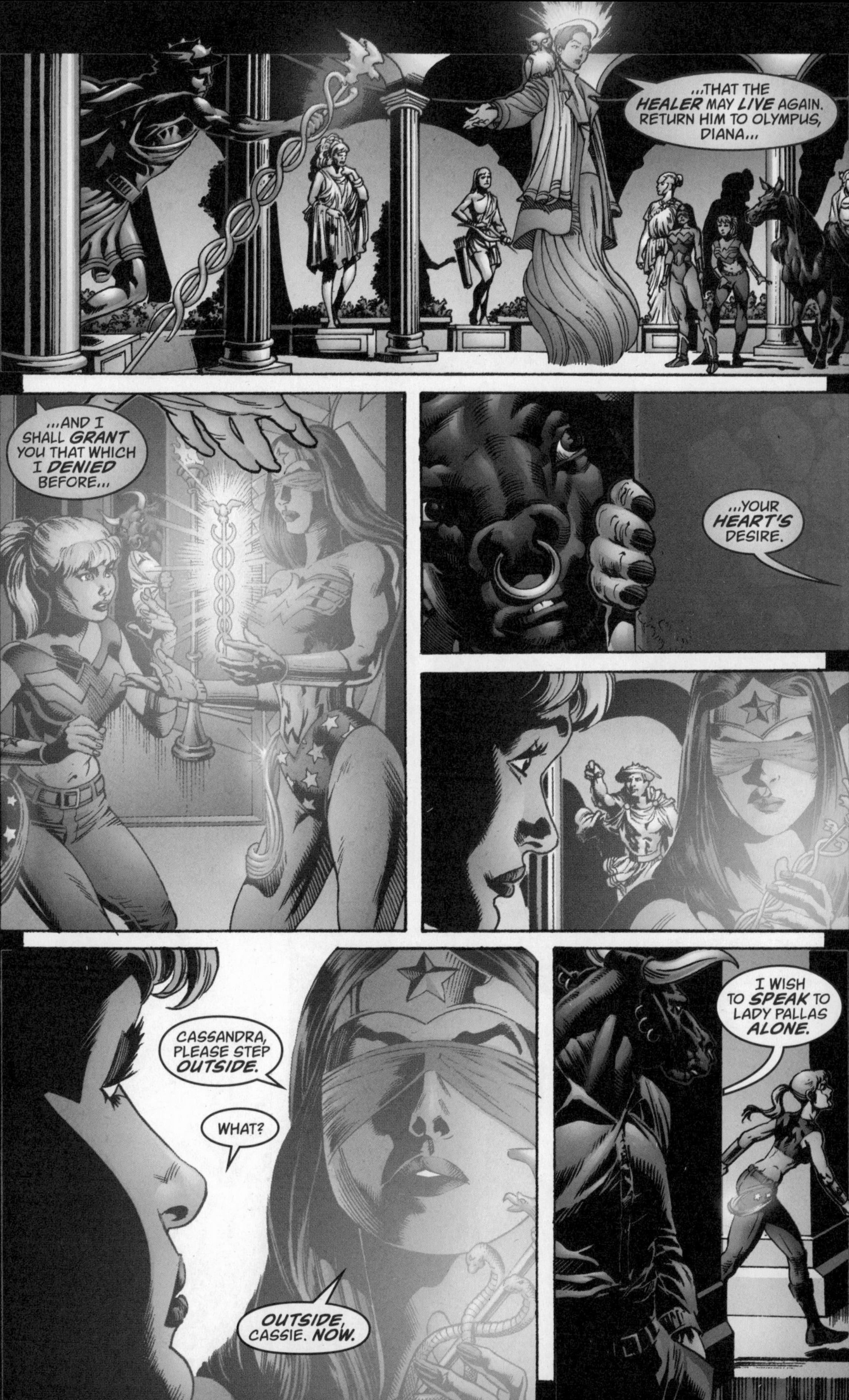
...THAT THE HEALER MAY LIVE AGAIN. RETURN HIM TO OLYMPUS, DIANA...
...AND I SHALL GRANT YOU THAT WHICH I DENIED BEFORE...
...YOUR HEART'S DESIRE.
CASSANDRA, PLEASE STEP OUTSIDE.
WHAT?
OUTSIDE, CASSIE. NOW.
I WISH TO SPEAK TO LADY PALLAS ALONE.

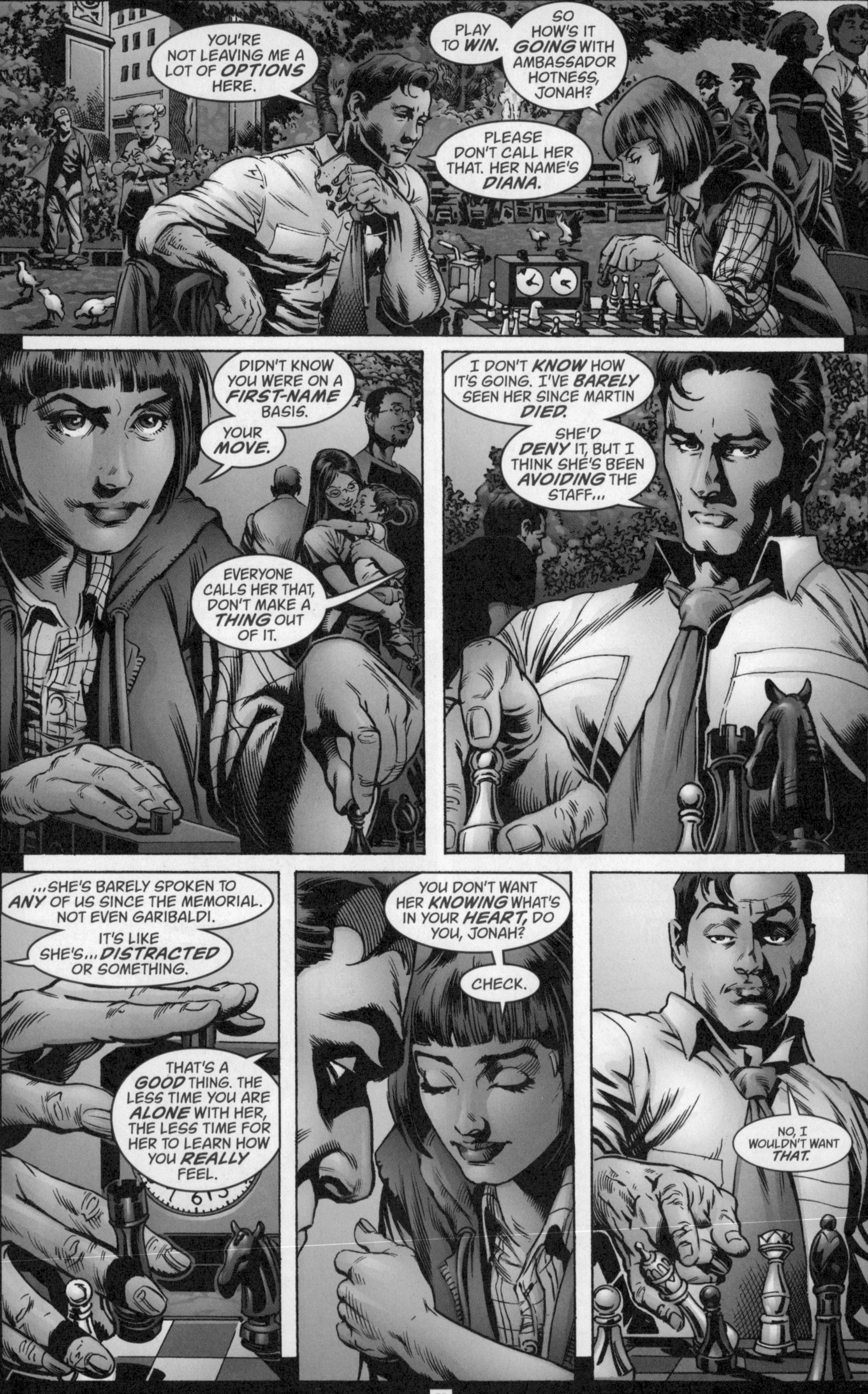

YOU'RE NOT LEAVING ME A LOT OF OPTIONS HERE.
PLAY TO WIN.
SO HOW'S IT GOING WITH AMBASSADOR HOTNESS, JONAH?
PLEASE DON'T CALL HER THAT. HER NAME'S DIANA.
DIDN'T KNOW YOU WERE ON A FIRST-NAME BASIS.
YOUR MOVE.
EVERYONE CALLS HER THAT, DON'T MAKE A THING OUT OF IT.
I DON'T KNOW HOW IT'S GOING. I'VE BARELY SEEN HER SINCE MARTIN DIED.
SHE'D DENY IT, BUT I THINK SHE'S BEEN AVOIDING THE STAFF...
...SHE'S BARELY SPOKEN TO ANY OF US SINCE THE MEMORIAL. NOT EVEN GARIBALDI.
IT'S LIKE SHE'S...DISTRACTED OR SOMETHING.
THAT'S A GOOD THING. THE LESS TIME YOU ARE ALONE WITH HER, THE LESS TIME FOR HER TO LEARN HOW YOU REALLY FEEL.
YOU DON'T WANT HER KNOWING WHAT'S IN YOUR HEART, DO YOU, JONAH?
CHECK.
NO, I WOULDN'T WANT THAT.

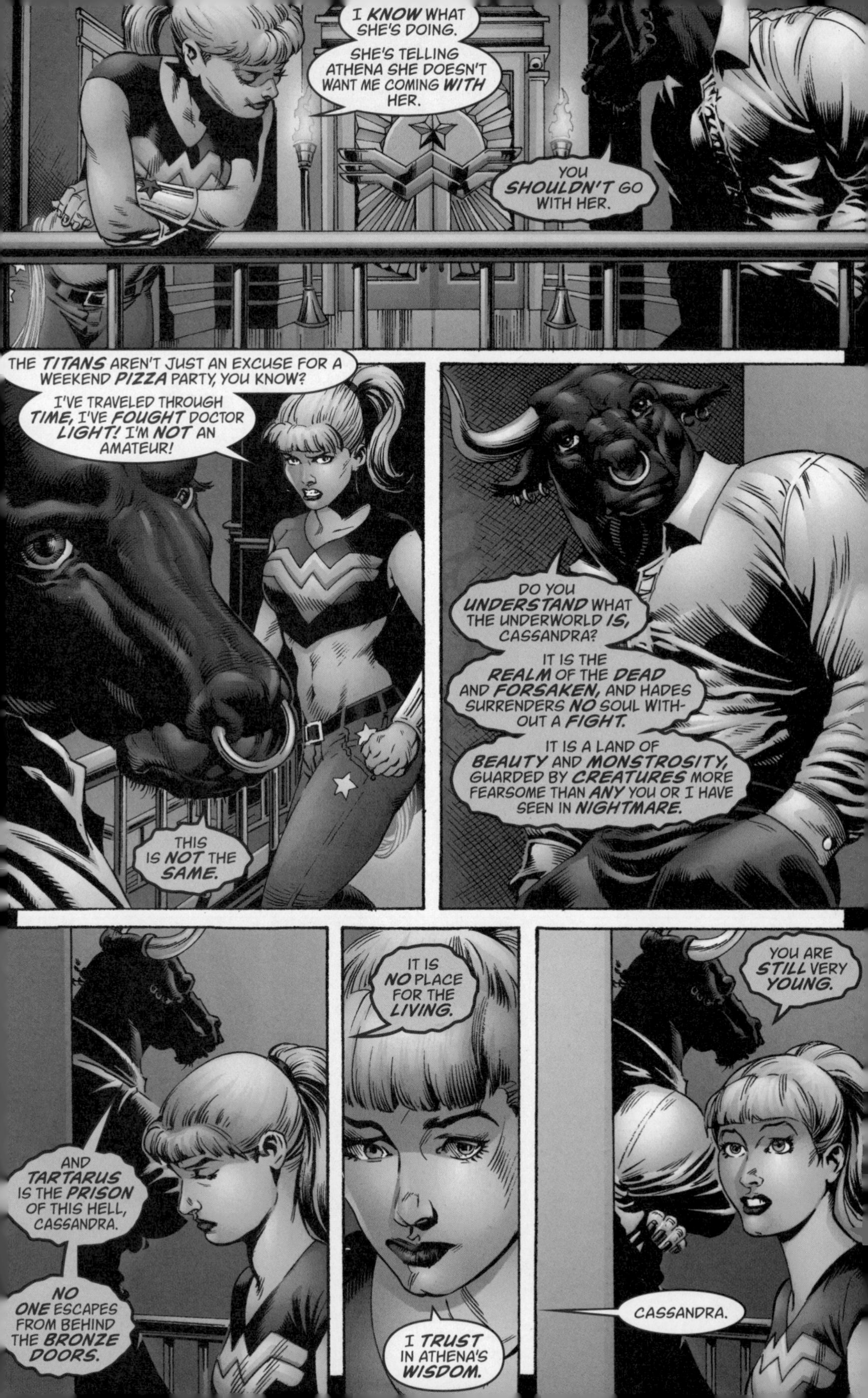
I KNOW WHAT SHE'S DOING.
SHE'S TELLING ATHENA SHE DOESN'T WANT ME COMING WITH HER.
YOU SHOULDN'T GO WITH HER.
THE TITANS AREN'T JUST AN EXCUSE FOR A WEEKEND PIZZA PARTY, YOU KNOW?
I'VE TRAVELED THROUGH TIME, I'VE FOUGHT DOCTOR LIGHT! I'M NOT AN AMATEUR!
THIS IS NOT THE SAME.
DO YOU UNDERSTAND WHAT THE UNDERWORLD IS, CASSANDRA?
IT IS THE REALM OF THE DEAD AND FORSAKEN, AND HADES SURRENDERS NO SOUL WITH-OUT A FIGHT.
IT IS A LAND OF BEAUTY AND MONSTROSITY, GUARDED BY CREATURES MORE FEARSOME THAN ANY YOU OR I HAVE SEEN IN NIGHTMARE.
AND TARTARUS IS THE PRISON OF THIS HELL, CASSANDRA.
NO ONE ESCAPES FROM BEHIND THE BRONZE DOORS.
IT IS NO PLACE FOR THE LIVING.
I TRUST IN ATHENA'S WISDOM.
YOU ARE STILL VERY YOUNG.
CASSANDRA.

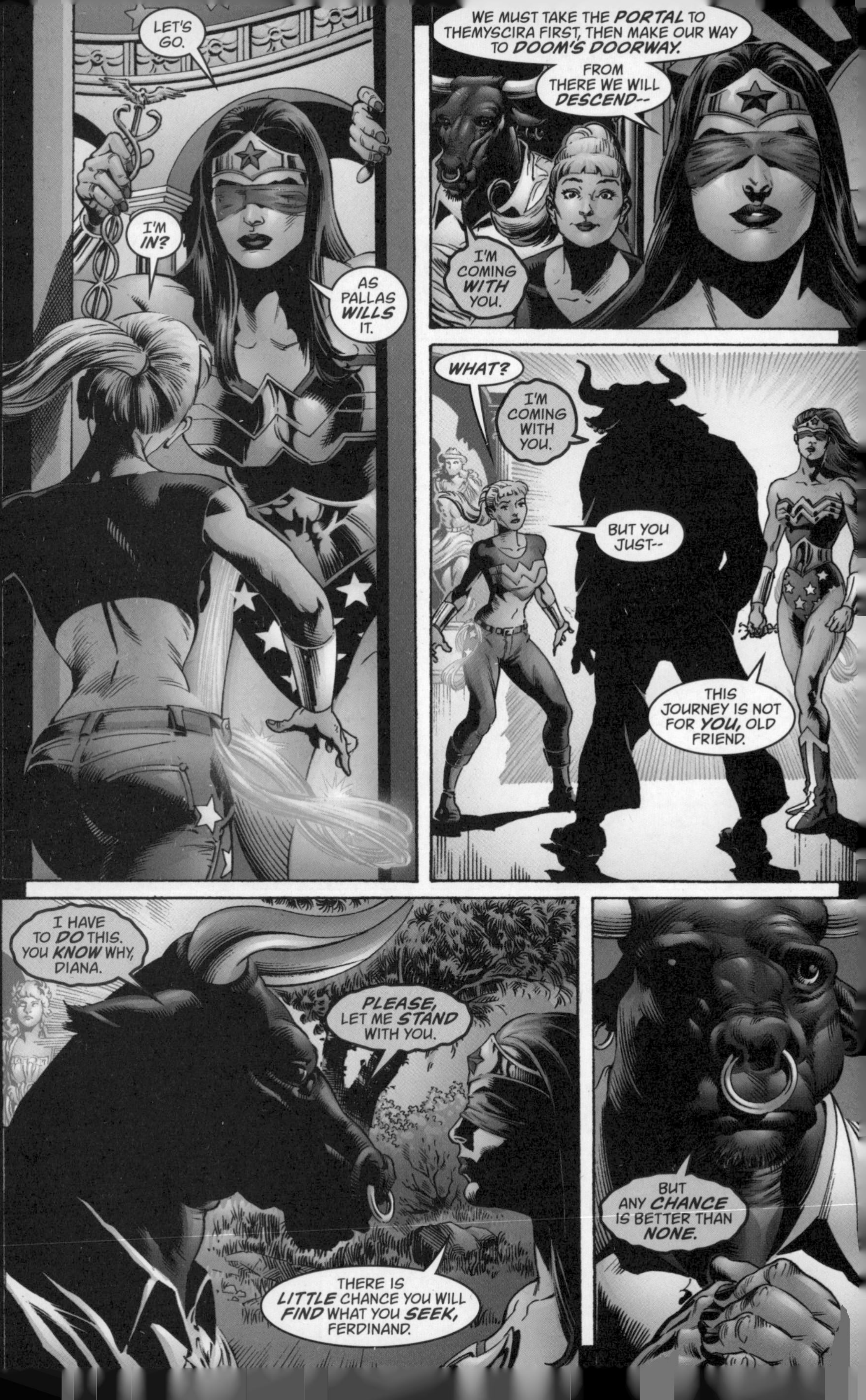
LET'S GO.
I'M IN?
AS PALLAS WILLS IT.
WE MUST TAKE THE PORTAL TO THEMYSCIRA FIRST, THEN MAKE OUR WAY TO DOOM'S DOORWAY.
FROM THERE WE WILL DESCEND--
I'M COMING WITH YOU.
WHAT?
I'M COMING WITH YOU.
BUT YOU JUST--
THIS JOURNEY IS NOT FOR YOU, OLD FRIEND.
I HAVE TO DO THIS. YOU KNOW WHY, DIANA.
PLEASE, LET ME STAND WITH YOU.
THERE IS LITTLE CHANCE YOU WILL FIND WHAT YOU SEEK, FERDINAND.
BUT ANY CHANCE IS BETTER THAN NONE.

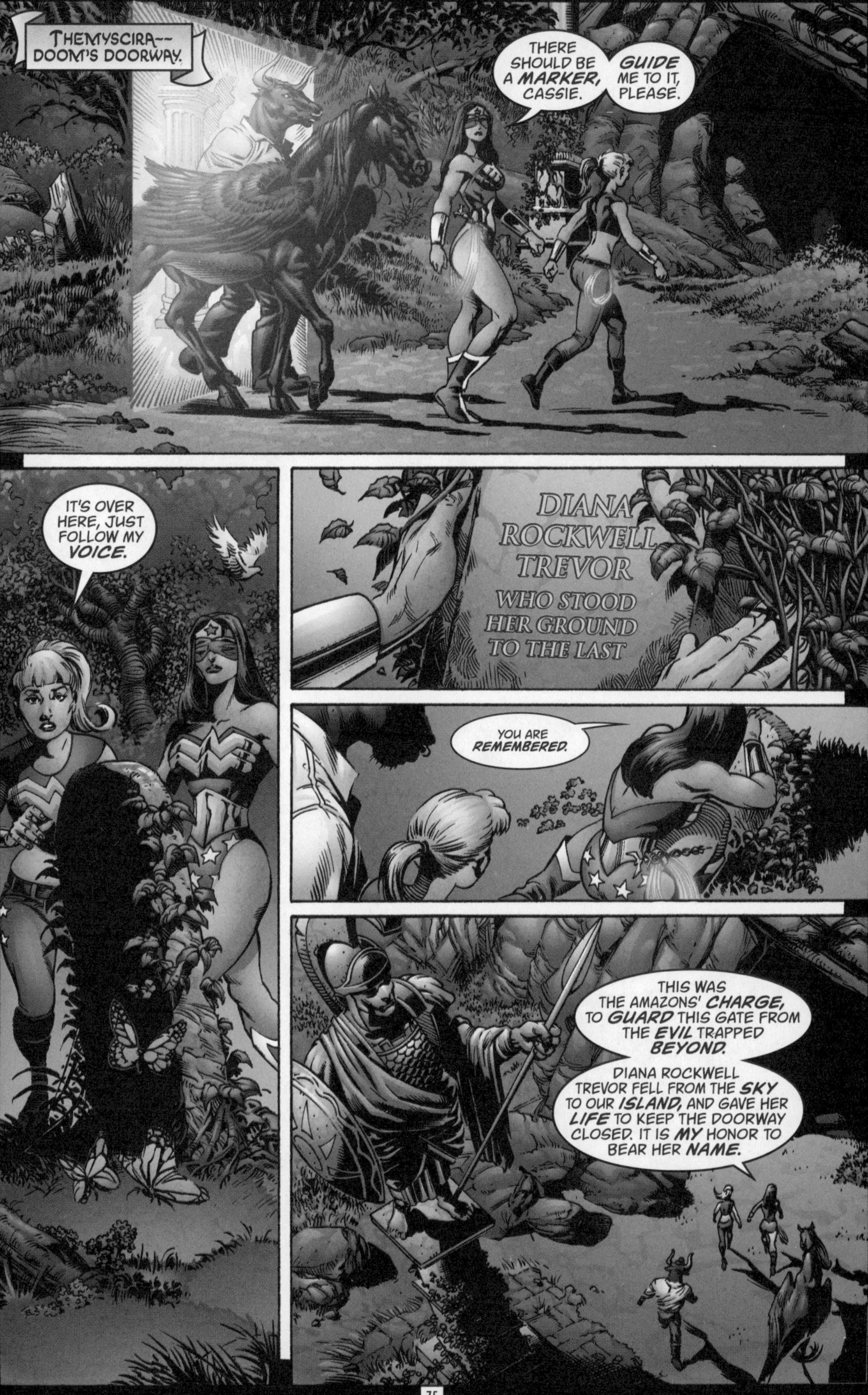
THEMYSCIRA--
DOOM'S DOORWAY.
THERE SHOULD BE A MARKER, CASSIE.
GUIDE ME TO IT, PLEASE.
IT'S OVER HERE, JUST FOLLOW MY VOICE.
DIANA ROCKWELL TREVOR
WHO STOOD HER GROUND TO THE LAST
YOU ARE REMEMBERED.
THIS WAS THE AMAZONS' CHARGE, TO GUARD THIS GATE FROM THE EVIL TRAPPED BEYOND.
DIANA ROCKWELL TREVOR FELL FROM THE SKY TO OUR ISLAND, AND GAVE HER LIFE TO KEEP THE DOORWAY CLOSED. IT IS MY HONOR TO BEAR HER NAME.

WHIMSICAL IS *NOT* ONE OF THEM.

SO IT'S *POSSIBLE,* THEN?

THE DOORWAY HAS BEEN *OPENED* SINCE, ALWAYS TO *SATISFY* THE *WHIM* OF THE *GODS.*

IS THAT WHAT *THIS* IS? ATHENA'S *WHIM?*

ATHENA IS *MANY* THINGS, CASSIE.

WHAT SHE'S COMMANDED OF US, IT *CAN* BE DONE?

WE CAN BRING HERMES BACK FROM THE *DEAD?*

YES.

WHAT ABOUT YOUR *MOTHER?* OR *DONNA?* ARE *THEY* TRAPPED IN THE UNDER-WORLD, TOO?

OR DO YOU GET YOUR *VISION* BACK FOR SAVING A *GOD* AND TO *HELL* WITH THE OTHERS?

THAT *IS* WHAT ATHENA'S *PROMISING* YOU, ISN'T IT? YOU DO HER *ERRAND,* YOU GET YOUR *EYESIGHT* BACK?

THAT *DOES* SEEM TO BE *IMPLIED,* DOESN'T IT?

BUT THAT IS *NOT* WHY WE ARE HERE.

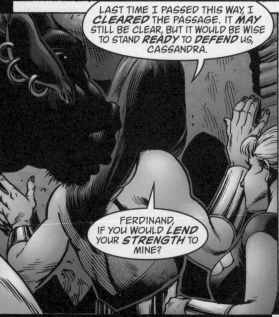

LAST TIME I PASSED THIS WAY, I *CLEARED* THE PASSAGE. IT *MAY* STILL BE CLEAR, BUT IT WOULD BE WISE TO STAND *READY* TO *DEFEND* US, CASSANDRA.

FERDINAND, IF YOU WOULD *LEND* YOUR *STRENGTH* TO MINE?

BE READY TO MOVE *QUICKLY*--

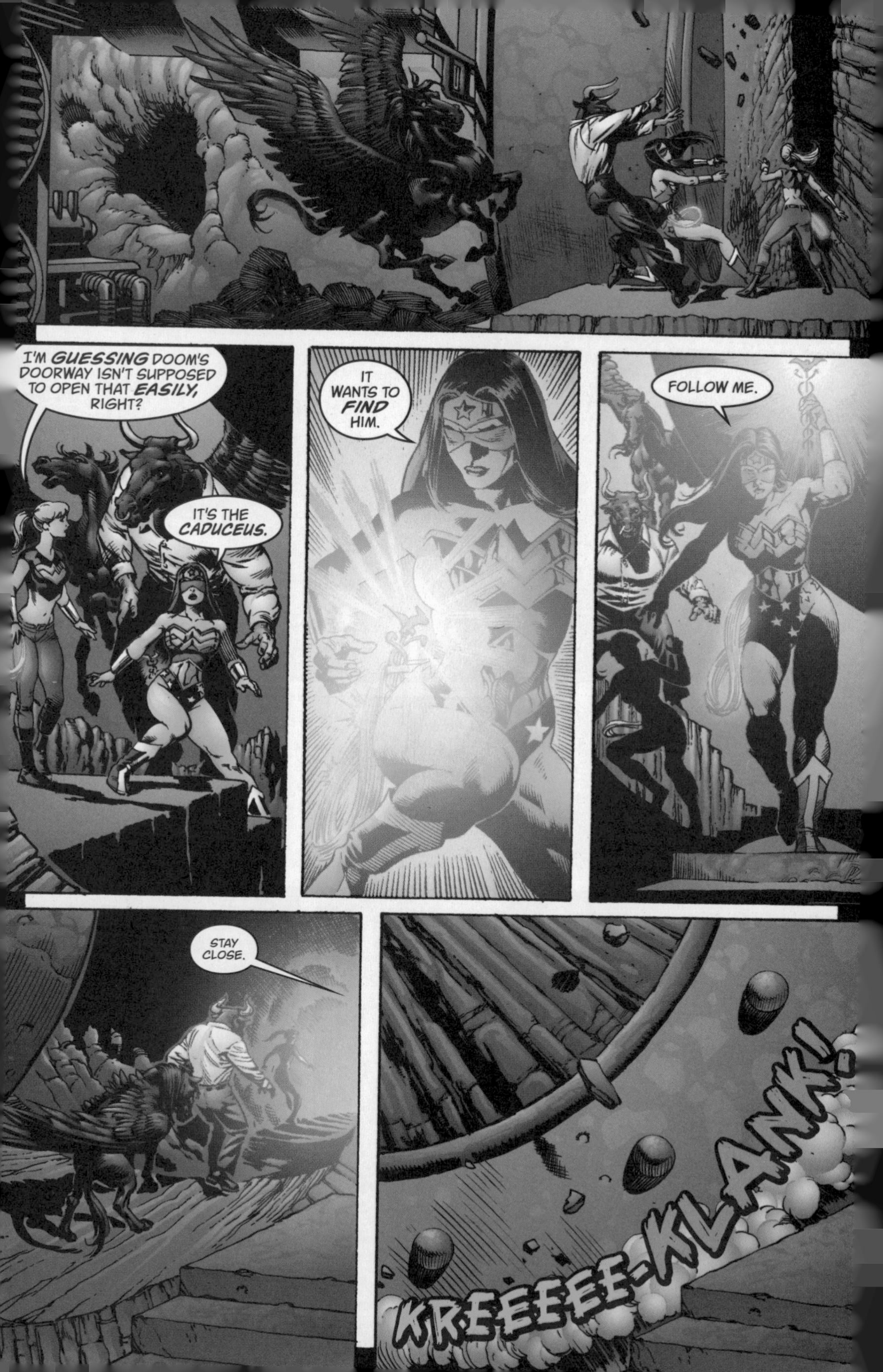
I'M GUESSING DOOM'S DOORWAY ISN'T SUPPOSED TO OPEN THAT EASILY, RIGHT?
IT'S THE CADUCEUS.
IT WANTS TO FIND HIM.
FOLLOW ME.
STAY CLOSE.
KREEEEEE-KLANK!

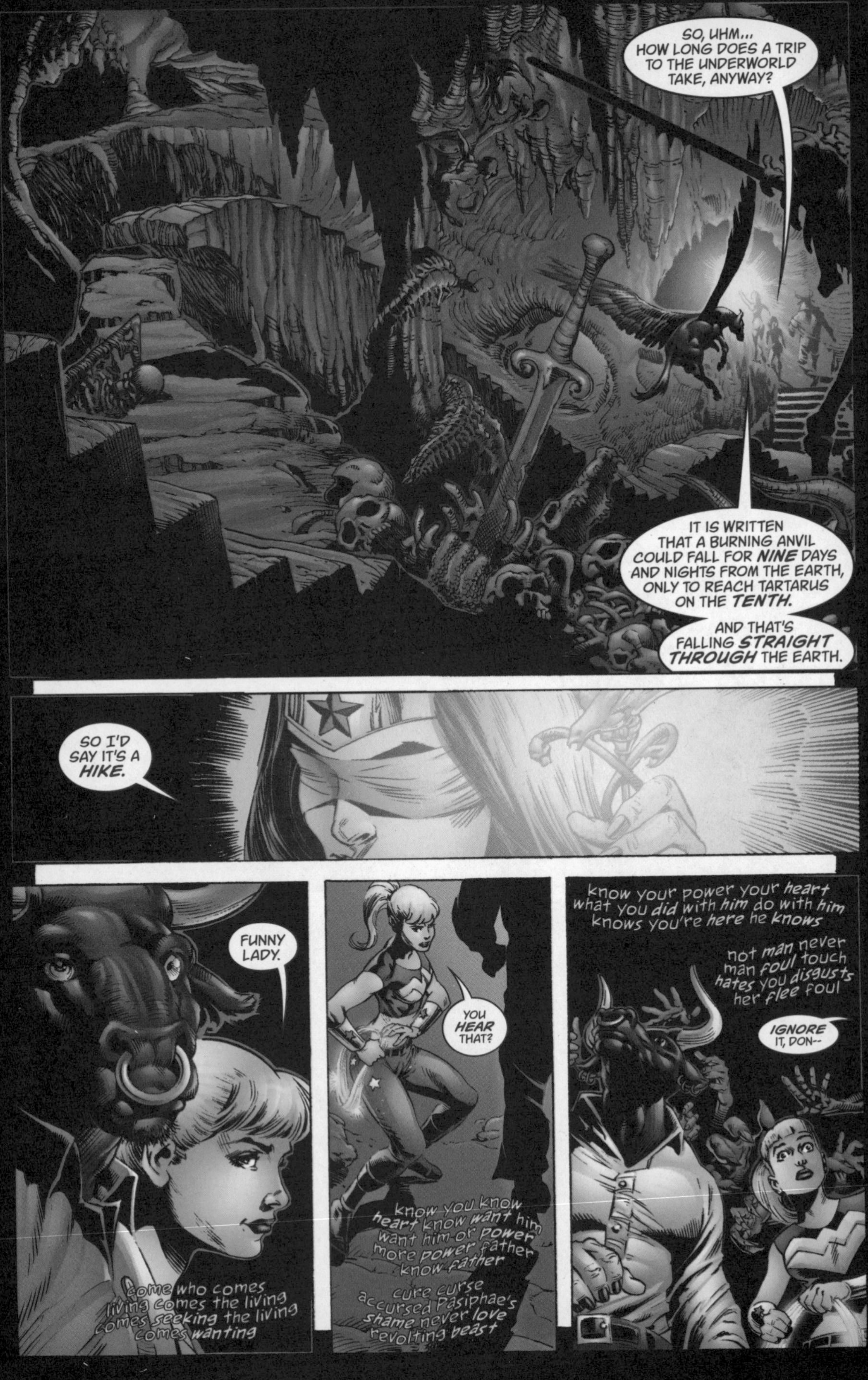
SO, UHM... HOW LONG DOES A TRIP TO THE UNDERWORLD TAKE, ANYWAY?
IT IS WRITTEN THAT A BURNING ANVIL COULD FALL FOR NINE DAYS AND NIGHTS FROM THE EARTH, ONLY TO REACH TARTARUS ON THE TENTH.
AND THAT'S FALLING STRAIGHT THROUGH THE EARTH.
SO I'D SAY IT'S A HIKE.
FUNNY LADY.
come who comes living comes the living comes seeking the living comes wanting
YOU HEAR THAT?
know you know heart know want him want him or power more power father know father
cure curse accursed Pasiphae's shame never love revolting beast
know your power your heart what you did with him do with him knows you're here he knows
not man never man foul touch hates you disgusts her flee foul
IGNORE IT, DON--

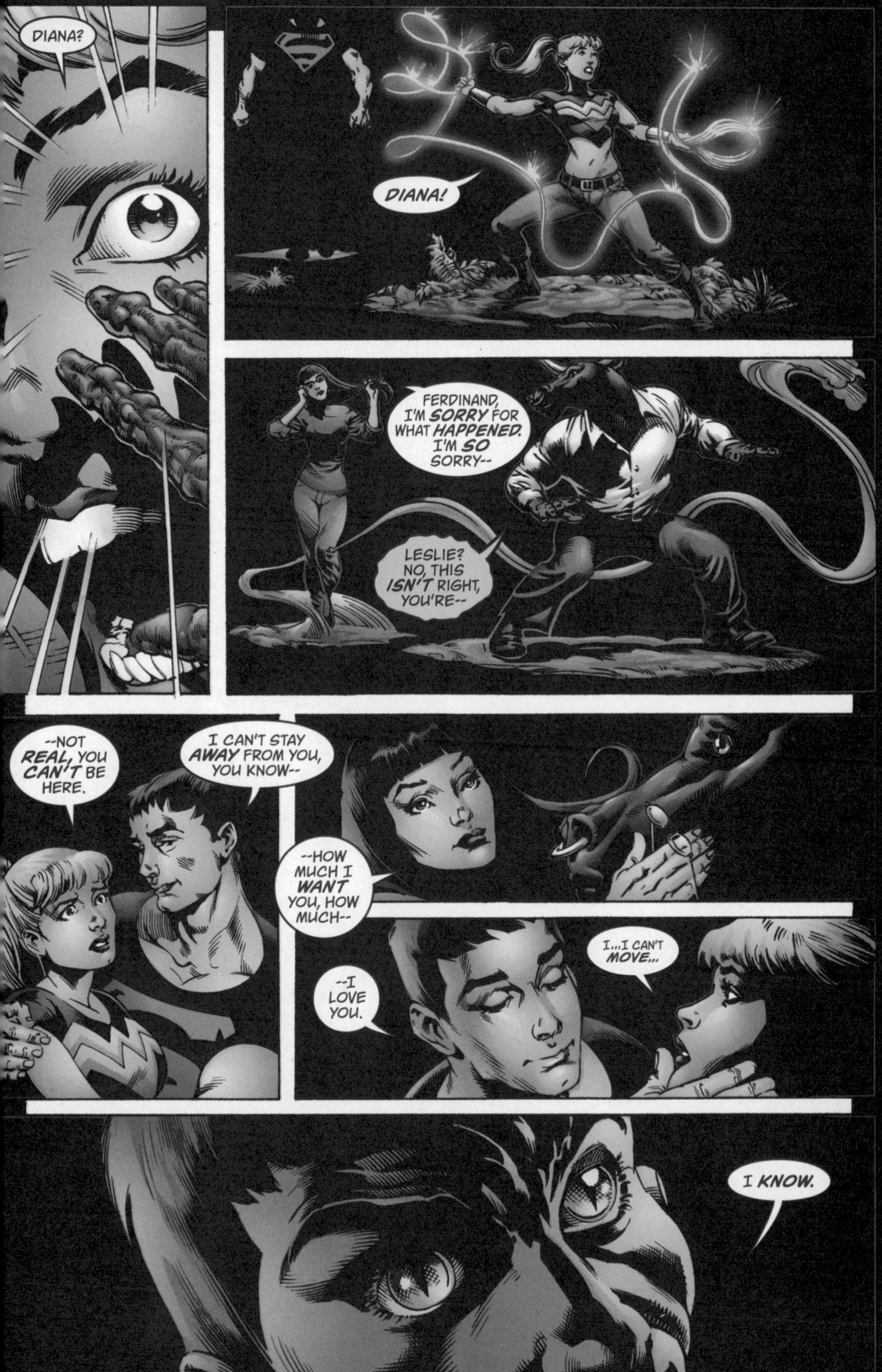
DIANA?
DIANA!
FERDINAND, I'M SORRY FOR WHAT HAPPENED. I'M SO SORRY--
LESLIE? NO, THIS ISN'T RIGHT, YOU'RE--
--NOT REAL, YOU CAN'T BE HERE.
I CAN'T STAY AWAY FROM YOU, YOU KNOW--
--HOW MUCH I WANT YOU, HOW MUCH--
--I LOVE YOU.
I...I CAN'T MOVE...
I KNOW.

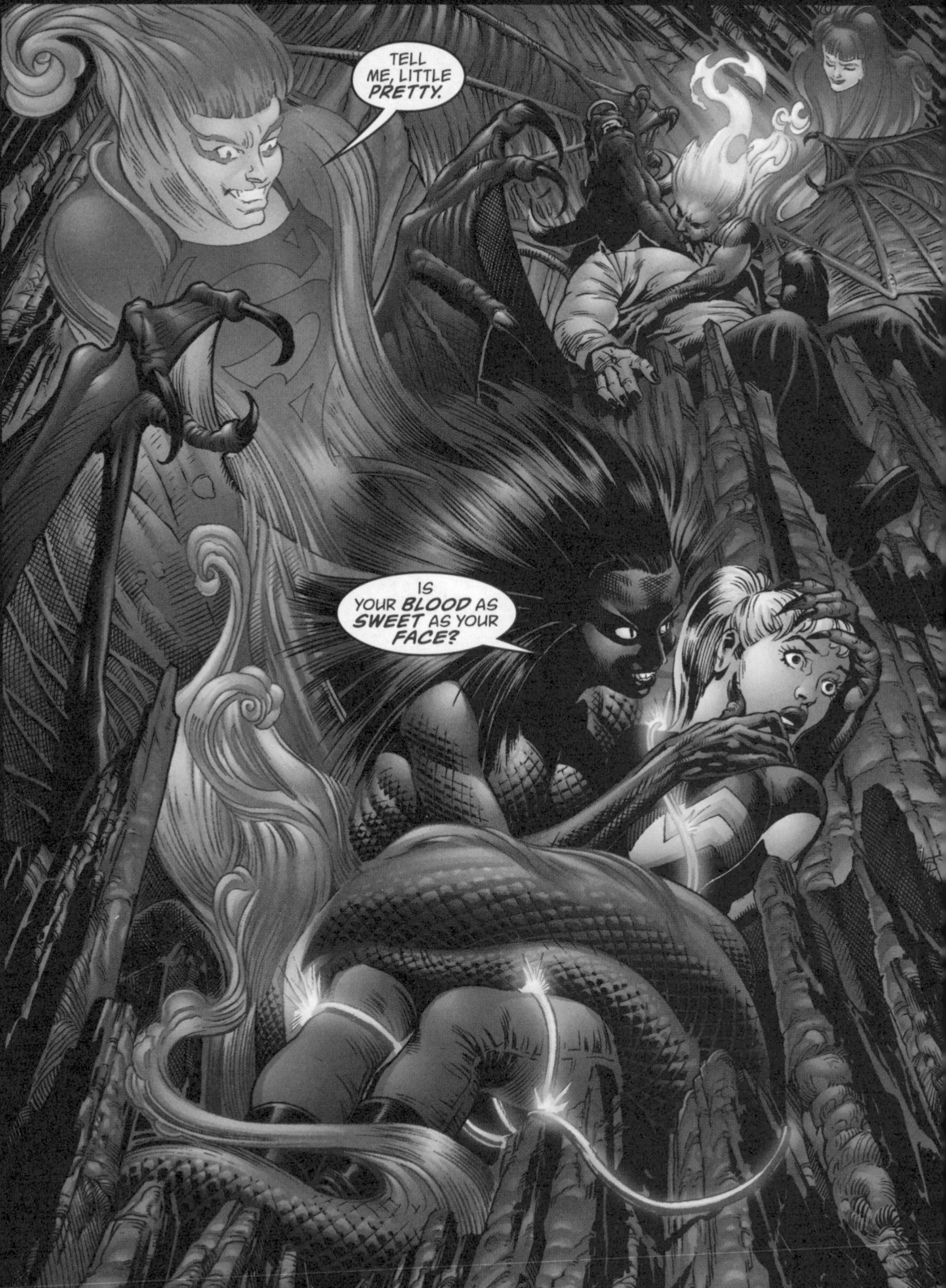
TELL ME, LITTLE PRETTY.
IS YOUR BLOOD AS SWEET AS YOUR FACE?

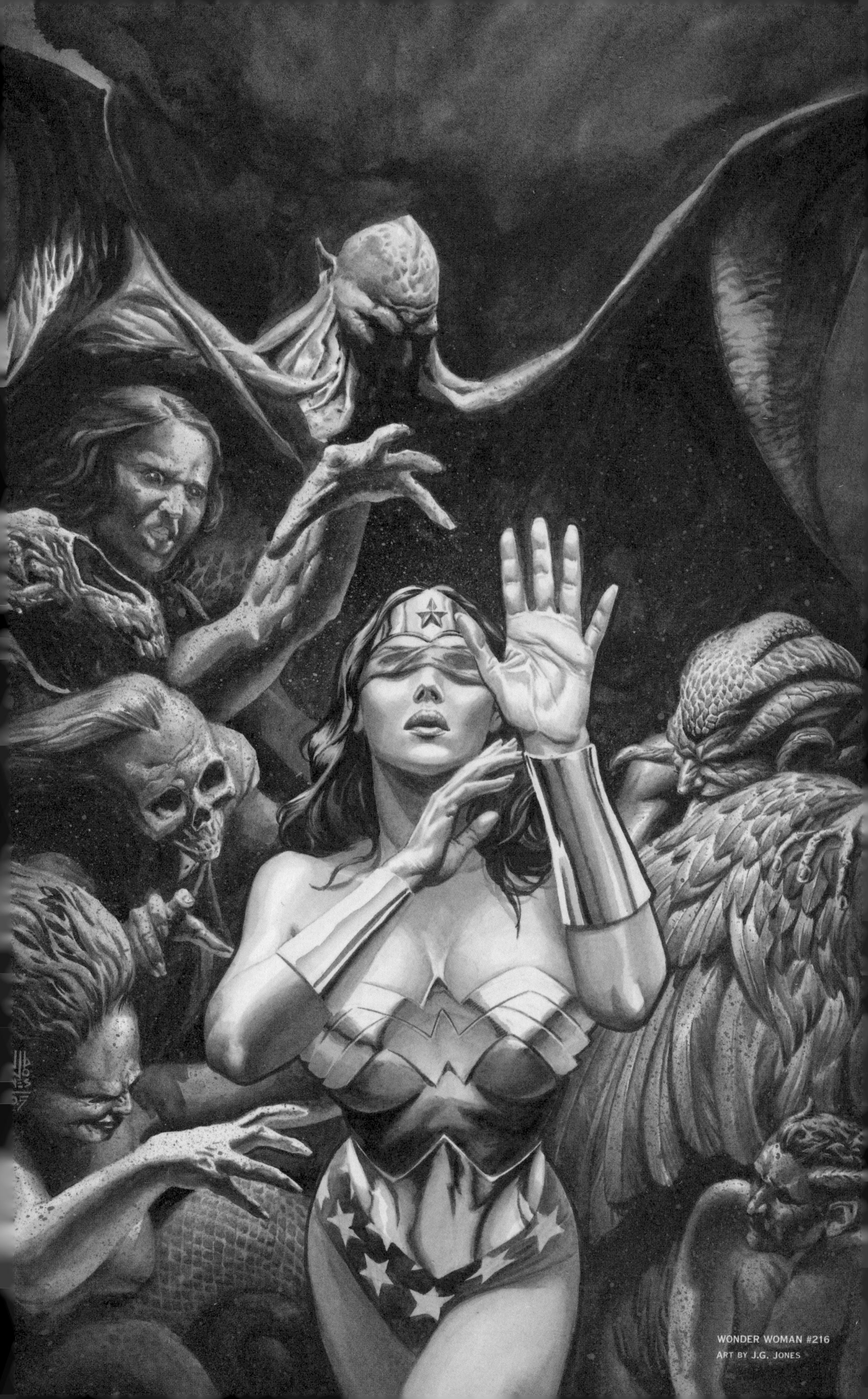

WONDER WOMAN #216
ART BY J.G. JONES

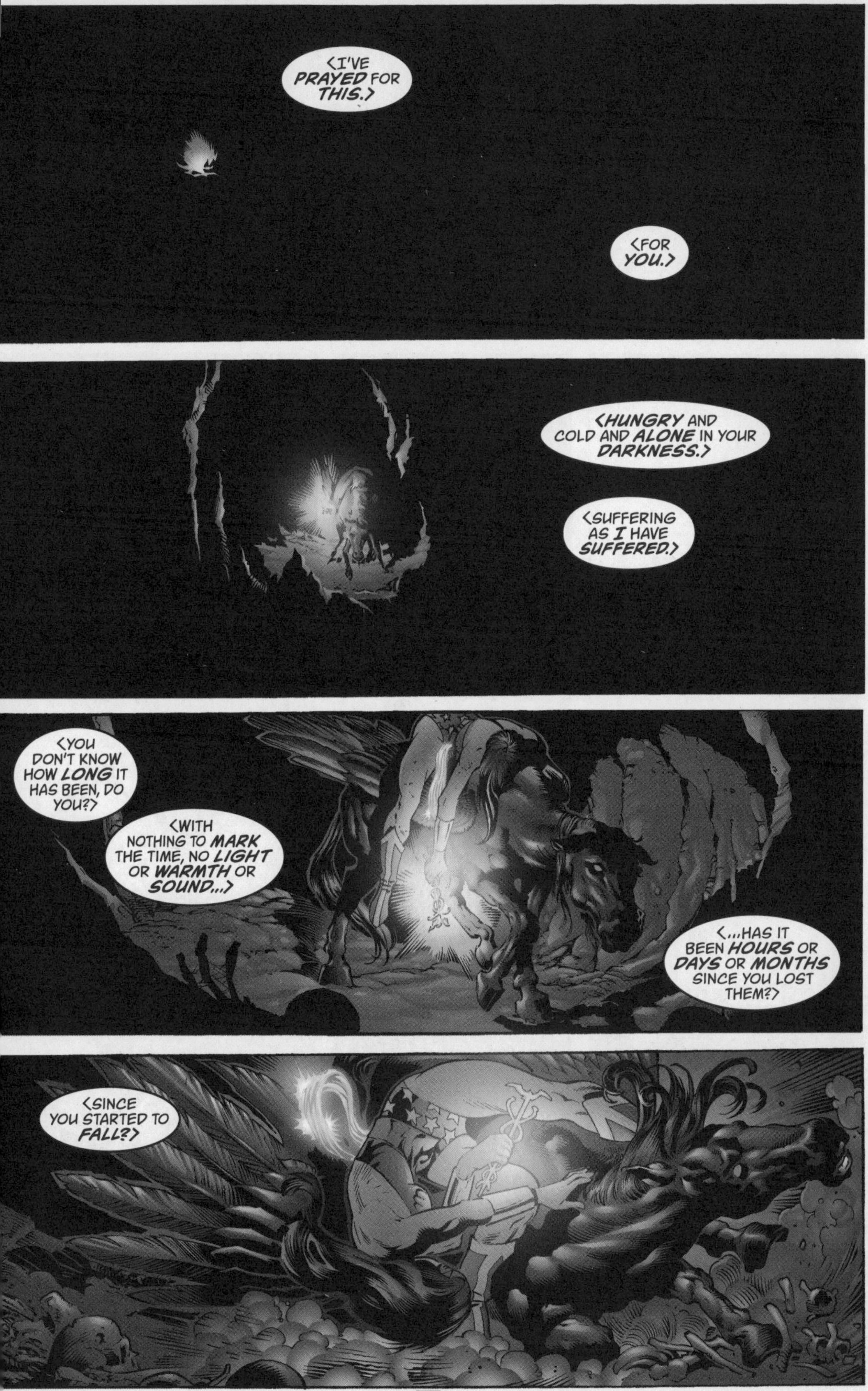
<I'VE PRAYED FOR THIS.>
<FOR YOU.>
<HUNGRY AND COLD AND ALONE IN YOUR DARKNESS.>
<SUFFERING AS I HAVE SUFFERED.>
<YOU DON'T KNOW HOW LONG IT HAS BEEN, DO YOU?>
<WITH NOTHING TO MARK THE TIME, NO LIGHT OR WARMTH OR SOUND...>
<...HAS IT BEEN HOURS OR DAYS OR MONTHS SINCE YOU LOST THEM?>
<SINCE YOU STARTED TO FALL?>

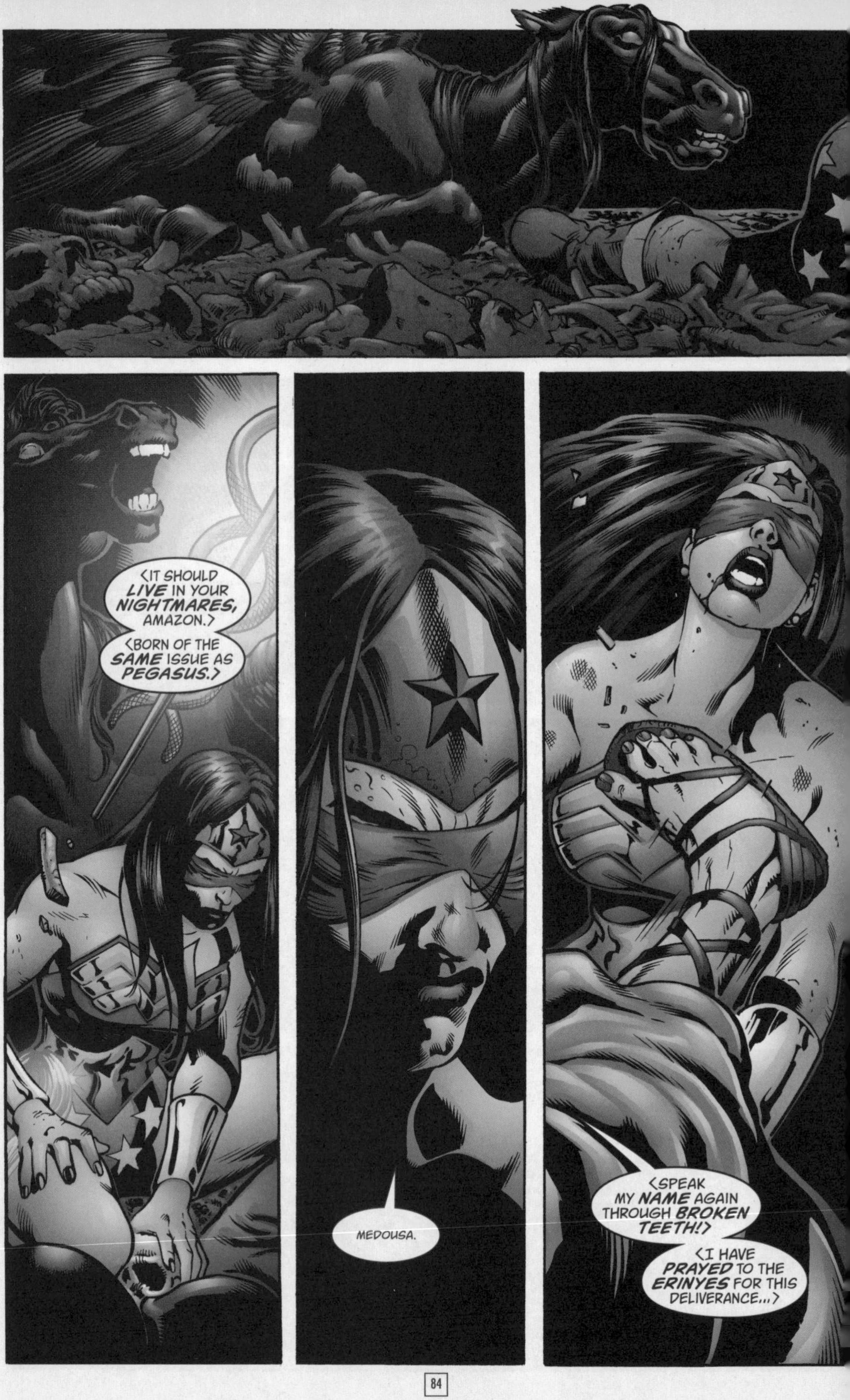

<IT SHOULD LIVE IN YOUR NIGHTMARES, AMAZON.>
<BORN OF THE SAME ISSUE AS PEGASUS.>
MEDOUSA.
<SPEAK MY NAME AGAIN THROUGH BROKEN TEETH!>
<I HAVE PRAYED TO THE ERINYES FOR THIS DELIVERANCE...>

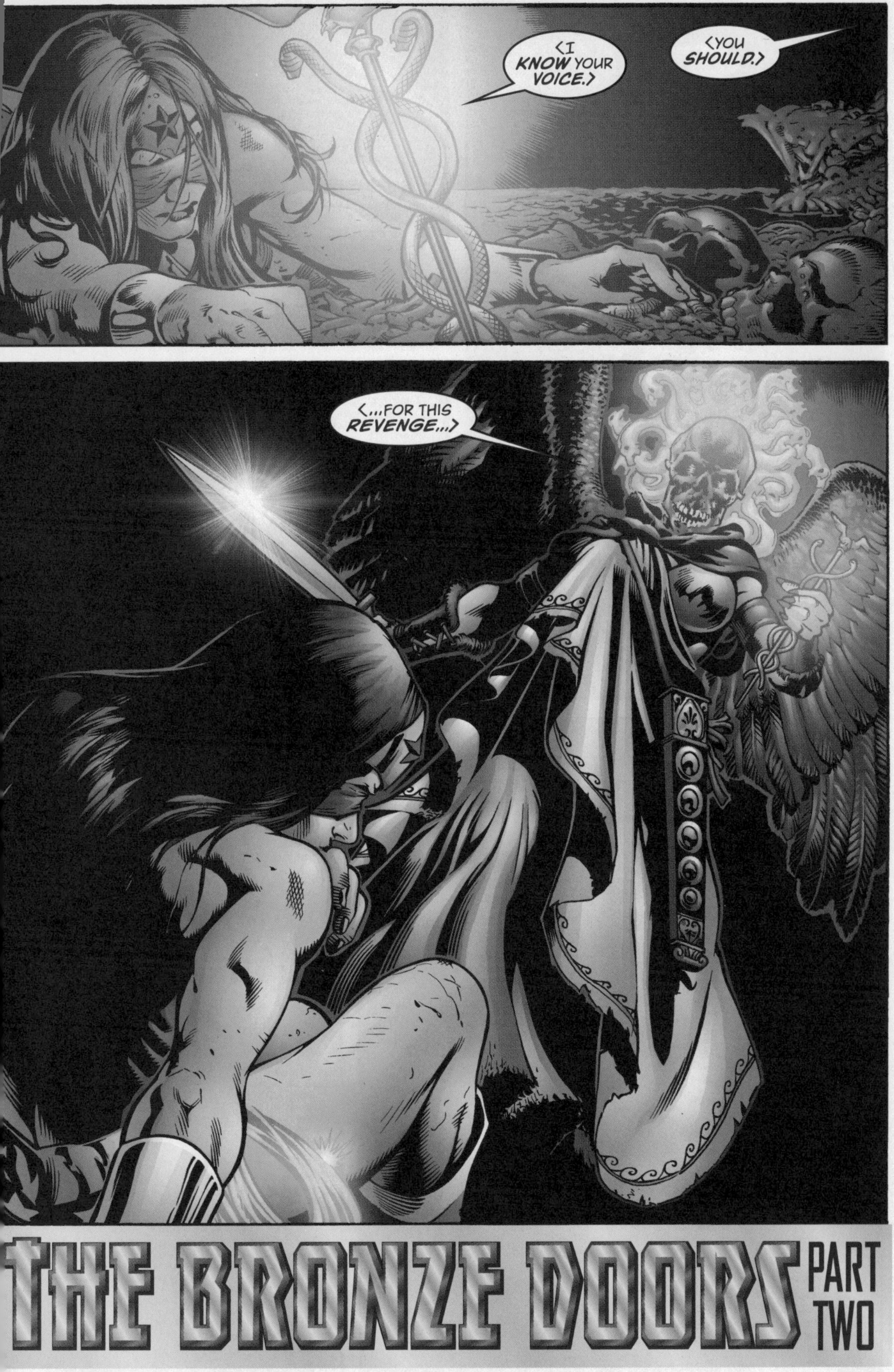
<I KNOW YOUR VOICE.>
<YOU SHOULD.>
<...FOR THIS REVENGE...>
THE BRONZE DOORS PART TWO

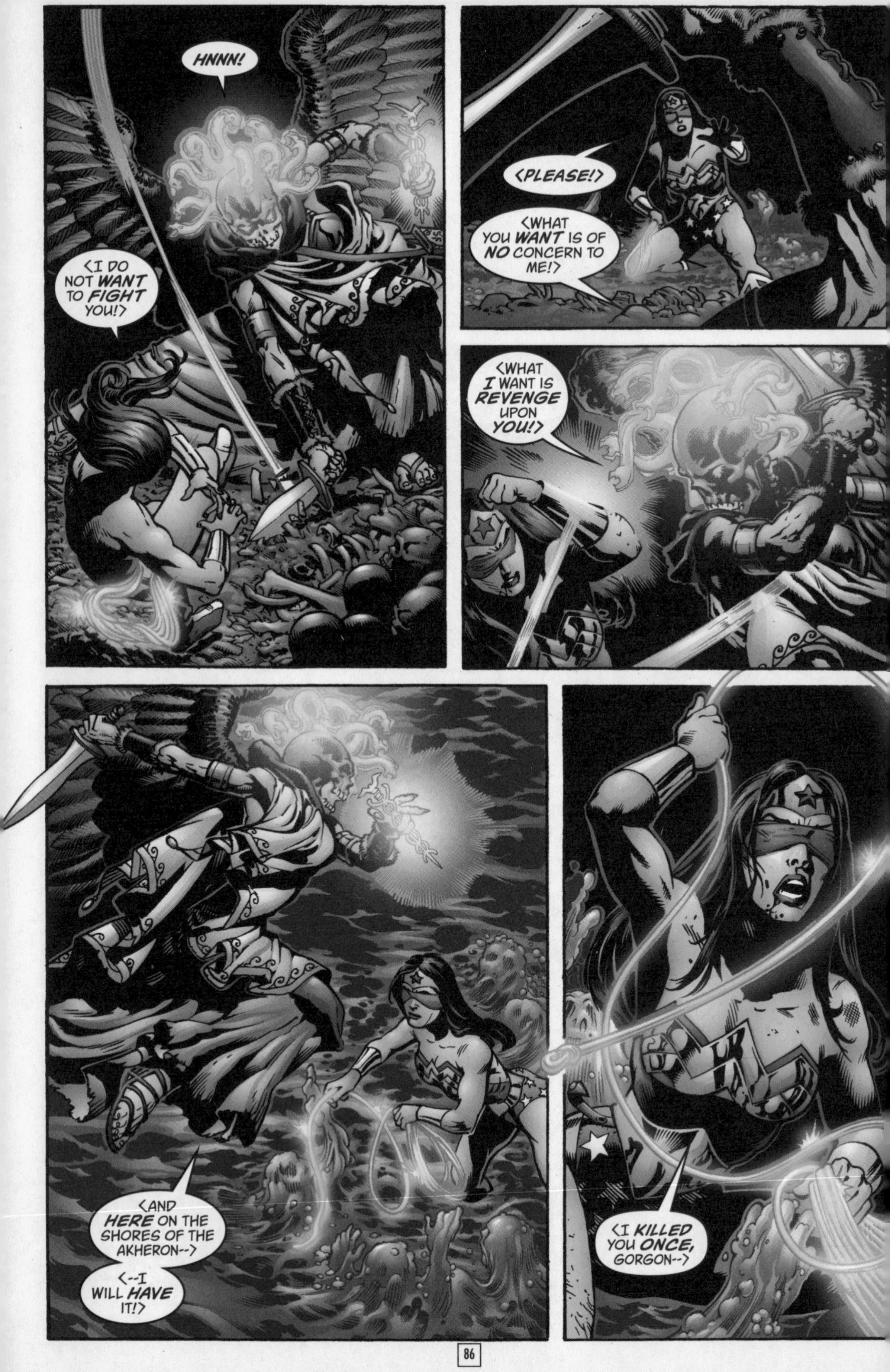
HNNN!
<I DO NOT WANT TO FIGHT YOU!>
<PLEASE!>
<WHAT YOU WANT IS OF NO CONCERN TO ME!>
<WHAT I WANT IS REVENGE UPON YOU!>
<AND HERE ON THE SHORES OF THE AKHERON-->
<--I WILL HAVE IT!>
<I KILLED YOU ONCE, GORGON-->

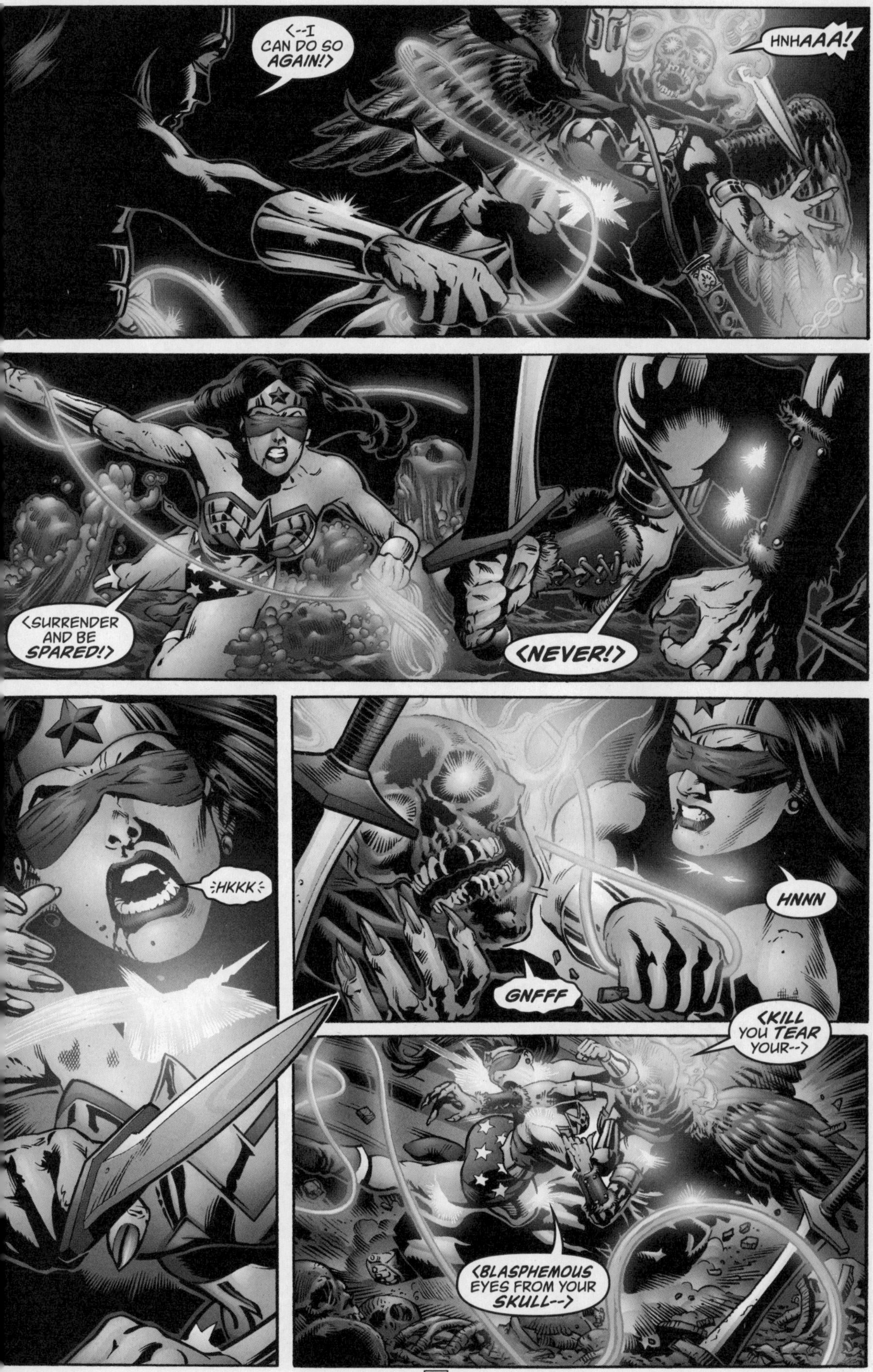

<--I CAN DO SO AGAIN!>
HNHAAA!
<SURRENDER AND BE SPARED!>
<NEVER!>
HKKK
HNNN
GNFFF
<KILL YOU TEAR YOUR-->
<BLASPHEMOUS EYES FROM YOUR SKULL-->

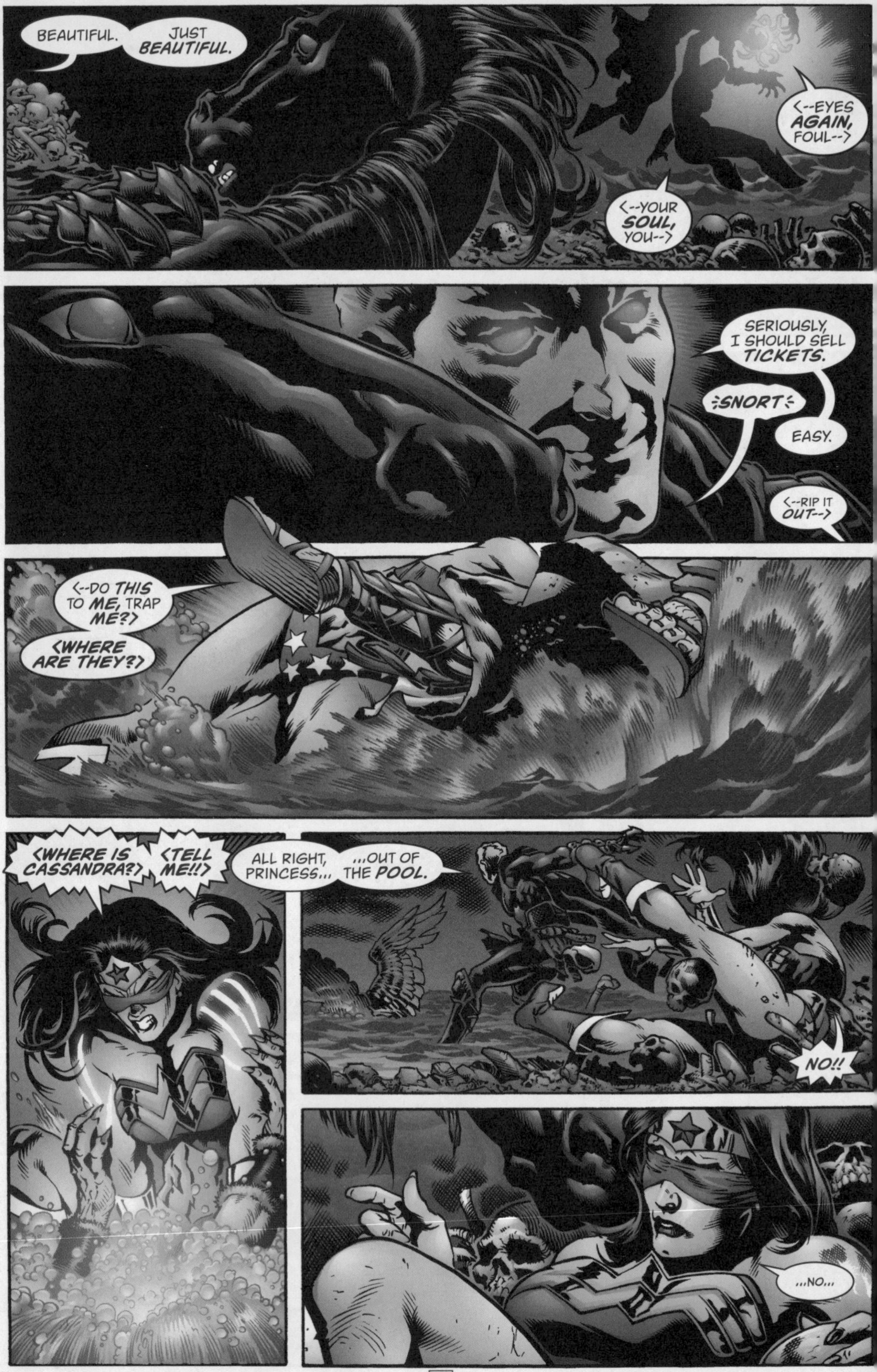
BEAUTIFUL.
JUST BEAUTIFUL.
<--EYES AGAIN, FOUL-->
<--YOUR SOUL, YOU-->
SERIOUSLY, I SHOULD SELL TICKETS.
SNORT
EASY.
<--RIP IT OUT-->
<--DO THIS TO ME, TRAP ME?>
<WHERE ARE THEY?>
<WHERE IS CASSANDRA?>
<TELL ME!!>
ALL RIGHT, PRINCESS...
...OUT OF THE POOL.
NO!!
...NO...

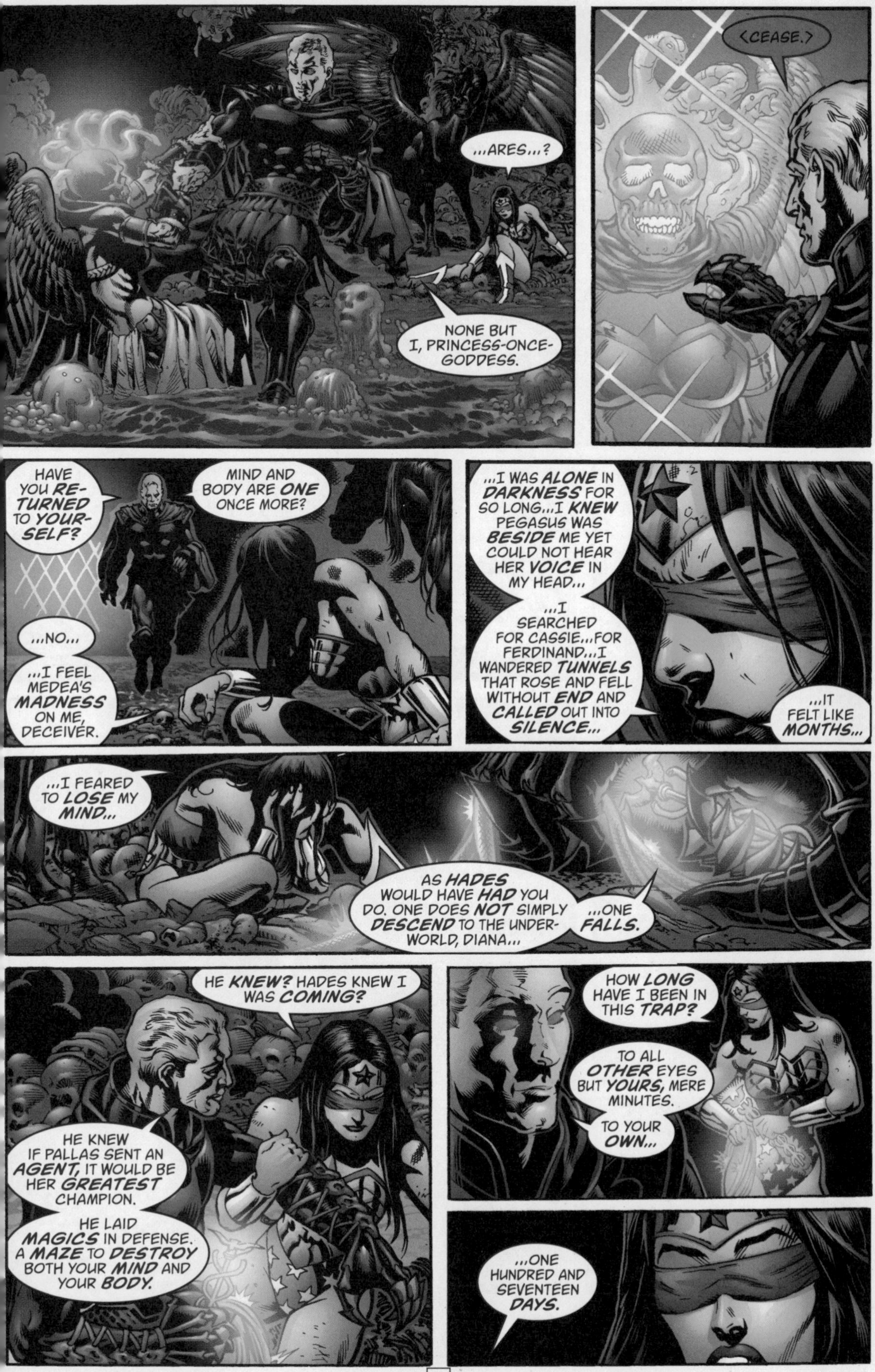

...ARES...?
NONE BUT I, PRINCESS-ONCE-GODDESS.
<CEASE.>
HAVE YOU RE-TURNED TO YOUR-SELF?
MIND AND BODY ARE ONE ONCE MORE?
...NO...
...I FEEL MEDEA'S MADNESS ON ME, DECEIVER.
...I WAS ALONE IN DARKNESS FOR SO LONG... I KNEW PEGASUS WAS BESIDE ME YET COULD NOT HEAR HER VOICE IN MY HEAD...
...I SEARCHED FOR CASSIE... FOR FERDINAND... I WANDERED TUNNELS THAT ROSE AND FELL WITHOUT END AND CALLED OUT INTO SILENCE...
...IT FELT LIKE MONTHS...
...I FEARED TO LOSE MY MIND...
AS HADES WOULD HAVE HAD YOU DO. ONE DOES NOT SIMPLY DESCEND TO THE UNDER-WORLD, DIANA...
...ONE FALLS.
HE KNEW? HADES KNEW I WAS COMING?
HE KNEW IF PALLAS SENT AN AGENT, IT WOULD BE HER GREATEST CHAMPION.
HE LAID MAGICS IN DEFENSE. A MAZE TO DESTROY BOTH YOUR MIND AND YOUR BODY.
HOW LONG HAVE I BEEN IN THIS TRAP?
TO ALL OTHER EYES BUT YOURS, MERE MINUTES.
TO YOUR OWN...
...ONE HUNDRED AND SEVENTEEN DAYS.

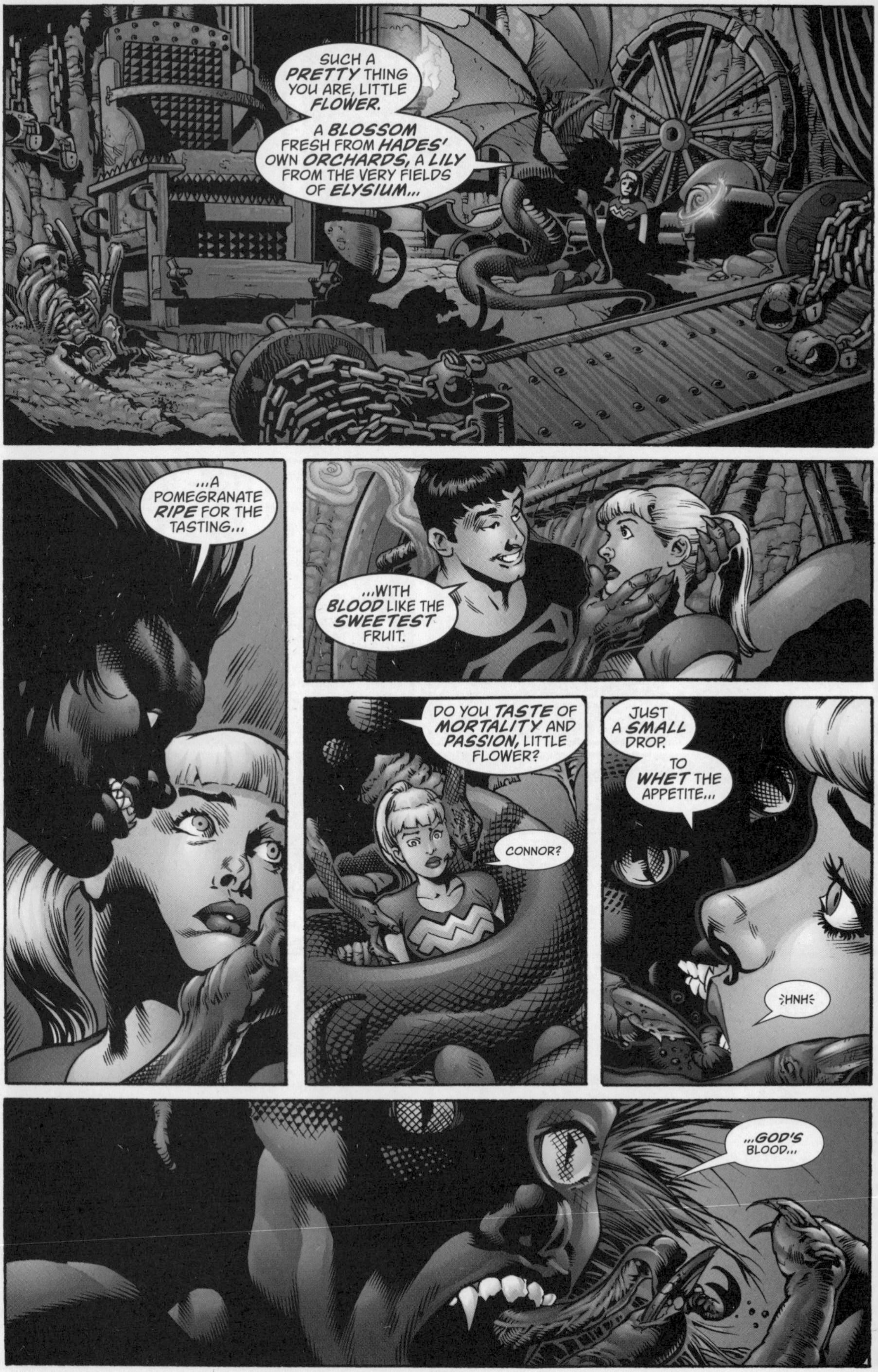
SUCH A PRETTY THING YOU ARE, LITTLE FLOWER.
A BLOSSOM FRESH FROM HADES' OWN ORCHARDS, A LILY FROM THE VERY FIELDS OF ELYSIUM...
...A POMEGRANATE RIPE FOR THE TASTING...
...WITH BLOOD LIKE THE SWEETEST FRUIT.
DO YOU TASTE OF MORTALITY AND PASSION, LITTLE FLOWER?
CONNOR?
JUST A SMALL DROP.
TO WHET THE APPETITE...
HNH
...GOD'S BLOOD...

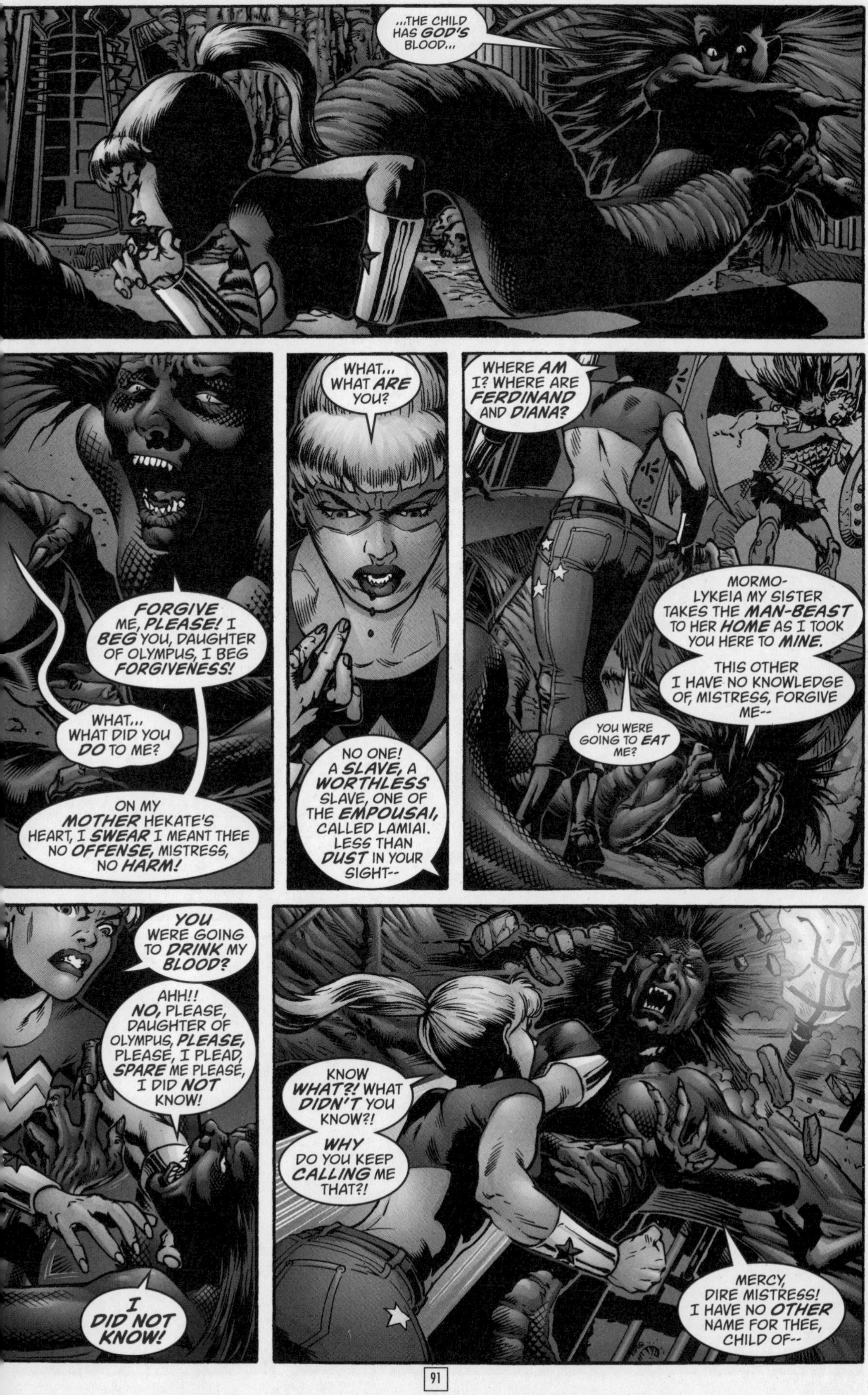

...THE CHILD HAS GOD'S BLOOD...
FORGIVE ME, PLEASE! I BEG YOU, DAUGHTER OF OLYMPUS, I BEG FORGIVENESS!
WHAT... WHAT DID YOU DO TO ME?
ON MY MOTHER HEKATE'S HEART, I SWEAR I MEANT THEE NO OFFENSE, MISTRESS, NO HARM!
WHAT... WHAT ARE YOU?
NO ONE! A SLAVE, A WORTHLESS SLAVE, ONE OF THE EMPOUSAI, CALLED LAMIAI. LESS THAN DUST IN YOUR SIGHT--
WHERE AM I? WHERE ARE FERDINAND AND DIANA?
MORMO-LYKEIA MY SISTER TAKES THE MAN-BEAST TO HER HOME AS I TOOK YOU HERE TO MINE.
THIS OTHER I HAVE NO KNOWLEDGE OF, MISTRESS, FORGIVE ME--
YOU WERE GOING TO EAT ME?
YOU WERE GOING TO DRINK MY BLOOD?
AHH!! NO, PLEASE, DAUGHTER OF OLYMPUS, PLEASE, PLEASE, I PLEAD, SPARE ME PLEASE, I DID NOT KNOW!
I DID NOT KNOW!
KNOW WHAT?! WHAT DIDN'T YOU KNOW?!
WHY DO YOU KEEP CALLING ME THAT?!
MERCY, DIRE MISTRESS! I HAVE NO OTHER NAME FOR THEE, CHILD OF--

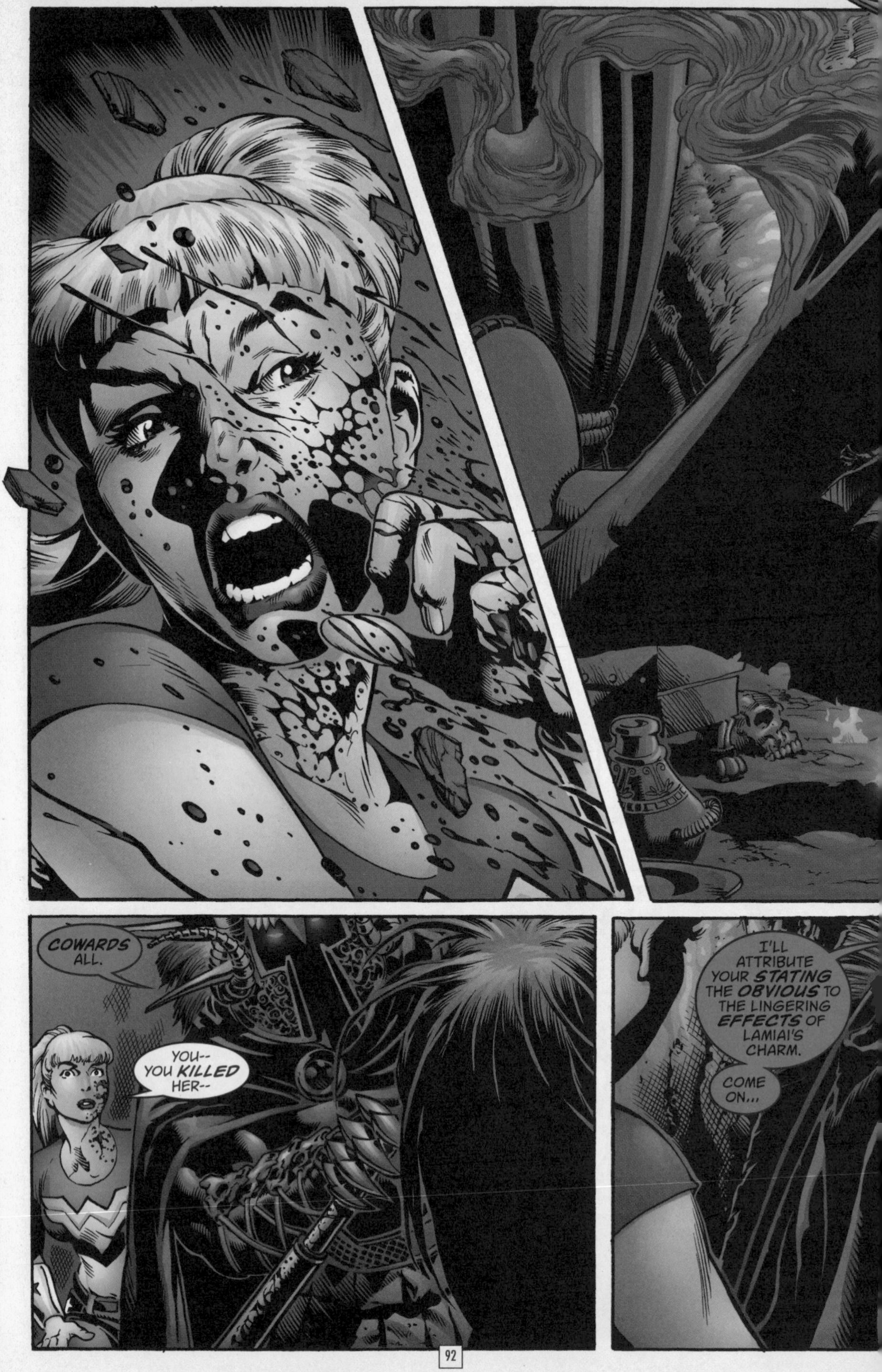
COWARDS ALL.
YOU-- YOU KILLED HER--
I'LL ATTRIBUTE YOUR STATING THE OBVIOUS TO THE LINGERING EFFECTS OF LAMIAI'S CHARM.
COME ON...

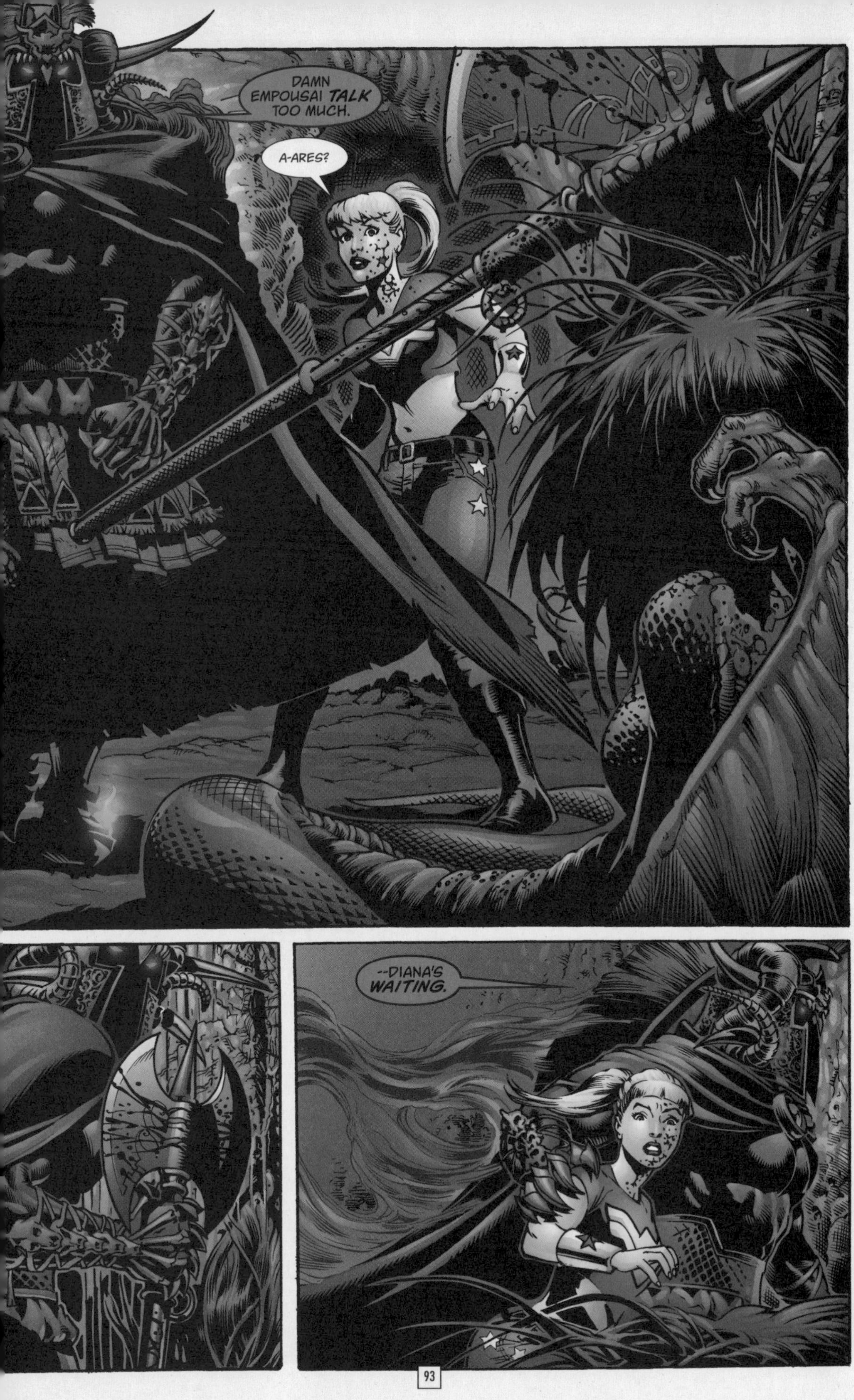
DAMN EMPOUSAI TALK TOO MUCH.
A-ARES?
--DIANA'S WAITING.

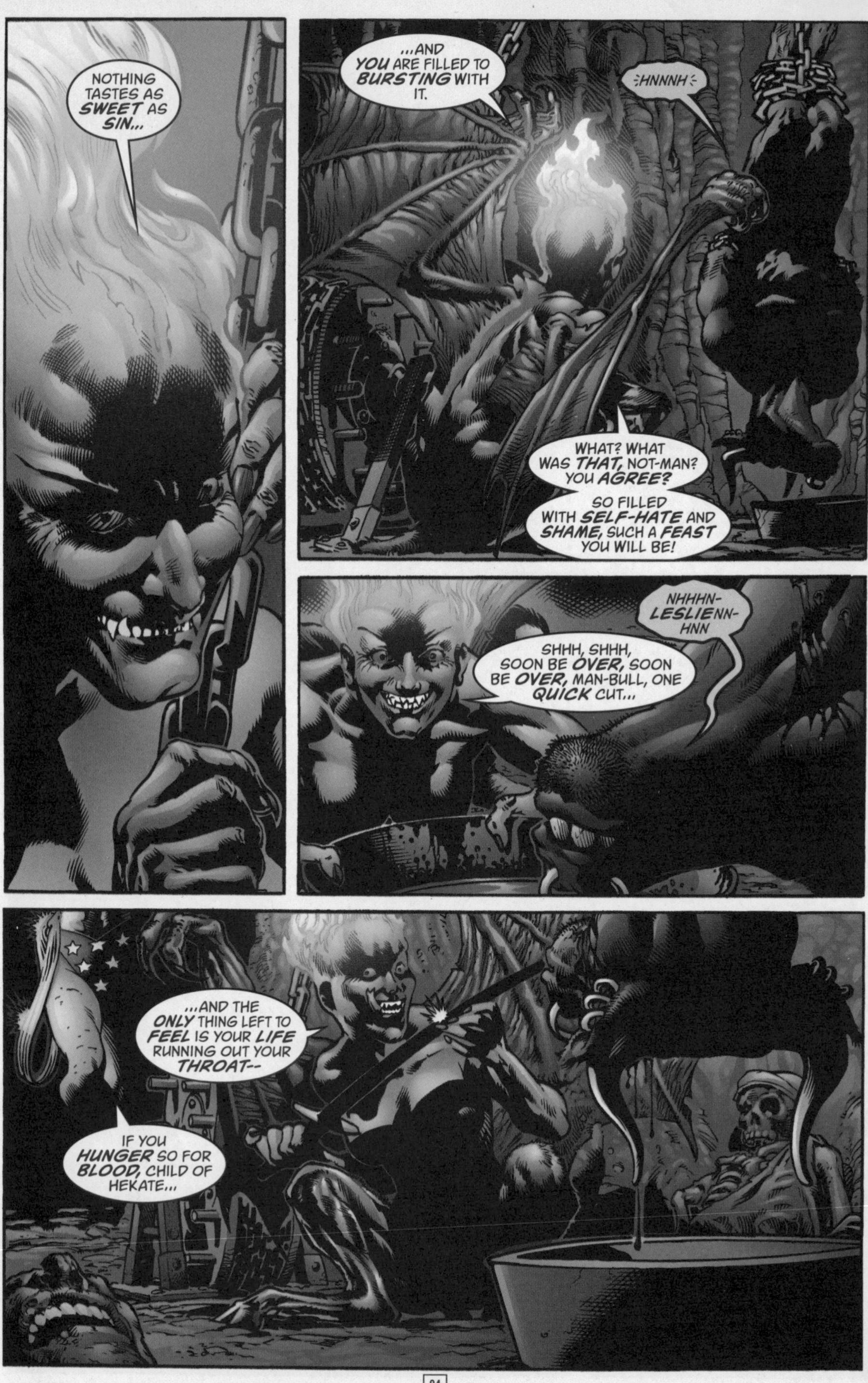
NOTHING TASTES AS SWEET AS SIN...
...AND YOU ARE FILLED TO BURSTING WITH IT.
HNNNH
WHAT? WHAT WAS THAT, NOT-MAN? YOU AGREE?
SO FILLED WITH SELF-HATE AND SHAME, SUCH A FEAST YOU WILL BE!
NHHHN-LESLIENN-HNN
SHHH, SHHH, SOON BE OVER, SOON BE OVER, MAN-BULL, ONE QUICK CUT...
...AND THE ONLY THING LEFT TO FEEL IS YOUR LIFE RUNNING OUT YOUR THROAT--
IF YOU HUNGER SO FOR BLOOD, CHILD OF HEKATE...

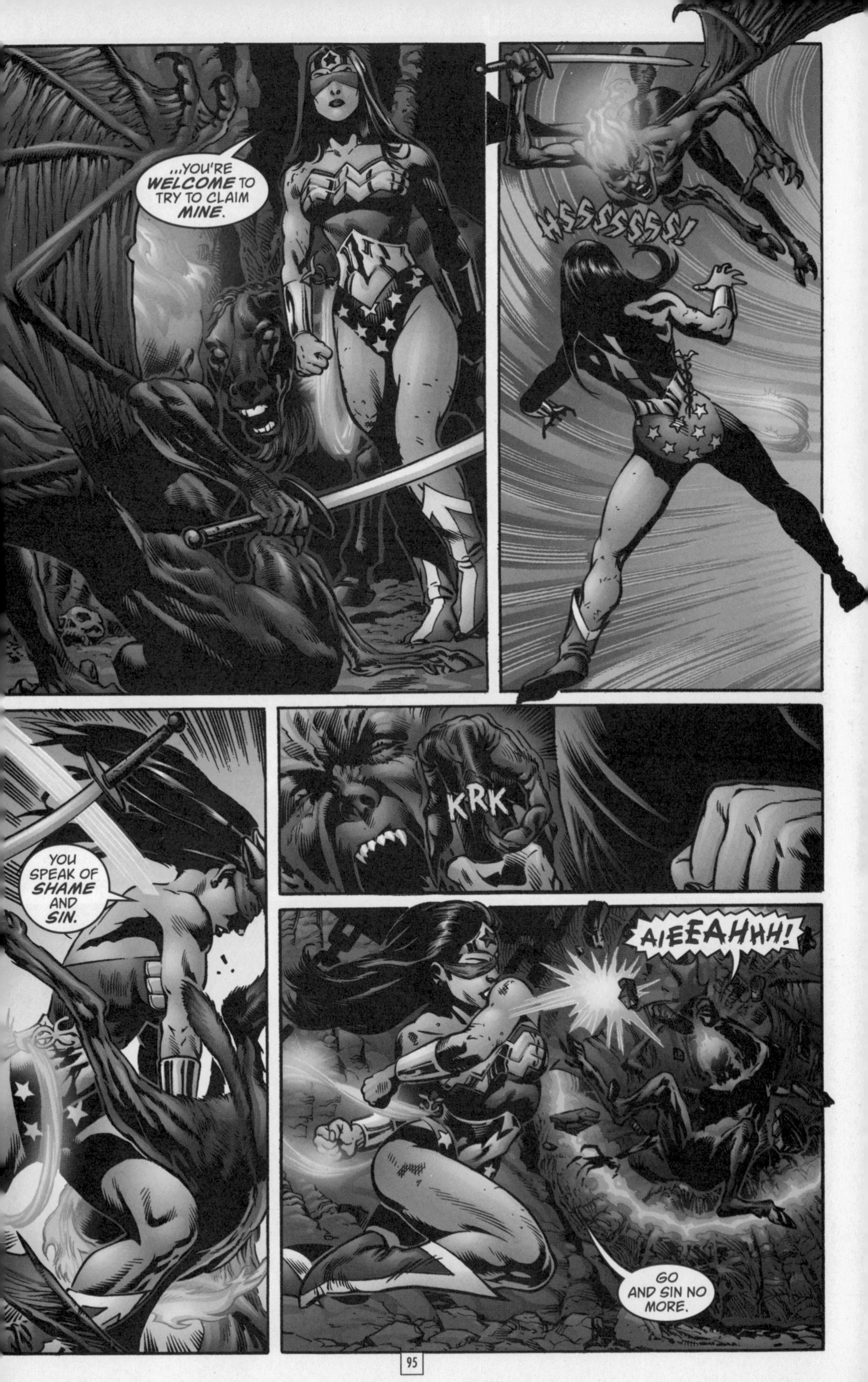

...YOU'RE WELCOME TO TRY TO CLAIM MINE.
HSSSSSSS!
YOU SPEAK OF SHAME AND SIN.
KRK
AIEEAHHH!
GO AND SIN NO MORE.

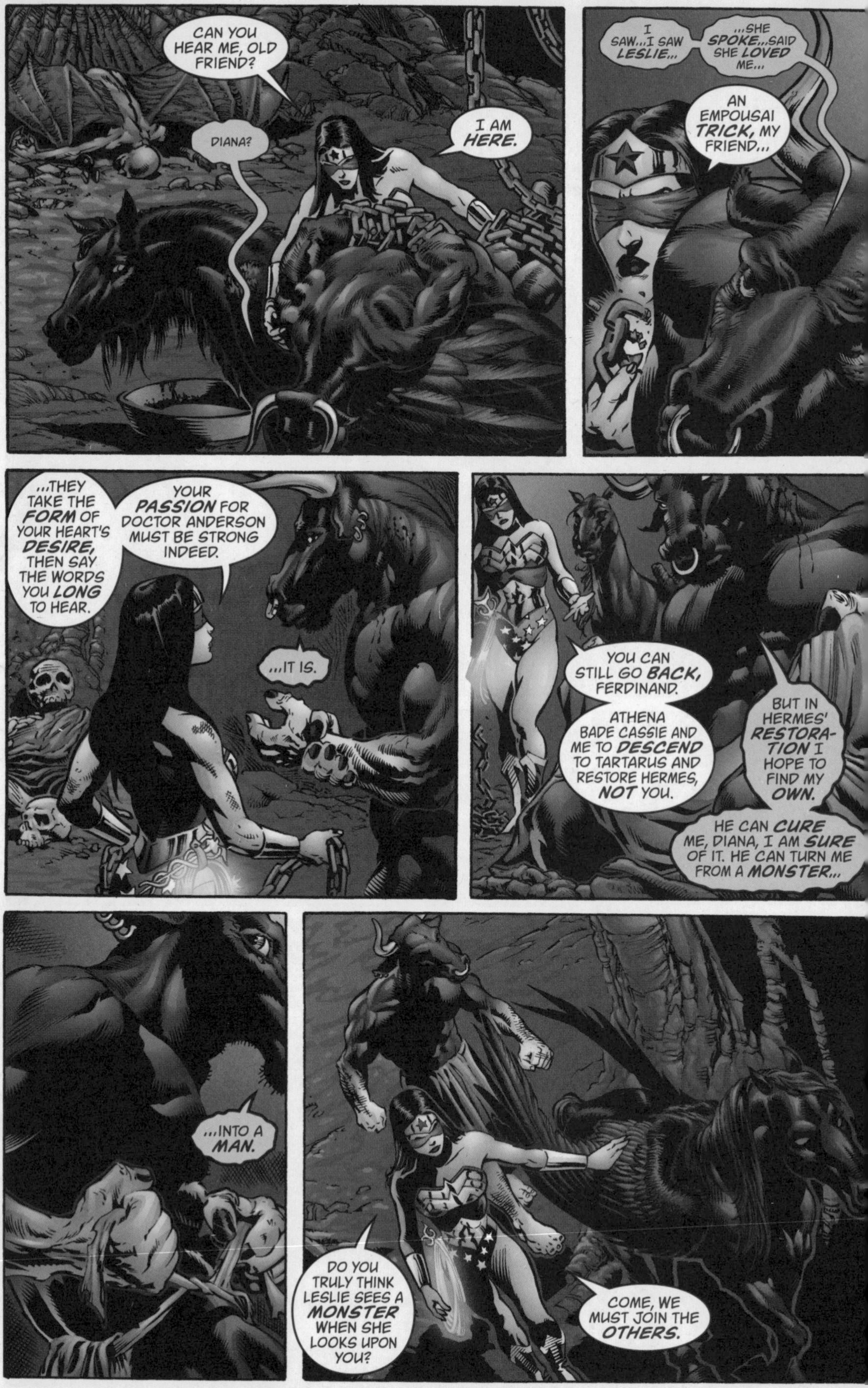
CAN YOU HEAR ME, OLD FRIEND?
DIANA?
I AM HERE.
I SAW... I SAW LESLIE...
...SHE SPOKE... SAID SHE LOVED ME...
AN EMPOUSAI TRICK, MY FRIEND...
...THEY TAKE THE FORM OF YOUR HEART'S DESIRE, THEN SAY THE WORDS YOU LONG TO HEAR.
YOUR PASSION FOR DOCTOR ANDERSON MUST BE STRONG INDEED.
...IT IS.
YOU CAN STILL GO BACK, FERDINAND.
ATHENA BADE CASSIE AND ME TO DESCEND TO TARTARUS AND RESTORE HERMES, NOT YOU.
BUT IN HERMES' RESTORATION I HOPE TO FIND MY OWN.
HE CAN CURE ME, DIANA, I AM SURE OF IT. HE CAN TURN ME FROM A MONSTER...
...INTO A MAN.
DO YOU TRULY THINK LESLIE SEES A MONSTER WHEN SHE LOOKS UPON YOU?
COME, WE MUST JOIN THE OTHERS.

...EYES GREW RED AGAIN, AND HE DANCED UP TO KARAIT WITH THE PECULIAR ROCKING, SWAYING MOTION THAT HE HAD INHERITED FROM HIS FAMILY.

IT LOOKS VERY FUNNY, BUT IS SO PERFECTLY BALANCED A GAIT THAT YOU CAN FLY OFF FROM IT AT ANY ANGLE YOU PLEASE...

MARTIN GABRIEL GARIBALDI
Brother, Son and Hero
b. 10-14-95 d. 11-10-04

...AND IN DEALING WITH SNAKES THIS IS AN ADVANTAGE.

IF RIKKI-TIKKI HAD ONLY KNOWN, HE WAS DOING A MUCH MORE DANGEROUS THING THAN FIGHTING NAG, FOR KARAIT IS SO SMALL, AND CAN TURN SO QUICKLY...

MARTIN GABRIEL GARIBALDI
Brother, Son and Hero
b. 10-14-95 d. 11-10-04

...UNLESS RIKKI BIT HIM CLOSE TO THE BACK OF THE HEAD, HE WOULD GET THE RETURN-STROKE IN HIS EYE OR LIP. BUT RIKKI DID NOT KNOW...

...HIS EYES WERE ALL RED, AND HE ROCKED BACK AND FORTH, LOOKING FOR A GOOD PLACE TO HOLD...

WHAT THE *HELL* ARE YOU DOING *HERE?*

DON'T DRAW *ATTENTION.*

HE *CAN'T* SEE US *TOGETHER.*

HE'S TOO *BUSY* PRETENDING HIS SON STILL *LIVES* TO BE OF ANY *CONCERN,* JONAH.

I'M HERE TO GIVE YOU A *MESSAGE.*

IT'S *ACTIVE,* JONAH.

ALL OF IT.

THE *NEXT* TIME YOU *SEE* ME BE READY TO *MOVE.*

...AND THE REST FOR *NEXT* TIME OKAY, SON?

MAYBE *DIANA* WILL COME AND READ TO YOU, TOO.

MARTIN GABRIEL GARIBALDI
Son and Hero

I LOVE YOU.

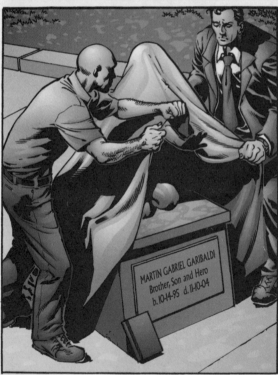

MARTIN GABRIEL GARIBALDI
Brother, Son and Hero
b. 10-14-95 d. 11-10-04

SHE DOESN'T COME TO SEE HIM.

I'M SORRY, PETER, WHAT?

THE AMBASSADOR, DIANA, SHE HASN'T BEEN HERE SINCE THE *MEMORIAL.*

AT LEAST, NOT THAT I *KNOW* OF.

SHE FEELS *GUILTY.*

SHE *SHOULD.*

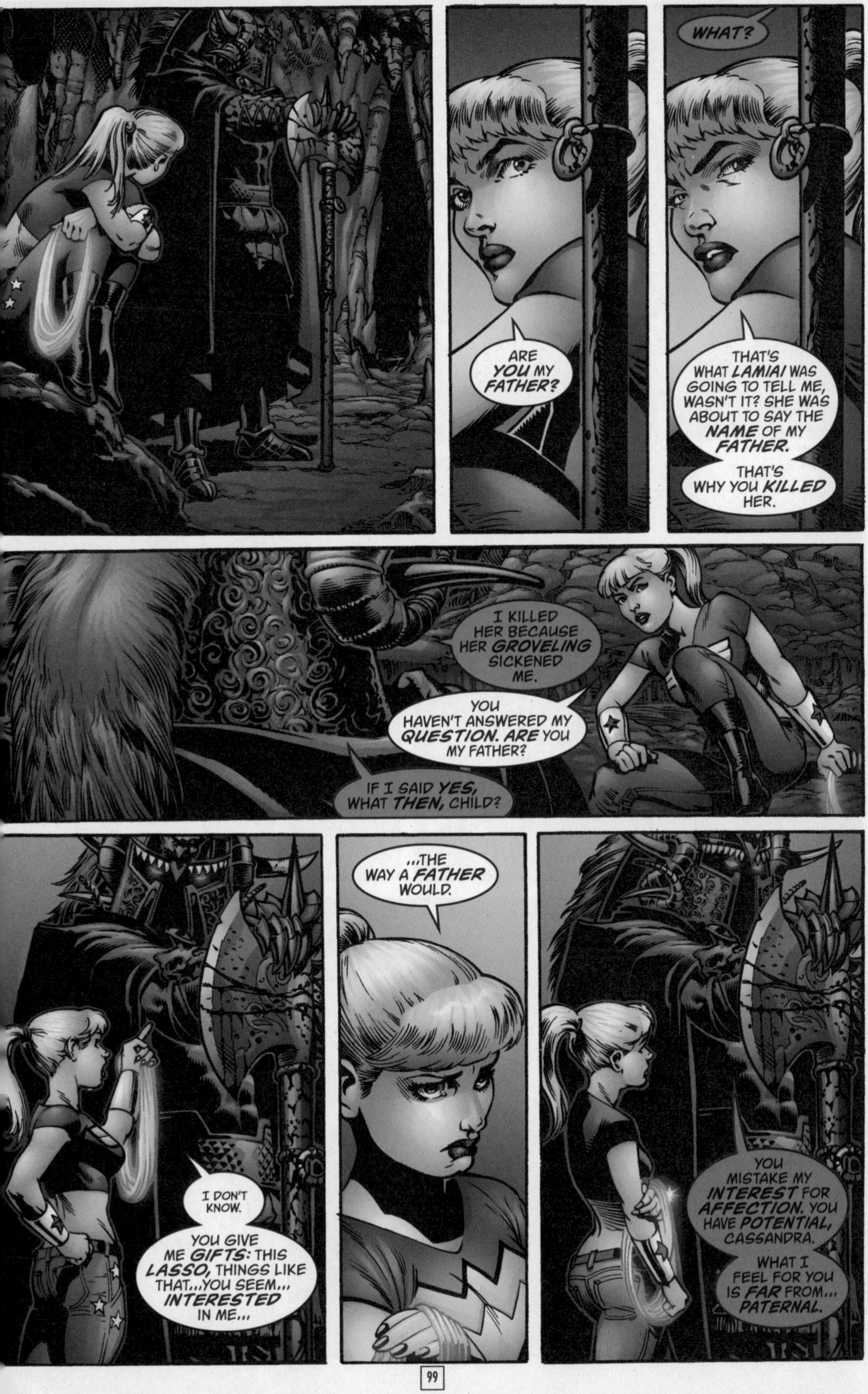
ARE YOU MY FATHER?
WHAT?
THAT'S WHAT LAMIAI WAS GOING TO TELL ME, WASN'T IT? SHE WAS ABOUT TO SAY THE NAME OF MY FATHER.
THAT'S WHY YOU KILLED HER.
I KILLED HER BECAUSE HER GROVELING SICKENED ME.
YOU HAVEN'T ANSWERED MY QUESTION. ARE YOU MY FATHER?
IF I SAID YES, WHAT THEN, CHILD?
I DON'T KNOW.
YOU GIVE ME GIFTS: THIS LASSO, THINGS LIKE THAT...YOU SEEM... INTERESTED IN ME...
...THE WAY A FATHER WOULD.
YOU MISTAKE MY INTEREST FOR AFFECTION. YOU HAVE POTENTIAL, CASSANDRA.
WHAT I FEEL FOR YOU IS FAR FROM... PATERNAL.

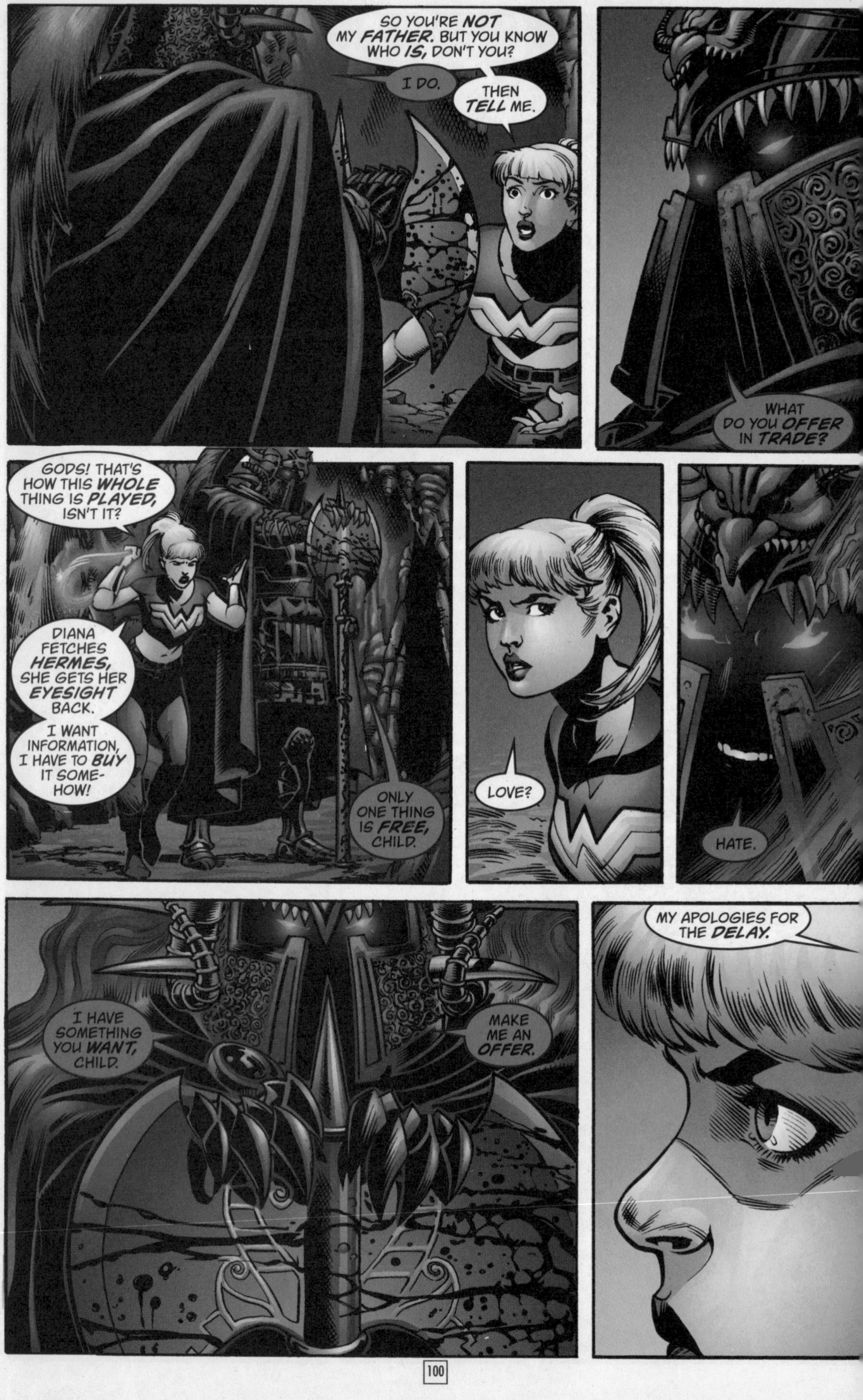
SO YOU'RE NOT MY FATHER. BUT YOU KNOW WHO IS, DON'T YOU?
I DO.
THEN TELL ME.
WHAT DO YOU OFFER IN TRADE?
GODS! THAT'S HOW THIS WHOLE THING IS PLAYED, ISN'T IT?
DIANA FETCHES HERMES, SHE GETS HER EYESIGHT BACK.
I WANT INFORMATION, I HAVE TO BUY IT SOME-HOW!
ONLY ONE THING IS FREE, CHILD.
LOVE?
HATE.
I HAVE SOMETHING YOU WANT, CHILD.
MAKE ME AN OFFER.
MY APOLOGIES FOR THE DELAY.

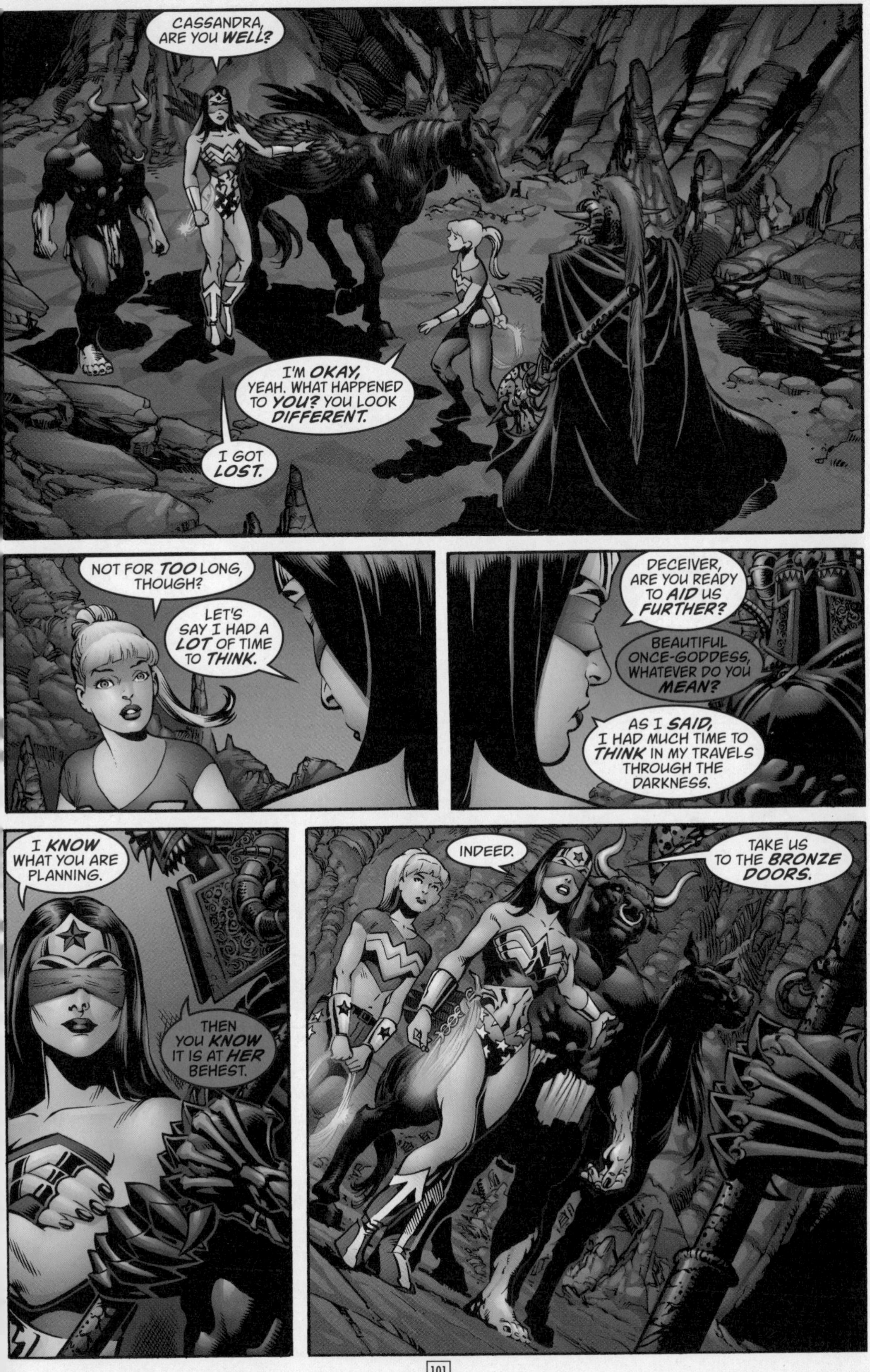
CASSANDRA, ARE YOU WELL?
I'M OKAY, YEAH. WHAT HAPPENED TO YOU? YOU LOOK DIFFERENT.
I GOT LOST.
NOT FOR TOO LONG, THOUGH?
LET'S SAY I HAD A LOT OF TIME TO THINK.
DECEIVER, ARE YOU READY TO AID US FURTHER?
BEAUTIFUL ONCE-GODDESS, WHATEVER DO YOU MEAN?
AS I SAID, I HAD MUCH TIME TO THINK IN MY TRAVELS THROUGH THE DARKNESS.
I KNOW WHAT YOU ARE PLANNING.
THEN YOU KNOW IT IS AT HER BEHEST.
INDEED.
TAKE US TO THE BRONZE DOORS.

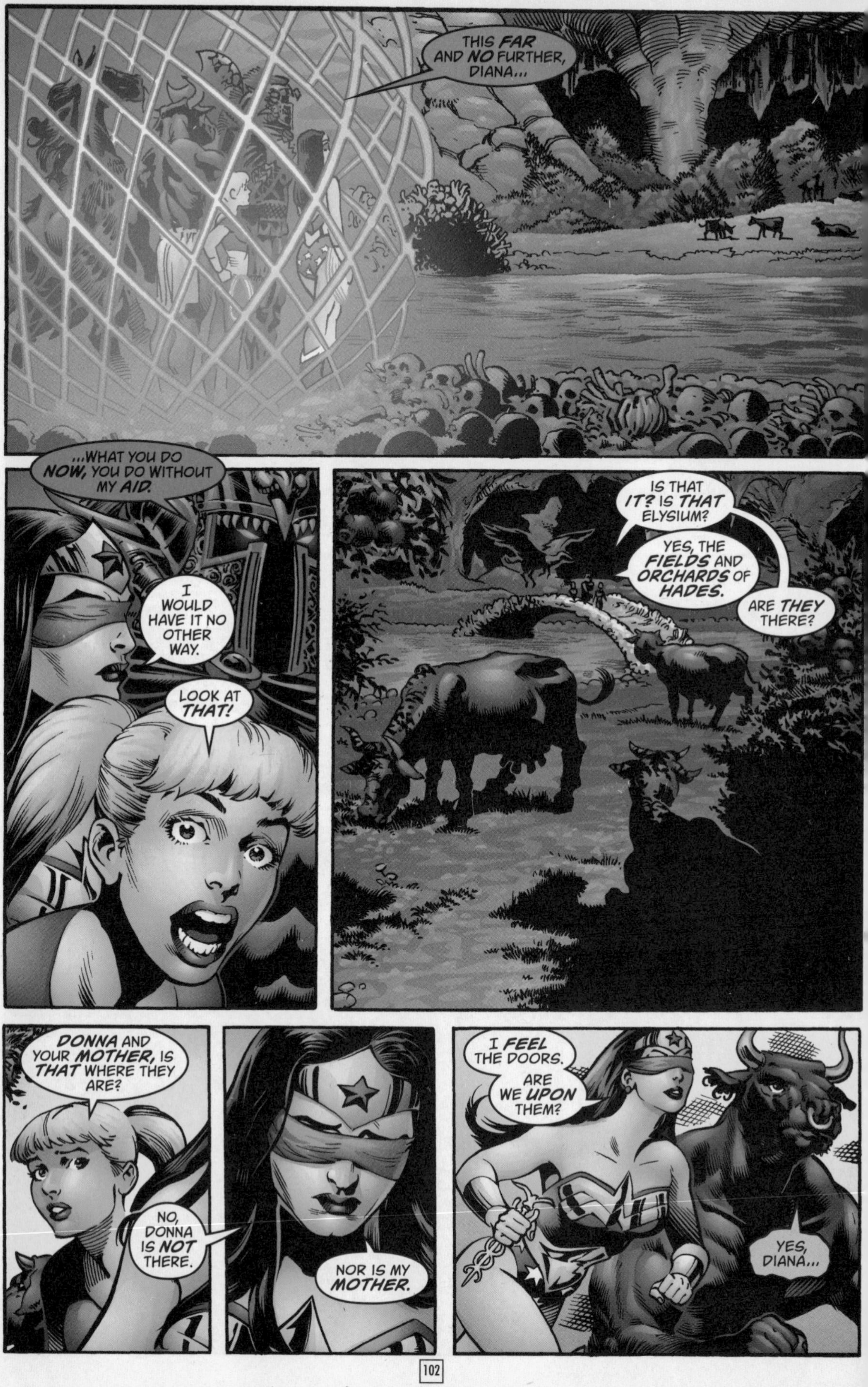
THIS FAR AND NO FURTHER, DIANA...
...WHAT YOU DO NOW, YOU DO WITHOUT MY AID.
I WOULD HAVE IT NO OTHER WAY.
LOOK AT THAT!
IS THAT IT? IS THAT ELYSIUM?
YES, THE FIELDS AND ORCHARDS OF HADES.
ARE THEY THERE?
DONNA AND YOUR MOTHER, IS THAT WHERE THEY ARE?
NO, DONNA IS NOT THERE.
NOR IS MY MOTHER.
I FEEL THE DOORS.
ARE WE UPON THEM?
YES, DIANA...

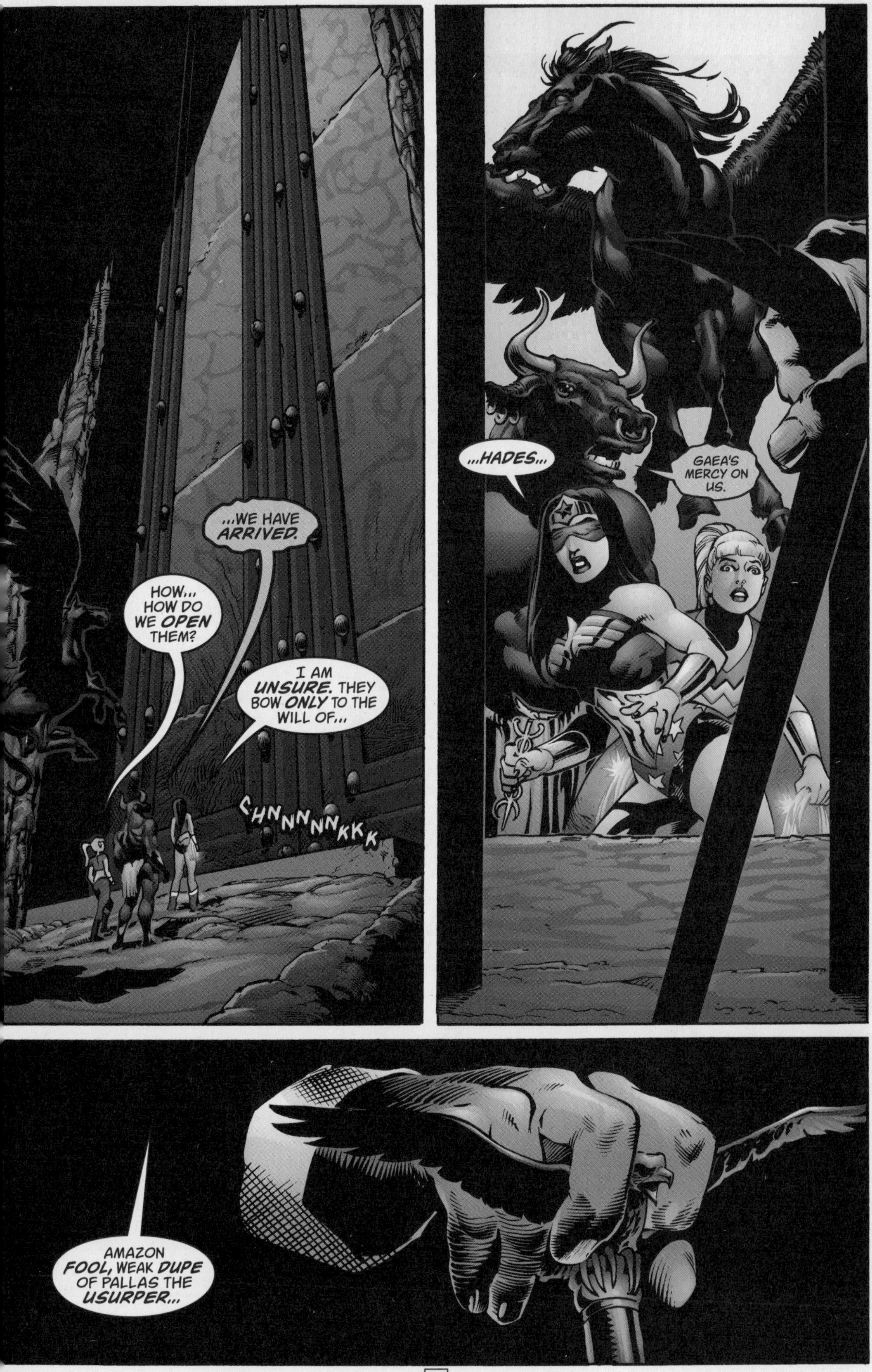
...WE HAVE ARRIVED.
HOW... HOW DO WE OPEN THEM?
I AM UNSURE. THEY BOW ONLY TO THE WILL OF...
CHNNNNNKKK
...HADES...
GAEA'S MERCY ON US.
AMAZON FOOL, WEAK DUPE OF PALLAS THE USURPER...

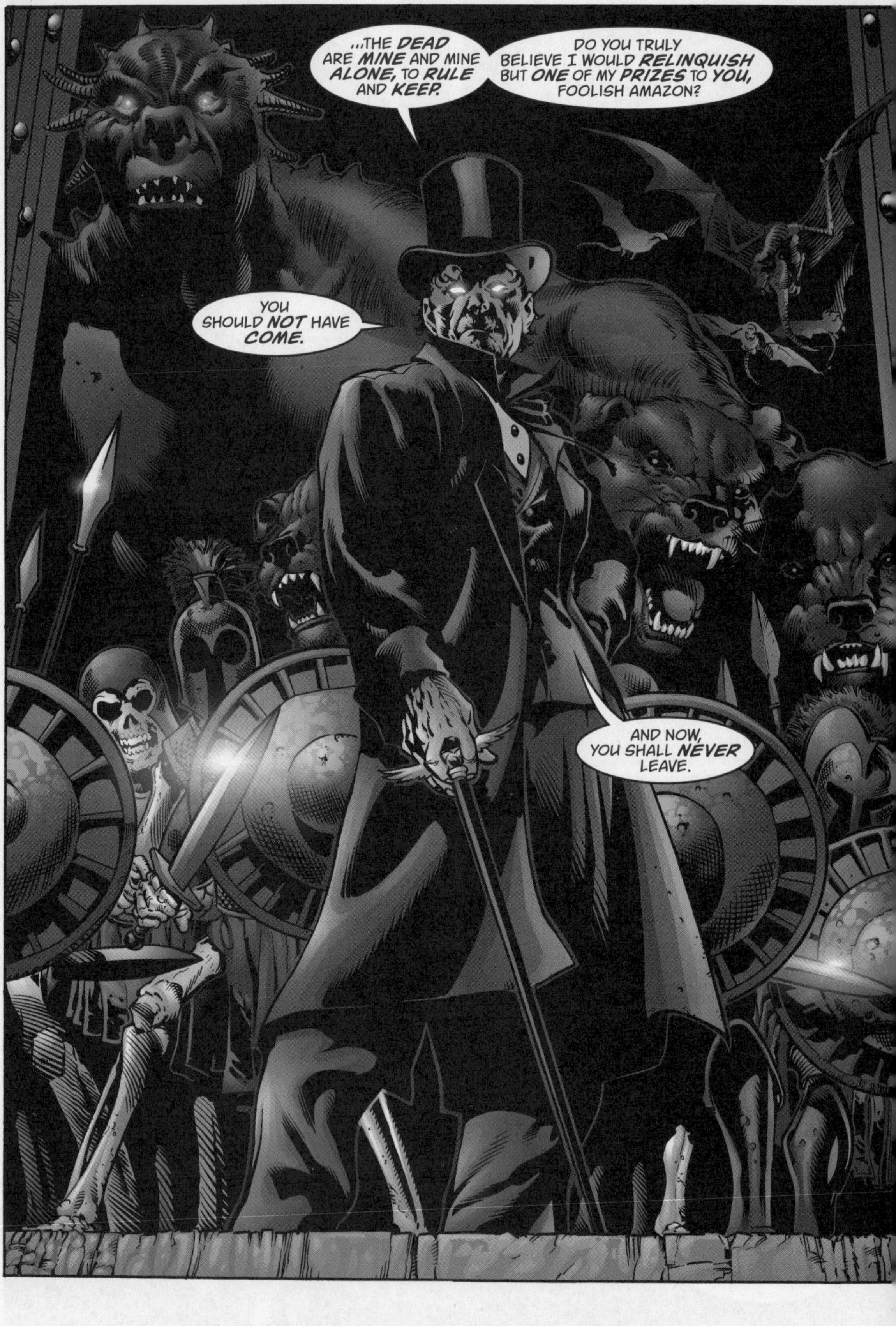
...THE DEAD ARE MINE AND MINE ALONE, TO RULE AND KEEP.
DO YOU TRULY BELIEVE I WOULD RELINQUISH BUT ONE OF MY PRIZES TO YOU, FOOLISH AMAZON?
YOU SHOULD NOT HAVE COME.
AND NOW, YOU SHALL NEVER LEAVE.

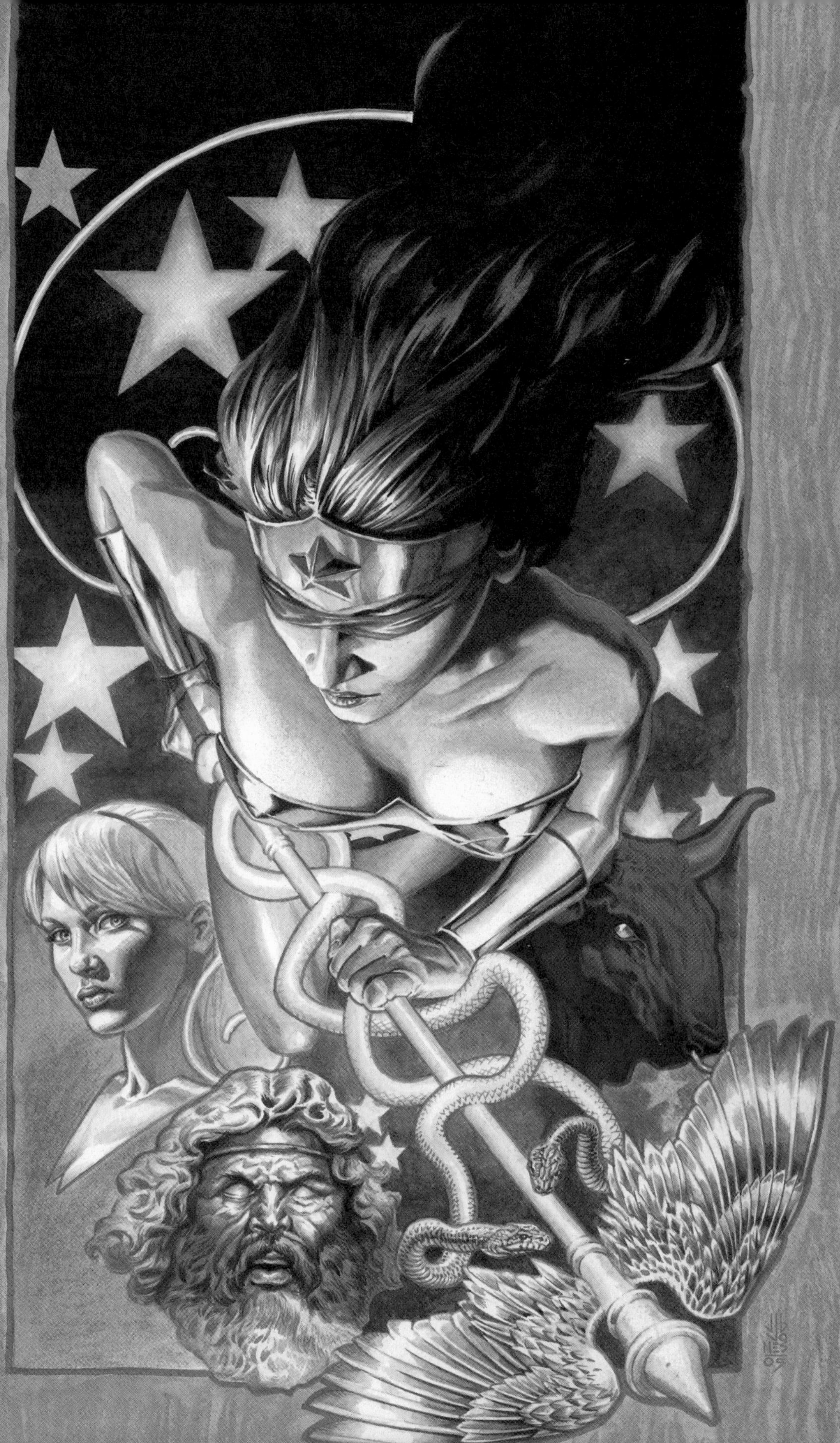

WONDER WOMAN #217
ART BY J.G. JONES

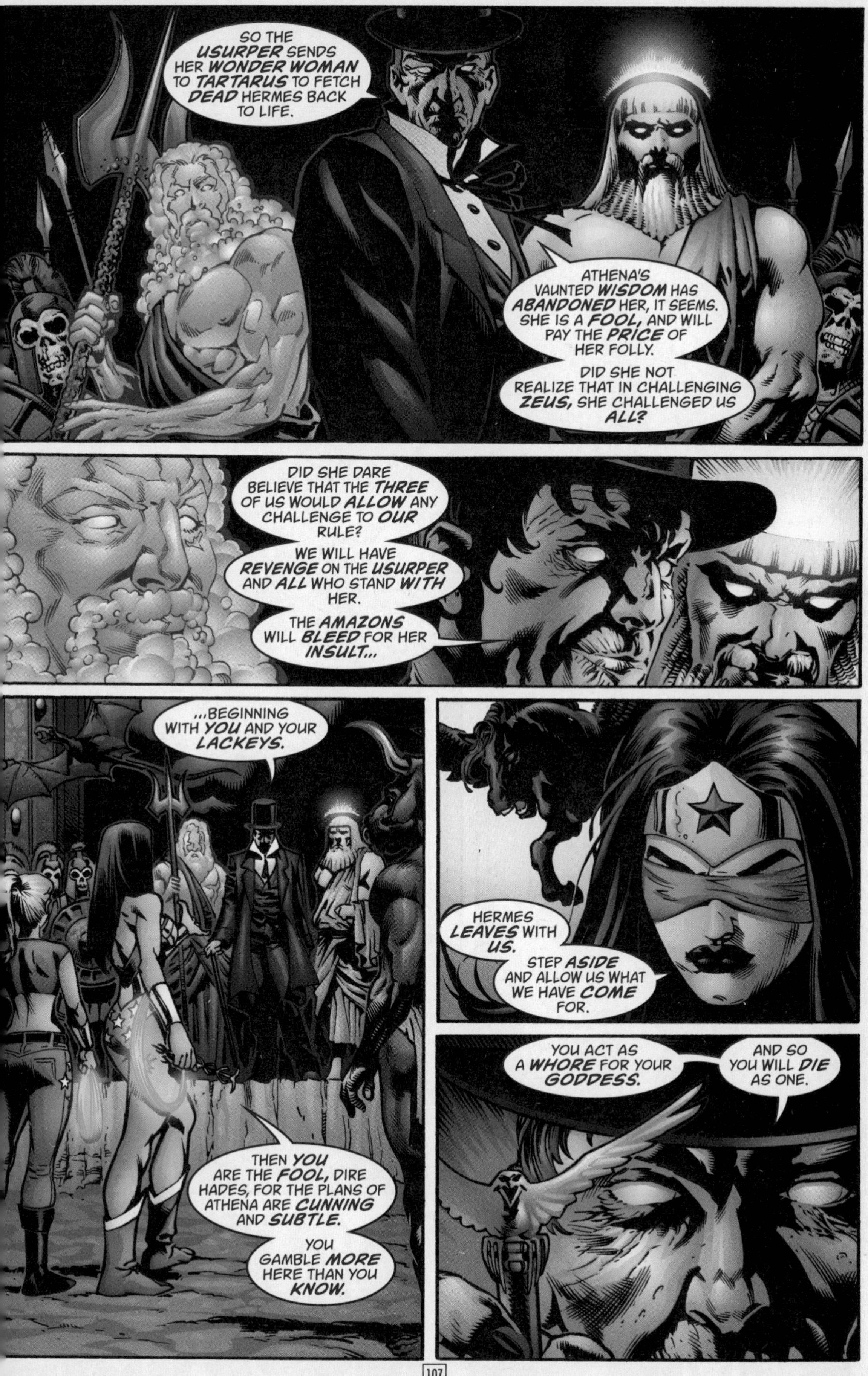
SO THE USURPER SENDS HER WONDER WOMAN TO TARTARUS TO FETCH DEAD HERMES BACK TO LIFE.
ATHENA'S VAUNTED WISDOM HAS ABANDONED HER, IT SEEMS. SHE IS A FOOL, AND WILL PAY THE PRICE OF HER FOLLY.
DID SHE NOT REALIZE THAT IN CHALLENGING ZEUS, SHE CHALLENGED US ALL?
DID SHE DARE BELIEVE THAT THE THREE OF US WOULD ALLOW ANY CHALLENGE TO OUR RULE?
WE WILL HAVE REVENGE ON THE USURPER AND ALL WHO STAND WITH HER.
THE AMAZONS WILL BLEED FOR HER INSULT...
...BEGINNING WITH YOU AND YOUR LACKEYS.
THEN YOU ARE THE FOOL, DIRE HADES, FOR THE PLANS OF ATHENA ARE CUNNING AND SUBTLE.
YOU GAMBLE MORE HERE THAN YOU KNOW.
HERMES LEAVES WITH US.
STEP ASIDE AND ALLOW US WHAT WE HAVE COME FOR.
YOU ACT AS A WHORE FOR YOUR GODDESS.
AND SO YOU WILL DIE AS ONE.

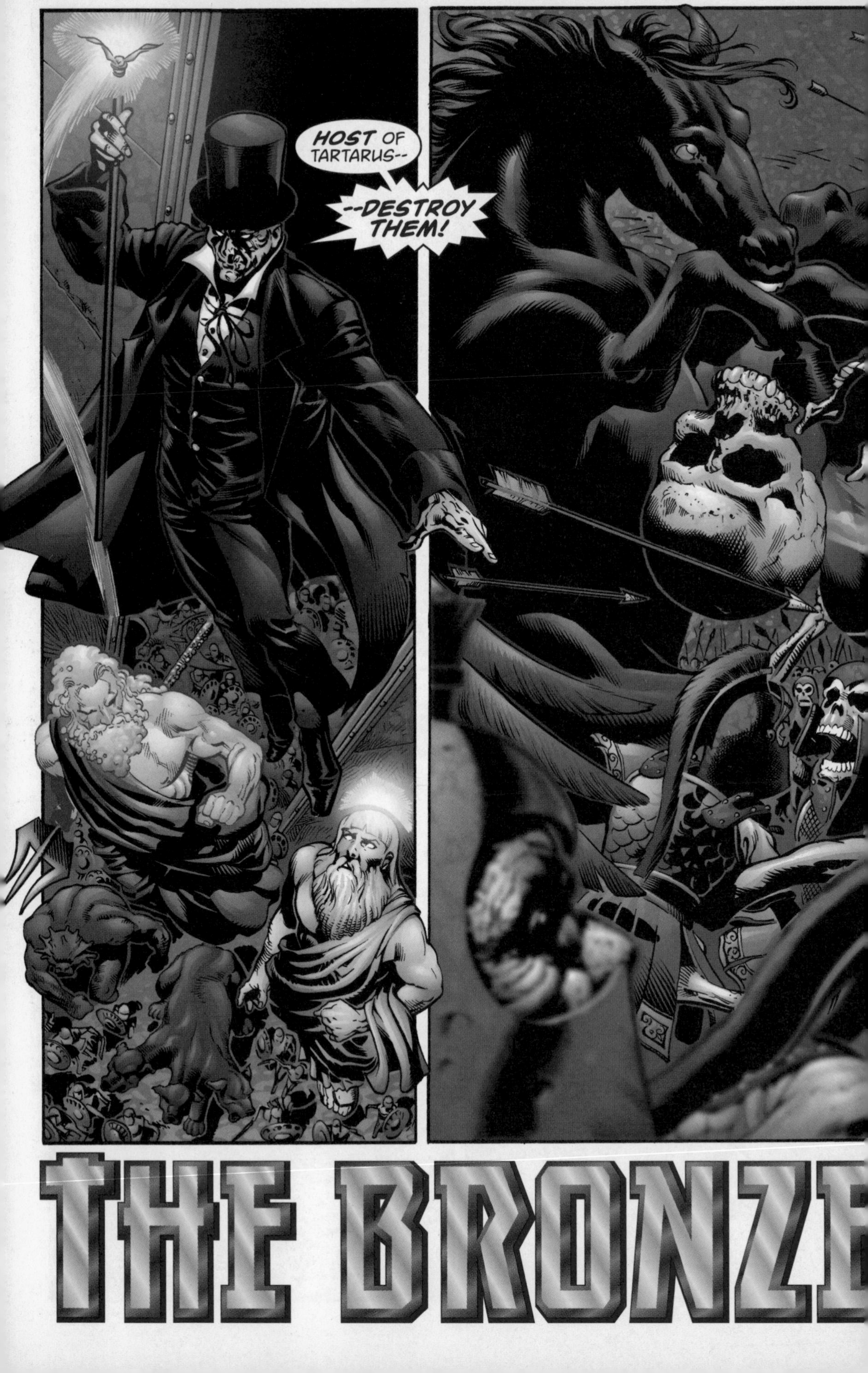
HOST OF TARTARUS--
--DESTROY THEM!
THE BRONZE

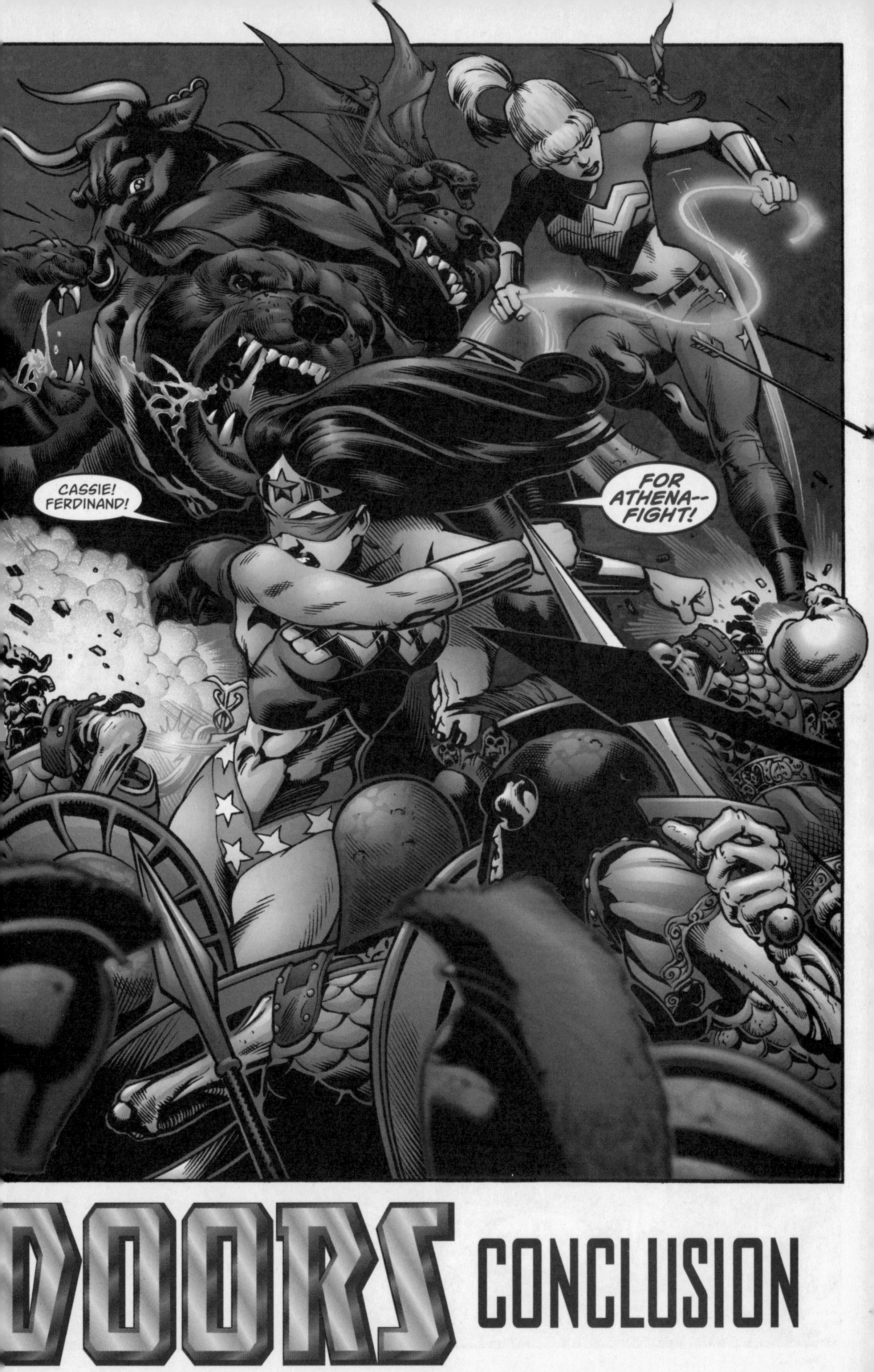
CASSIE! FERDINAND!
FOR ATHENA-- FIGHT!

DOORS CONCLUSION

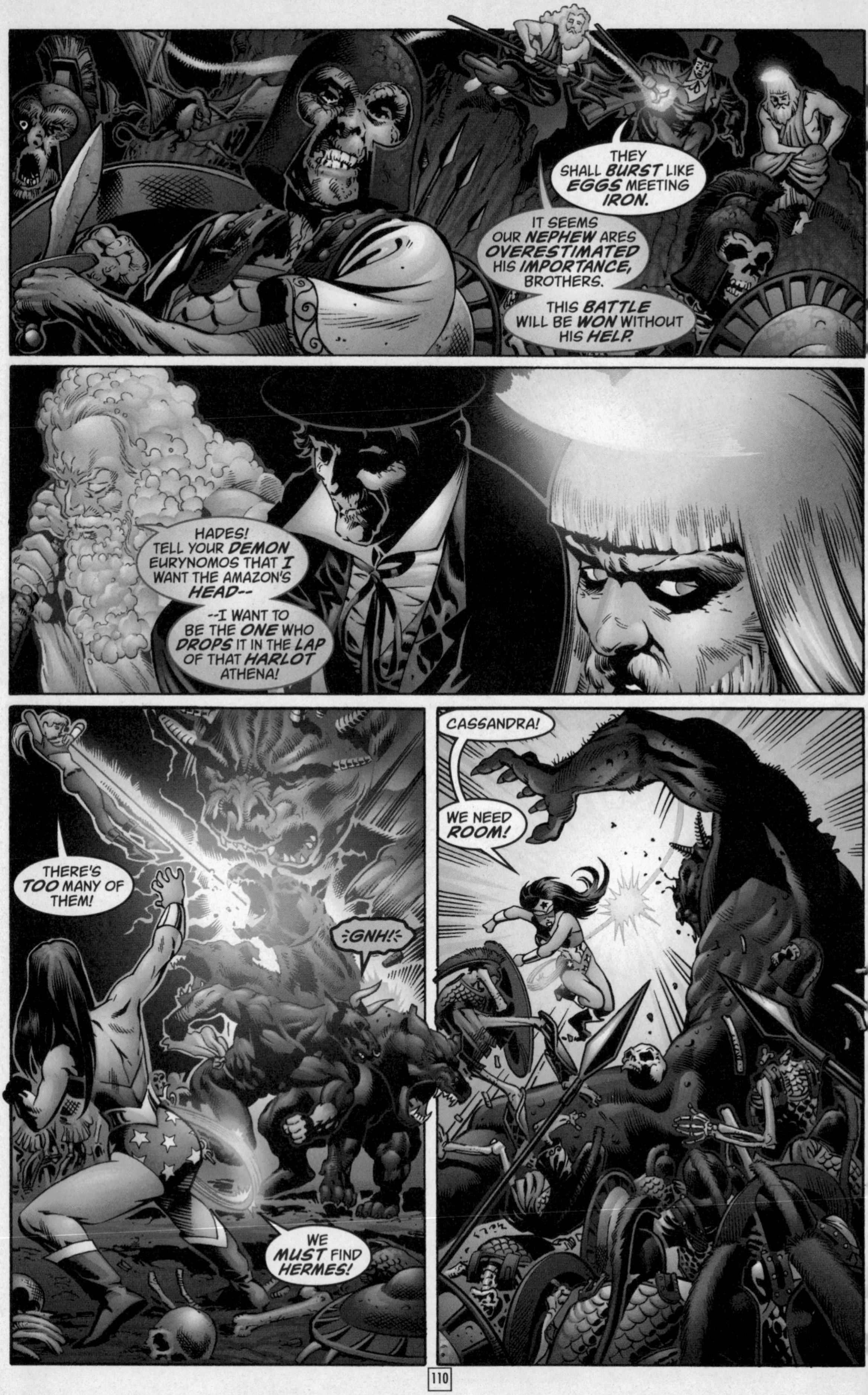
THEY SHALL BURST LIKE EGGS MEETING IRON.
IT SEEMS OUR NEPHEW ARES OVERESTIMATED HIS IMPORTANCE, BROTHERS.
THIS BATTLE WILL BE WON WITHOUT HIS HELP.
HADES! TELL YOUR DEMON EURYNOMOS THAT I WANT THE AMAZON'S HEAD--
--I WANT TO BE THE ONE WHO DROPS IT IN THE LAP OF THAT HARLOT ATHENA!
THERE'S TOO MANY OF THEM!
GNH!
WE MUST FIND HERMES!
CASSANDRA!
WE NEED ROOM!

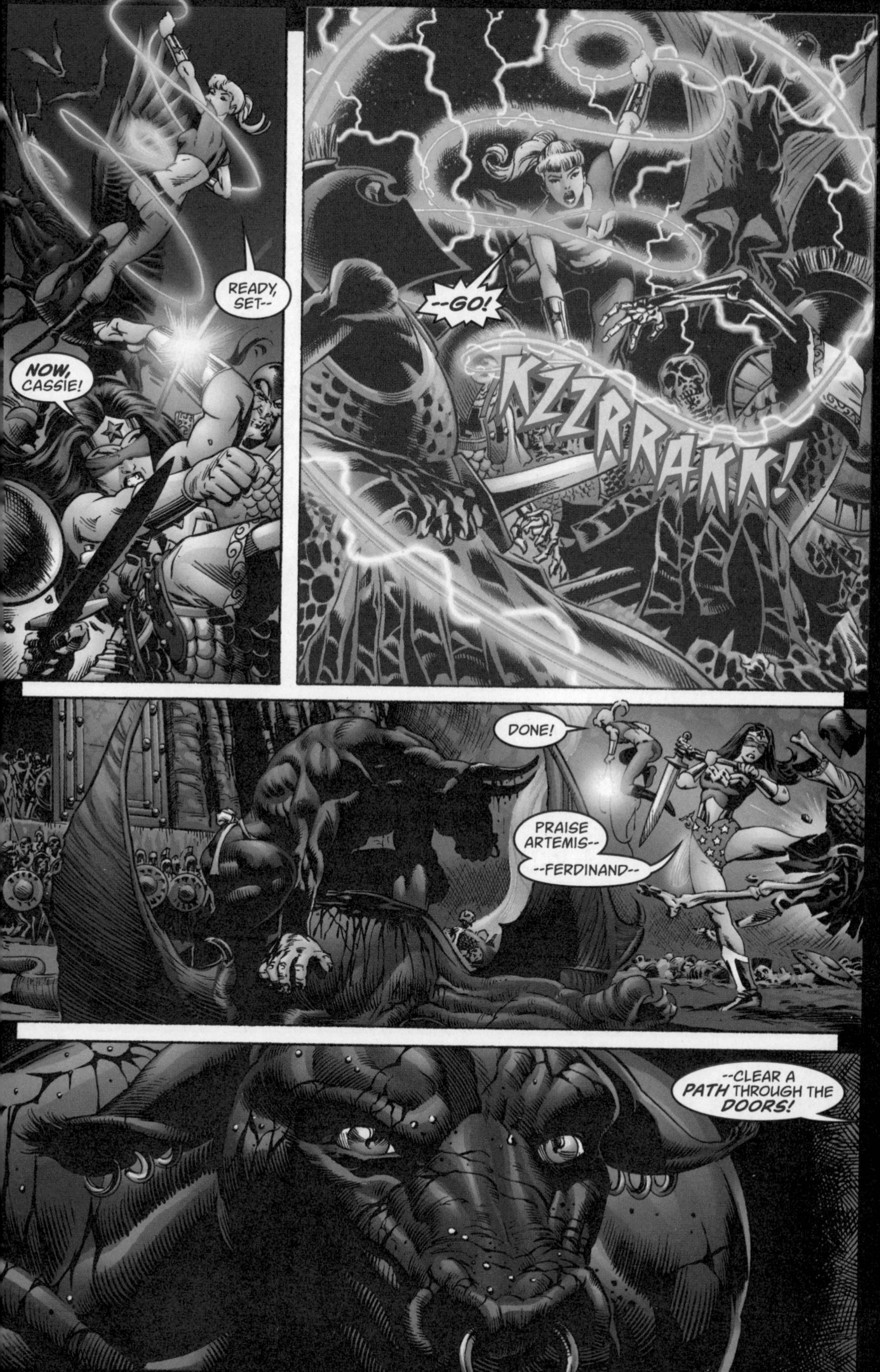

READY, SET--
NOW, CASSIE!
--GO!
KZZRRAKK!
DONE!
PRAISE ARTEMIS--
--FERDINAND--
--CLEAR A PATH THROUGH THE DOORS!

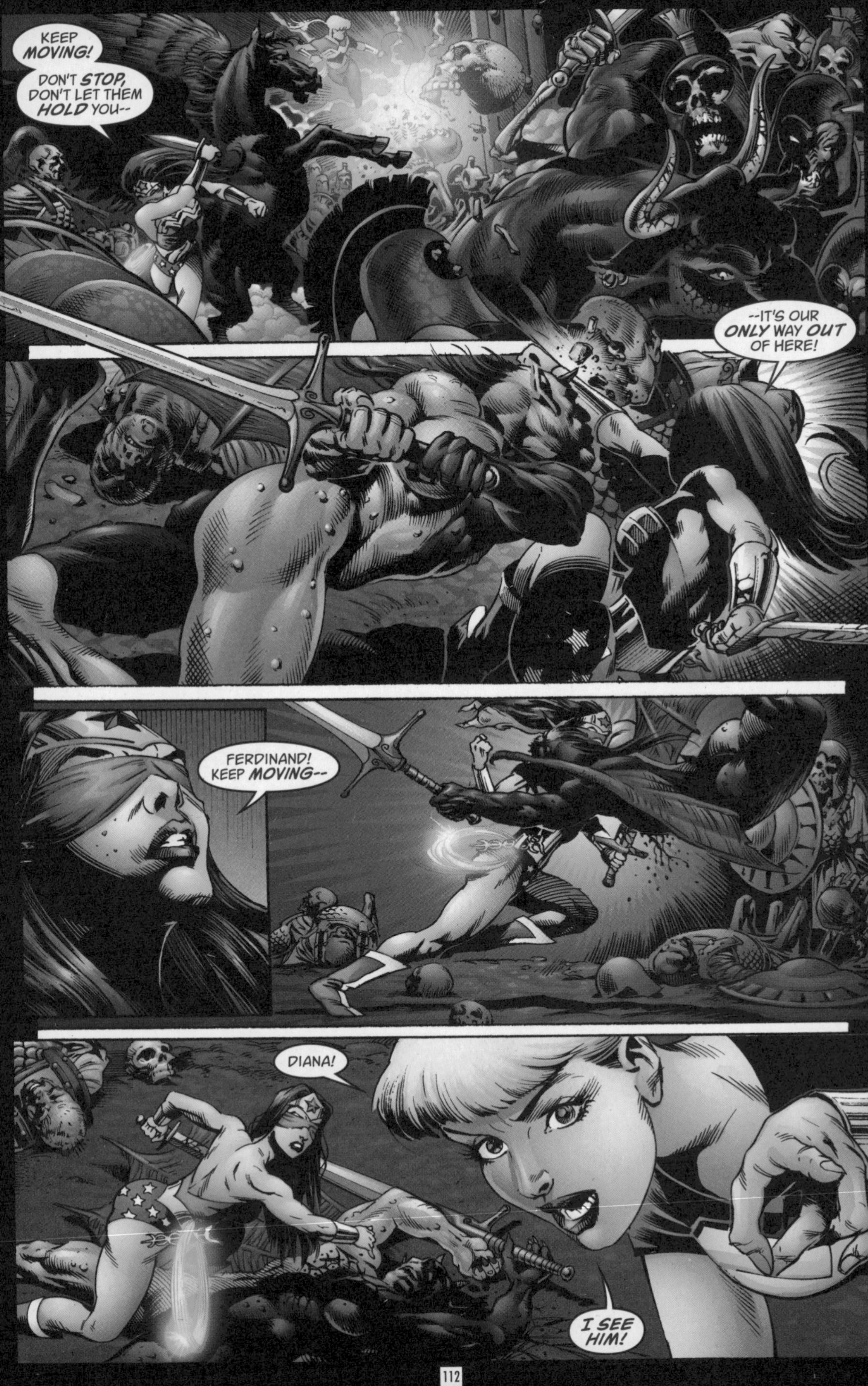
KEEP MOVING!
DON'T STOP, DON'T LET THEM HOLD YOU--
--IT'S OUR ONLY WAY OUT OF HERE!
FERDINAND! KEEP MOVING--
DIANA!
I SEE HIM!

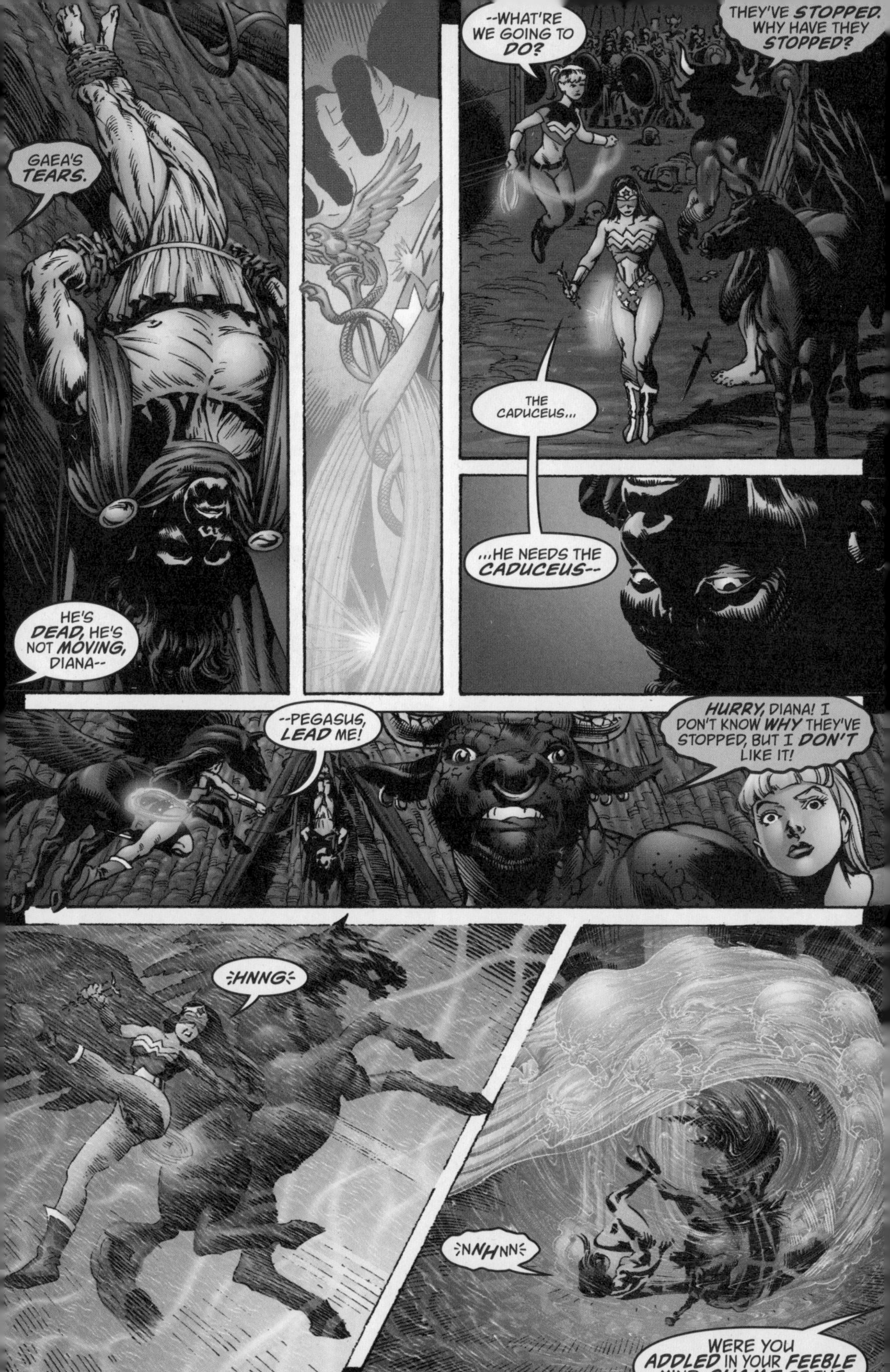
GAEA'S TEARS.
HE'S DEAD, HE'S NOT MOVING, DIANA--
--WHAT'RE WE GOING TO DO?
THEY'VE STOPPED. WHY HAVE THEY STOPPED?
THE CADUCEUS...
...HE NEEDS THE CADUCEUS--
--PEGASUS, LEAD ME!
HURRY, DIANA! I DON'T KNOW WHY THEY'VE STOPPED, BUT I DON'T LIKE IT!
HNNG
NNHNN
WERE YOU ADDLED IN YOUR FEEBLE MIND, SHAME OF THE

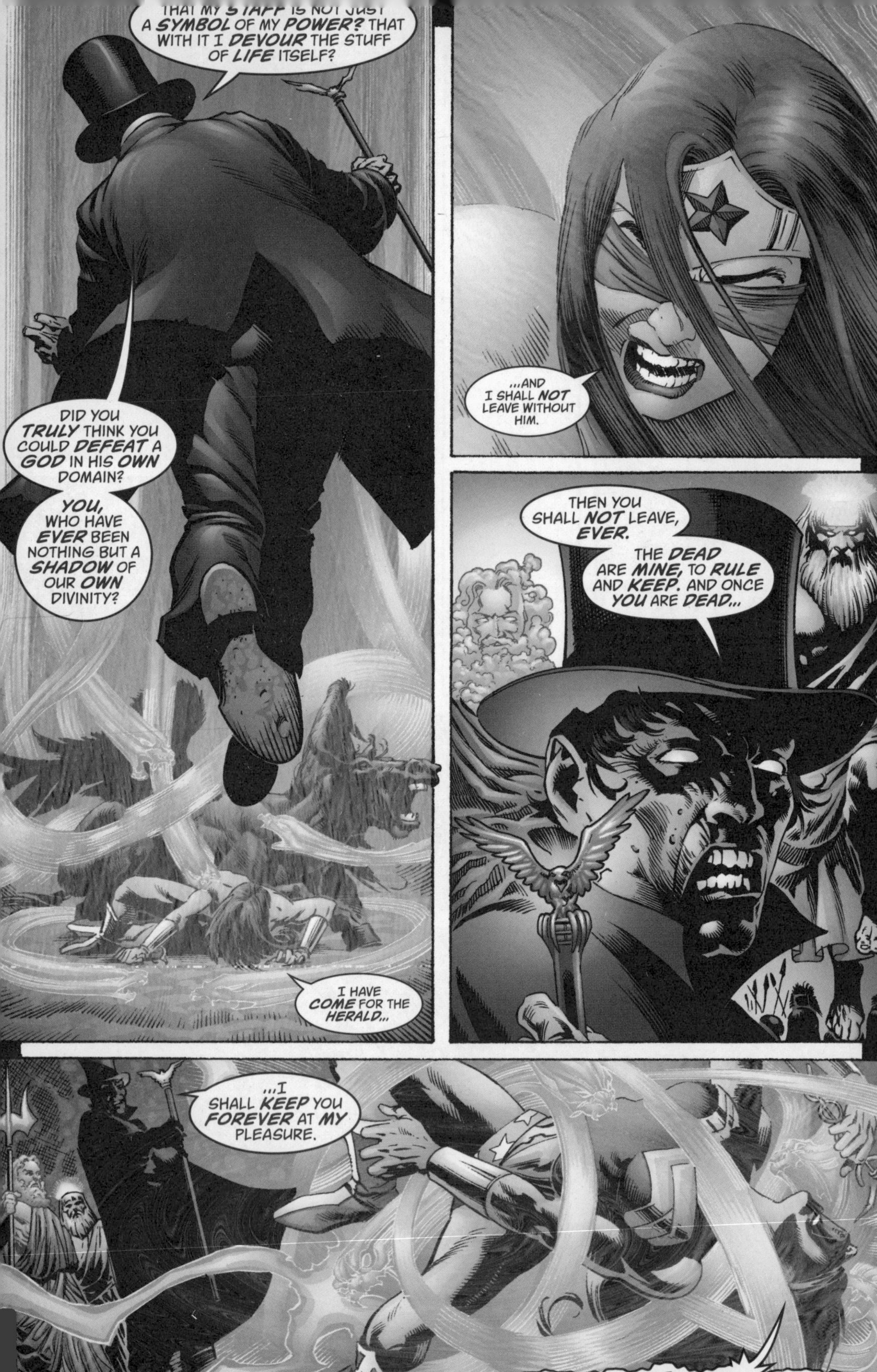

THAT MY STAFF IS NOT JUST A SYMBOL OF MY POWER? THAT WITH IT I DEVOUR THE STUFF OF LIFE ITSELF?
DID YOU TRULY THINK YOU COULD DEFEAT A GOD IN HIS OWN DOMAIN?
YOU, WHO HAVE EVER BEEN NOTHING BUT A SHADOW OF OUR OWN DIVINITY?
I HAVE COME FOR THE HERALD...
...AND I SHALL NOT LEAVE WITHOUT HIM.
THEN YOU SHALL NOT LEAVE, EVER.
THE DEAD ARE MINE, TO RULE AND KEEP. AND ONCE YOU ARE DEAD...
...I SHALL KEEP YOU FOREVER AT MY PLEASURE.

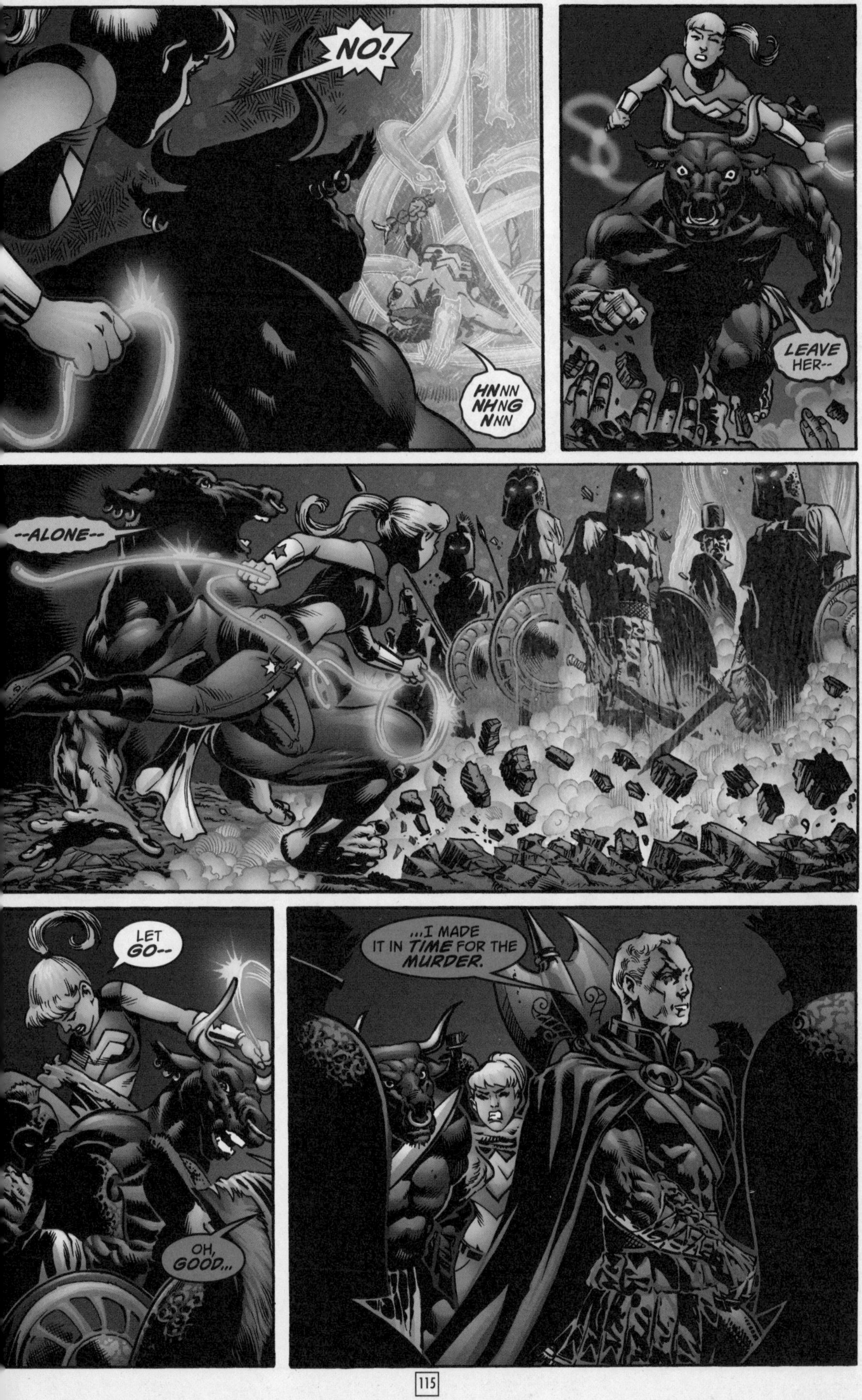
NO!
HNNN
NHNG
NNN
LEAVE
HER--
--ALONE--
LET
GO--
OH,
GOOD...
...I MADE
IT IN TIME FOR THE
MURDER.

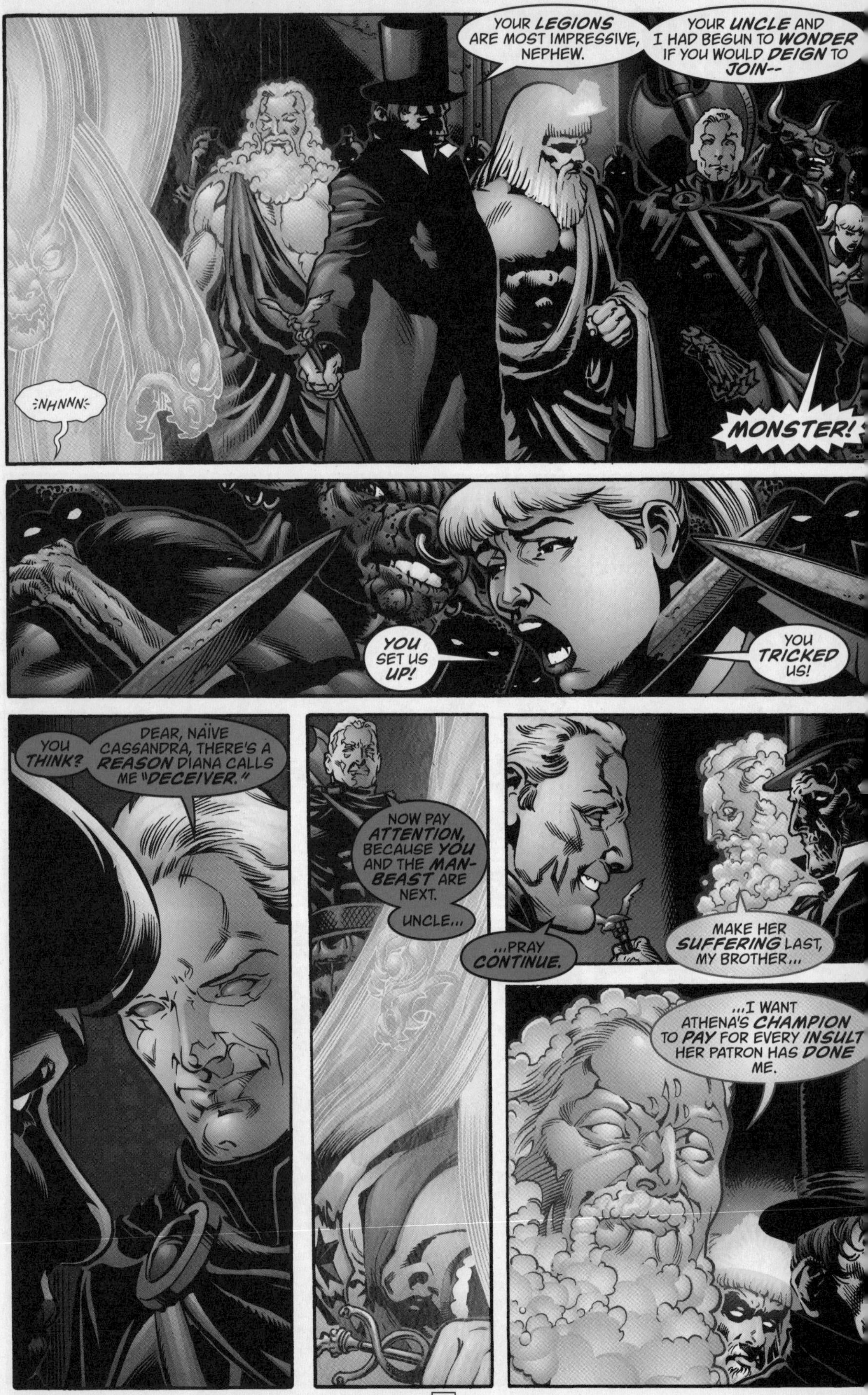

YOUR LEGIONS ARE MOST IMPRESSIVE, NEPHEW.
YOUR UNCLE AND I HAD BEGUN TO WONDER IF YOU WOULD DEIGN TO JOIN--
NHNNN
MONSTER!
YOU SET US UP!
YOU TRICKED US!
YOU THINK?
DEAR, NAÏVE CASSANDRA, THERE'S A REASON DIANA CALLS ME "DECEIVER."
NOW PAY ATTENTION, BECAUSE YOU AND THE MAN-BEAST ARE NEXT.
UNCLE...
...PRAY CONTINUE.
MAKE HER SUFFERING LAST, MY BROTHER...
...I WANT ATHENA'S CHAMPION TO PAY FOR EVERY INSULT HER PATRON HAS DONE ME.

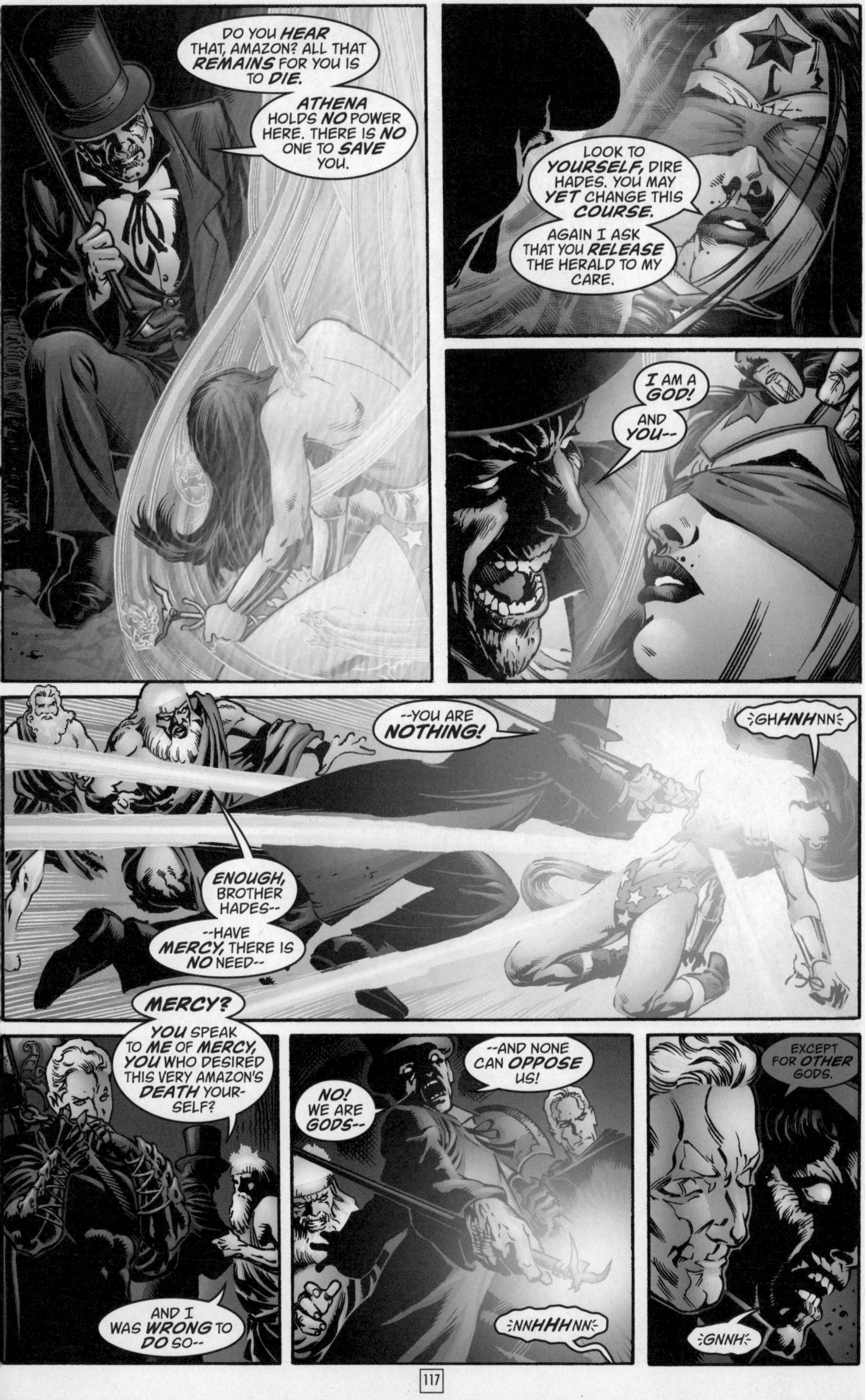
DO YOU HEAR THAT, AMAZON? ALL THAT REMAINS FOR YOU IS TO DIE.
ATHENA HOLDS NO POWER HERE. THERE IS NO ONE TO SAVE YOU.
LOOK TO YOURSELF, DIRE HADES. YOU MAY YET CHANGE THIS COURSE.
AGAIN I ASK THAT YOU RELEASE THE HERALD TO MY CARE.
I AM A GOD!
AND YOU--
--YOU ARE NOTHING!
GHHNHNN
ENOUGH, BROTHER HADES--
--HAVE MERCY, THERE IS NO NEED--
MERCY?
YOU SPEAK TO ME OF MERCY, YOU WHO DESIRED THIS VERY AMAZON'S DEATH YOURSELF?
AND I WAS WRONG TO DO SO--
NO! WE ARE GODS--
--AND NONE CAN OPPOSE US!
NNHHHNN
EXCEPT FOR OTHER GODS.
GNNH

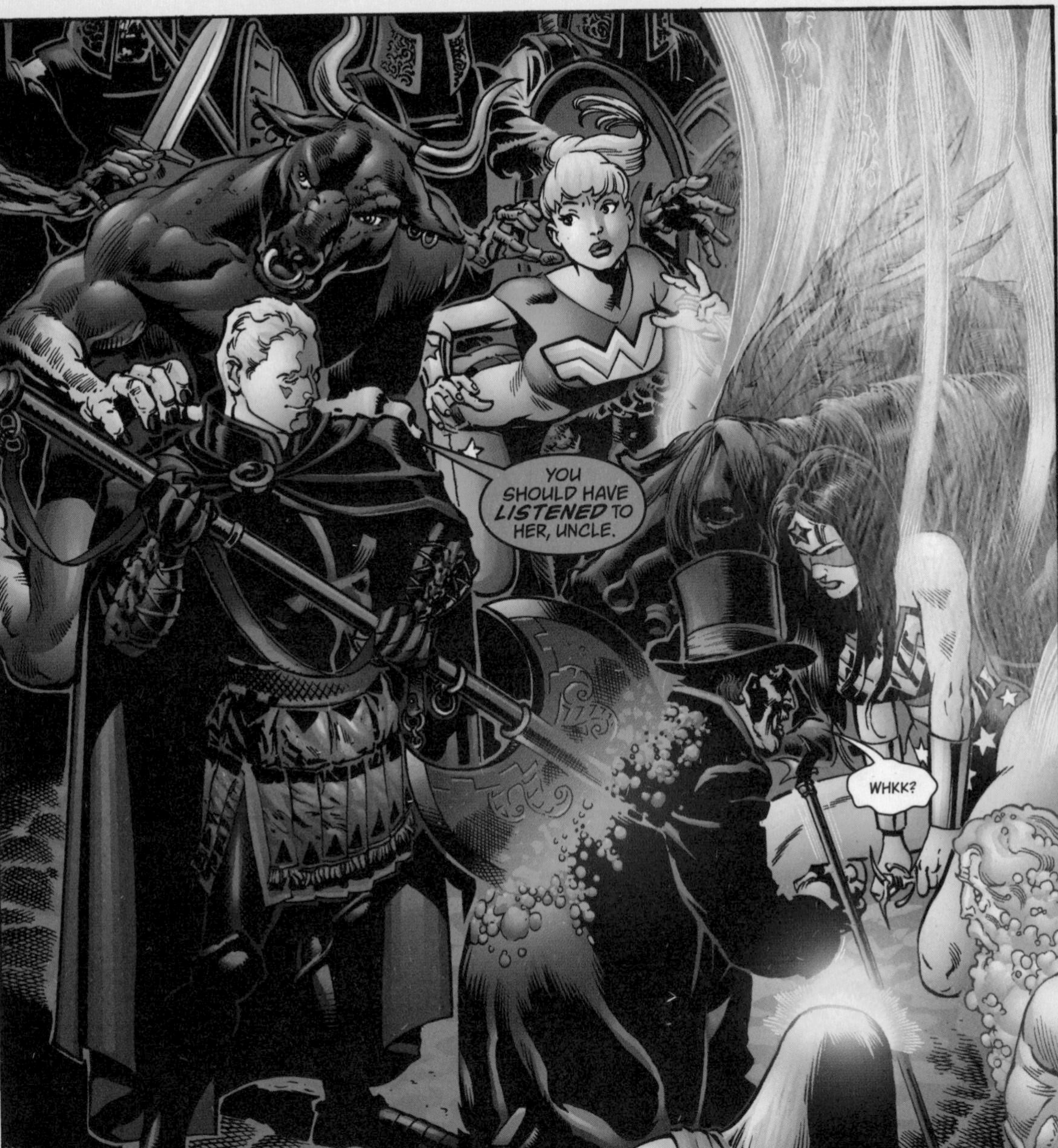
YOU SHOULD HAVE LISTENED TO HER, UNCLE.
WHKK?

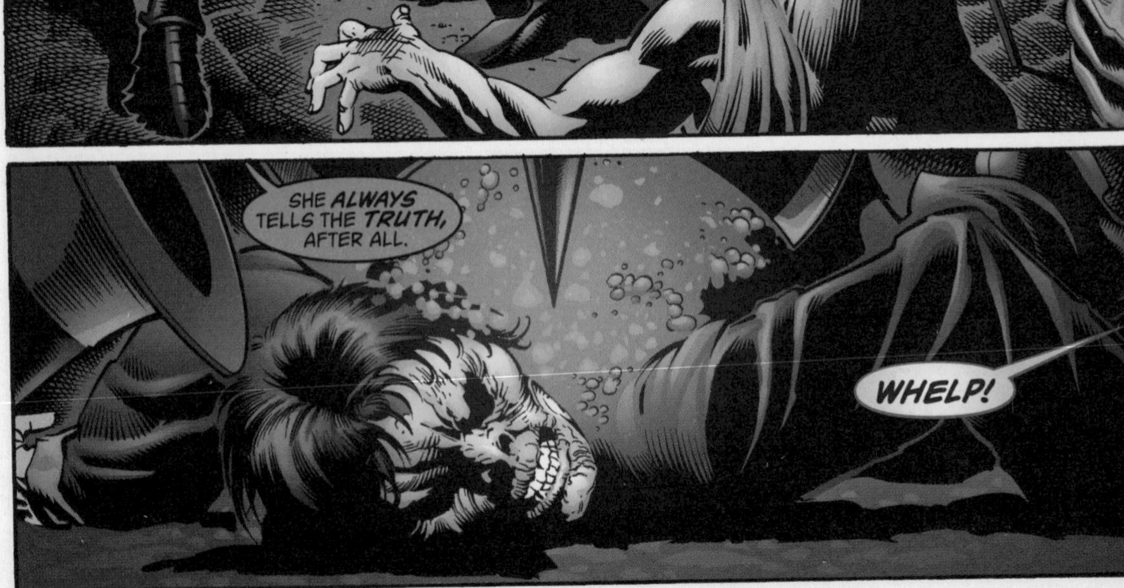
SHE ALWAYS TELLS THE TRUTH, AFTER ALL.
WHELP!

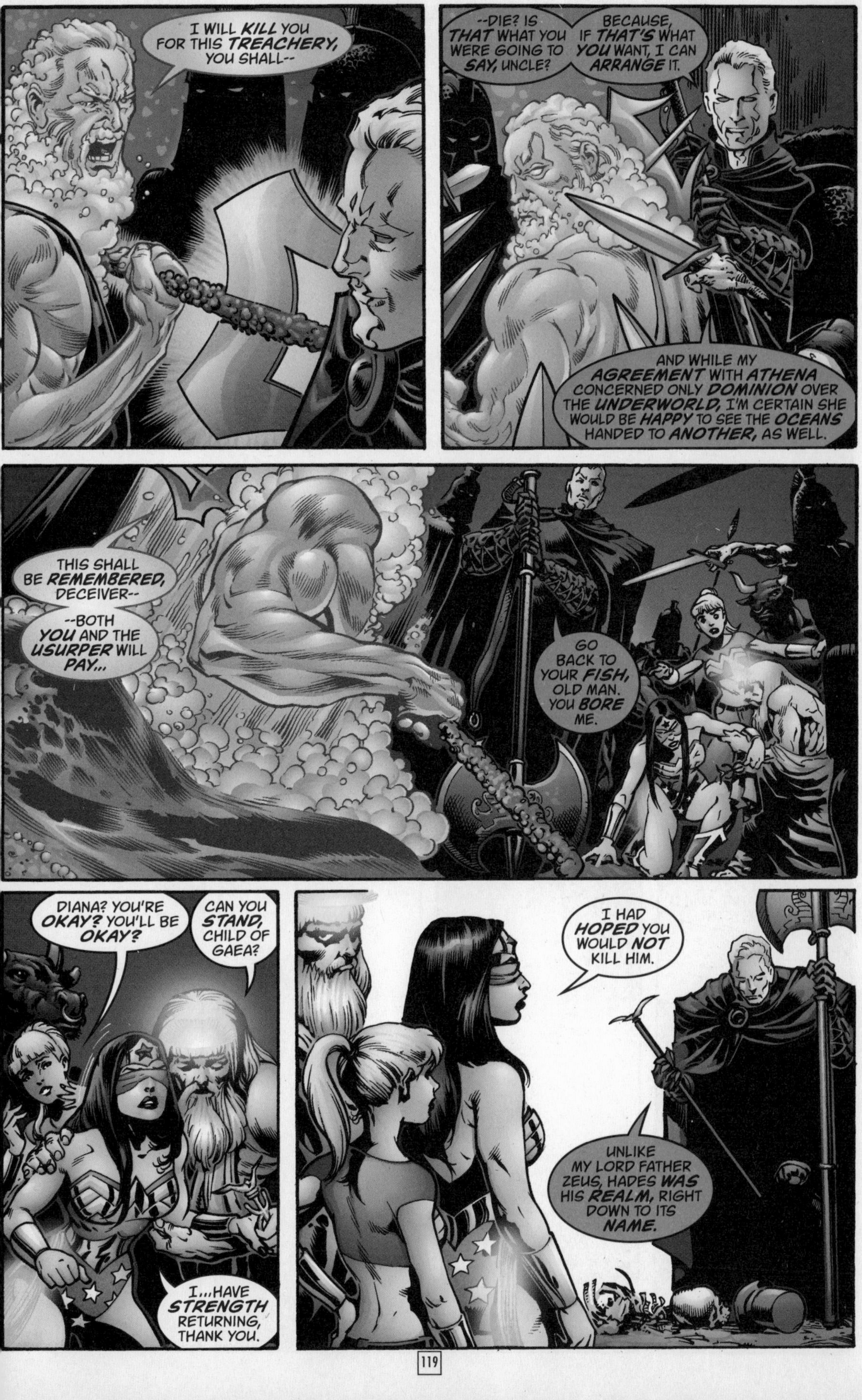

I WILL KILL YOU FOR THIS TREACHERY, YOU SHALL--
--DIE? IS THAT WHAT YOU WERE GOING TO SAY, UNCLE?
BECAUSE, IF THAT'S WHAT YOU WANT, I CAN ARRANGE IT.
AND WHILE MY AGREEMENT WITH ATHENA CONCERNED ONLY DOMINION OVER THE UNDERWORLD, I'M CERTAIN SHE WOULD BE HAPPY TO SEE THE OCEANS HANDED TO ANOTHER, AS WELL.
THIS SHALL BE REMEMBERED, DECEIVER--
--BOTH YOU AND THE USURPER WILL PAY...
GO BACK TO YOUR FISH, OLD MAN. YOU BORE ME.
DIANA? YOU'RE OKAY? YOU'LL BE OKAY?
CAN YOU STAND, CHILD OF GAEA?
I...HAVE STRENGTH RETURNING, THANK YOU.
I HAD HOPED YOU WOULD NOT KILL HIM.
UNLIKE MY LORD FATHER ZEUS, HADES WAS HIS REALM, RIGHT DOWN TO ITS NAME.

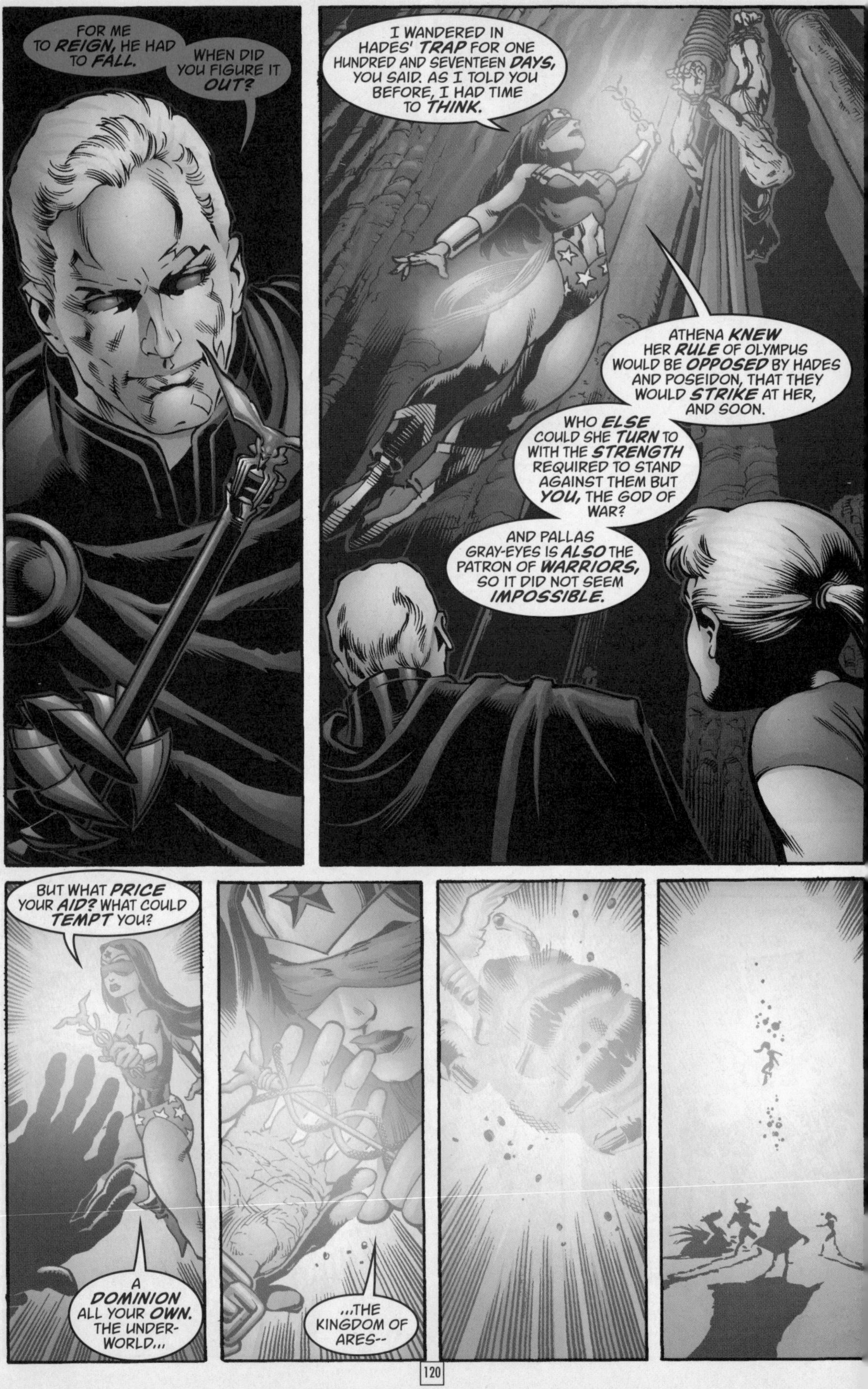
FOR ME TO REIGN, HE HAD TO FALL.
WHEN DID YOU FIGURE IT OUT?
I WANDERED IN HADES' TRAP FOR ONE HUNDRED AND SEVENTEEN DAYS, YOU SAID. AS I TOLD YOU BEFORE, I HAD TIME TO THINK.
ATHENA KNEW HER RULE OF OLYMPUS WOULD BE OPPOSED BY HADES AND POSEIDON, THAT THEY WOULD STRIKE AT HER, AND SOON.
WHO ELSE COULD SHE TURN TO WITH THE STRENGTH REQUIRED TO STAND AGAINST THEM BUT YOU, THE GOD OF WAR?
AND PALLAS GRAY-EYES IS ALSO THE PATRON OF WARRIORS, SO IT DID NOT SEEM IMPOSSIBLE.
BUT WHAT PRICE YOUR AID? WHAT COULD TEMPT YOU?
A DOMINION ALL YOUR OWN. THE UNDER-WORLD...
...THE KINGDOM OF ARES--

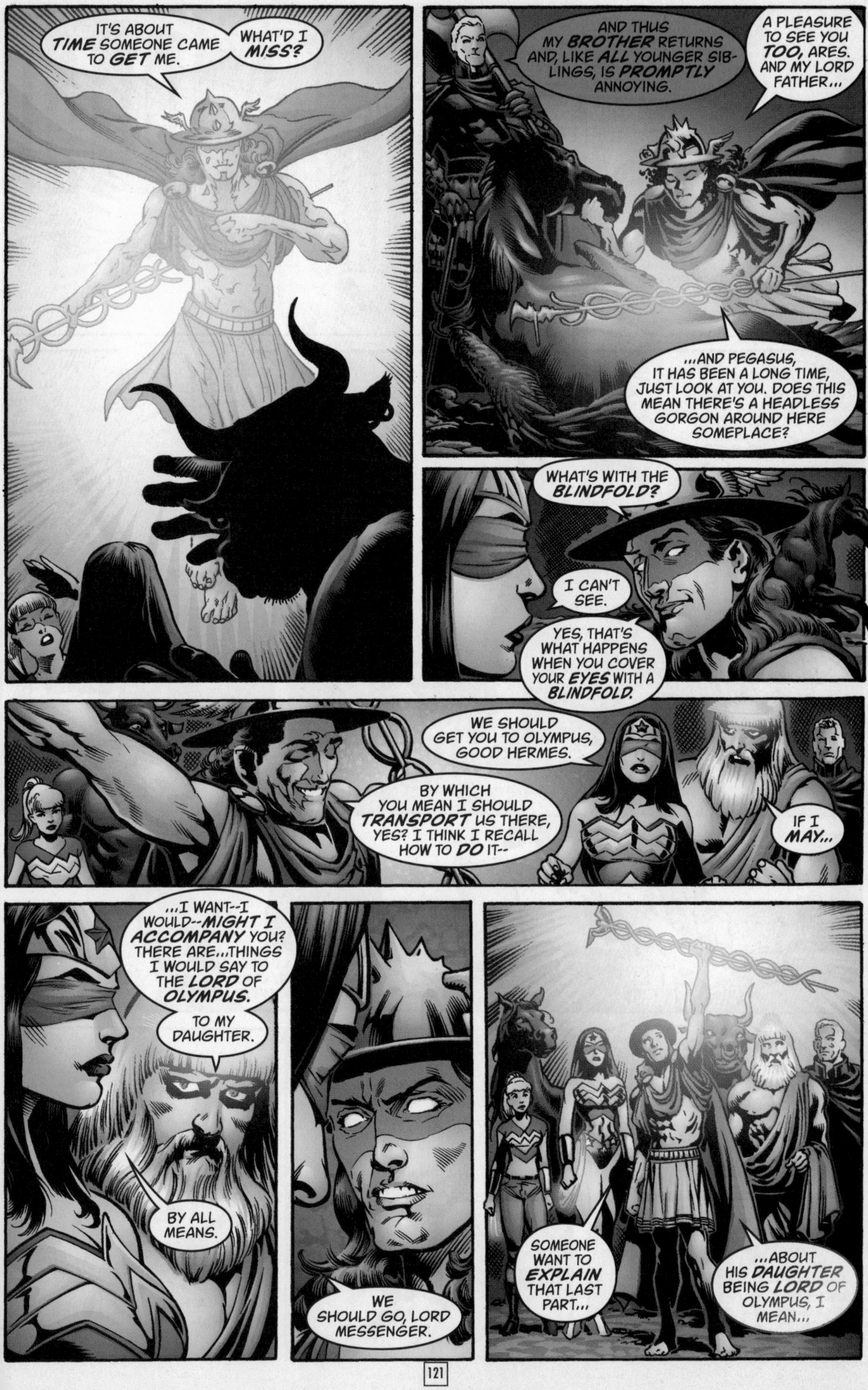
IT'S ABOUT TIME SOMEONE CAME TO GET ME.
WHAT'D I MISS?
AND THUS MY BROTHER RETURNS AND, LIKE ALL YOUNGER SIBLINGS, IS PROMPTLY ANNOYING.
A PLEASURE TO SEE YOU TOO, ARES. AND MY LORD FATHER...
...AND PEGASUS, IT HAS BEEN A LONG TIME, JUST LOOK AT YOU. DOES THIS MEAN THERE'S A HEADLESS GORGON AROUND HERE SOMEPLACE?
WHAT'S WITH THE BLINDFOLD?
I CAN'T SEE.
YES, THAT'S WHAT HAPPENS WHEN YOU COVER YOUR EYES WITH A BLINDFOLD.
WE SHOULD GET YOU TO OLYMPUS, GOOD HERMES.
BY WHICH YOU MEAN I SHOULD TRANSPORT US THERE, YES? I THINK I RECALL HOW TO DO IT--
IF I MAY...
...I WANT--I WOULD--MIGHT I ACCOMPANY YOU? THERE ARE...THINGS I WOULD SAY TO THE LORD OF OLYMPUS.
TO MY DAUGHTER.
BY ALL MEANS.
WE SHOULD GO, LORD MESSENGER.
SOMEONE WANT TO EXPLAIN THAT LAST PART...
...ABOUT HIS DAUGHTER BEING LORD OF OLYMPUS, I MEAN...

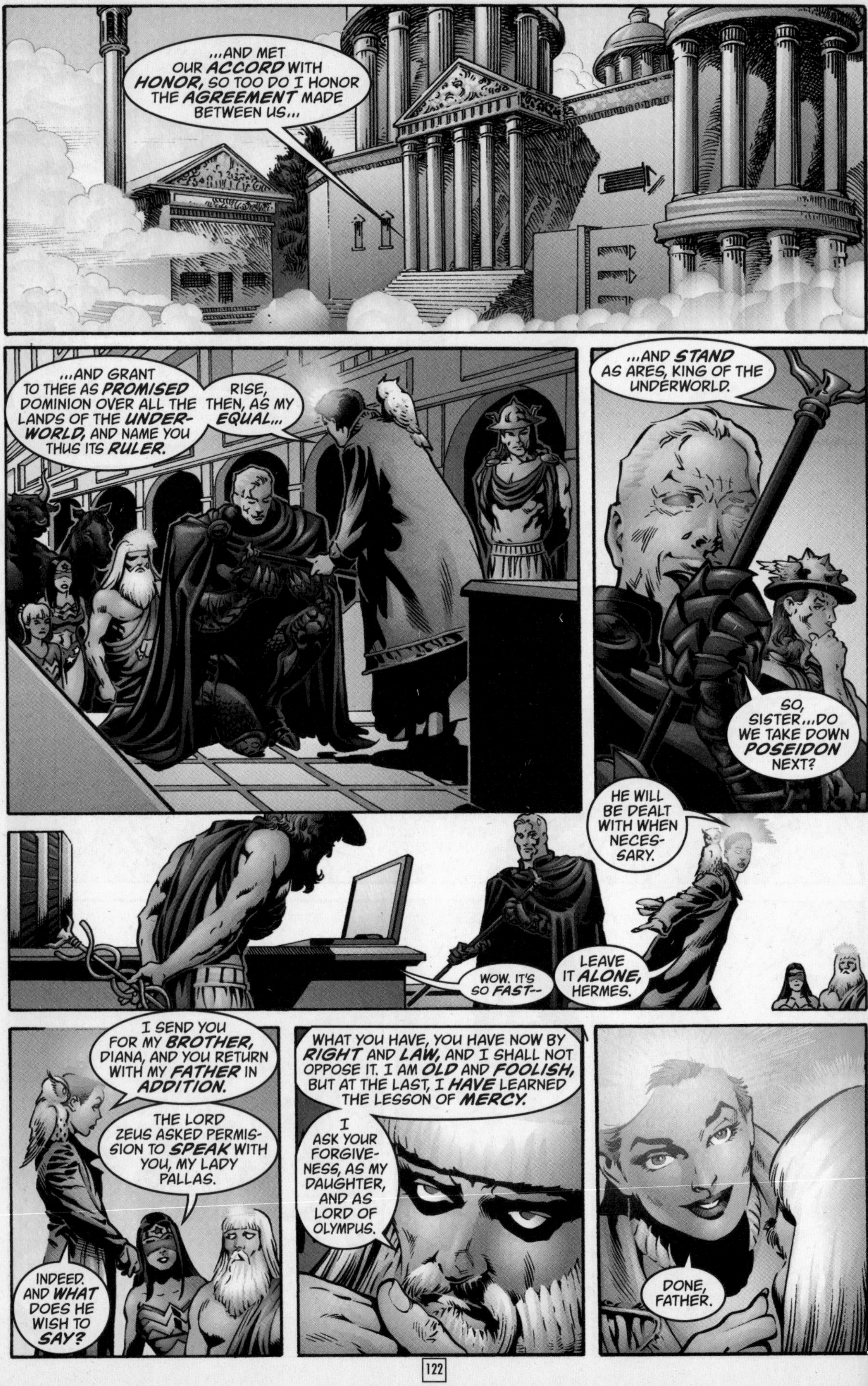
...AND MET OUR ACCORD WITH HONOR, SO TOO DO I HONOR THE AGREEMENT MADE BETWEEN US...
...AND GRANT TO THEE AS PROMISED DOMINION OVER ALL THE LANDS OF THE UNDER-WORLD, AND NAME YOU THUS ITS RULER.
RISE, THEN, AS MY EQUAL...
...AND STAND AS ARES, KING OF THE UNDERWORLD.
SO, SISTER...DO WE TAKE DOWN POSEIDON NEXT?
HE WILL BE DEALT WITH WHEN NECES-SARY.
WOW. IT'S SO FAST--
LEAVE IT ALONE, HERMES.
I SEND YOU FOR MY BROTHER, DIANA, AND YOU RETURN WITH MY FATHER IN ADDITION.
THE LORD ZEUS ASKED PERMIS-SION TO SPEAK WITH YOU, MY LADY PALLAS.
INDEED. AND WHAT DOES HE WISH TO SAY?
WHAT YOU HAVE, YOU HAVE NOW BY RIGHT AND LAW, AND I SHALL NOT OPPOSE IT. I AM OLD AND FOOLISH, BUT AT THE LAST, I HAVE LEARNED THE LESSON OF MERCY.
I ASK YOUR FORGIVE-NESS, AS MY DAUGHTER, AND AS LORD OF OLYMPUS.
DONE, FATHER.

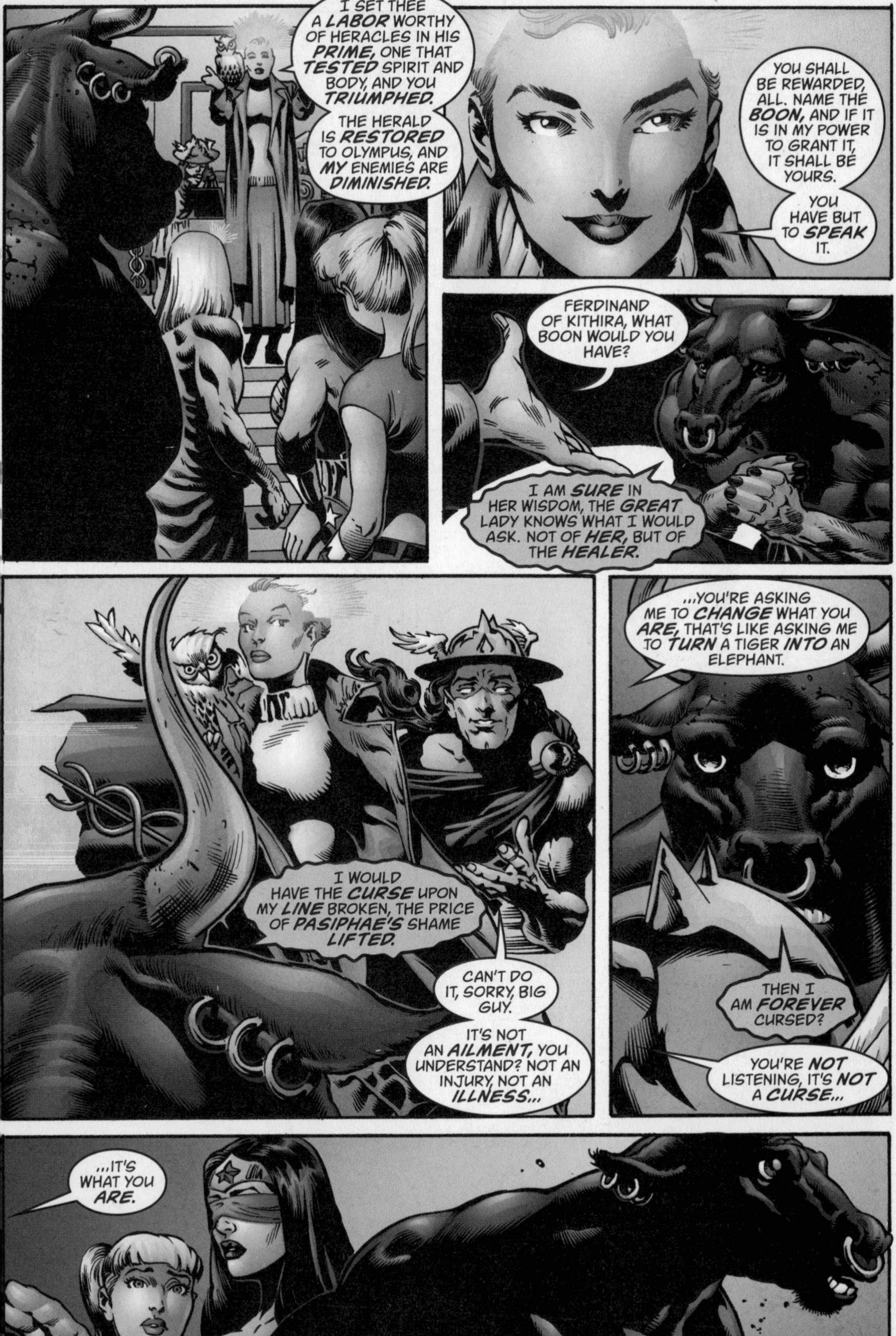
I SET THEE A LABOR WORTHY OF HERACLES IN HIS PRIME, ONE THAT TESTED SPIRIT AND BODY, AND YOU TRIUMPHED.
THE HERALD IS RESTORED TO OLYMPUS, AND MY ENEMIES ARE DIMINISHED.
YOU SHALL BE REWARDED, ALL. NAME THE BOON, AND IF IT IS IN MY POWER TO GRANT IT, IT SHALL BE YOURS.
YOU HAVE BUT TO SPEAK IT.
FERDINAND OF KITHIRA, WHAT BOON WOULD YOU HAVE?
I AM SURE IN HER WISDOM, THE GREAT LADY KNOWS WHAT I WOULD ASK. NOT OF HER, BUT OF THE HEALER.
I WOULD HAVE THE CURSE UPON MY LINE BROKEN, THE PRICE OF PASIPHAE'S SHAME LIFTED.
CAN'T DO IT, SORRY, BIG GUY.
IT'S NOT AN AILMENT, YOU UNDERSTAND? NOT AN INJURY, NOT AN ILLNESS...
...YOU'RE ASKING ME TO CHANGE WHAT YOU ARE, THAT'S LIKE ASKING ME TO TURN A TIGER INTO AN ELEPHANT.
THEN I AM FOREVER CURSED?
YOU'RE NOT LISTENING, IT'S NOT A CURSE...
...IT'S WHAT YOU ARE.

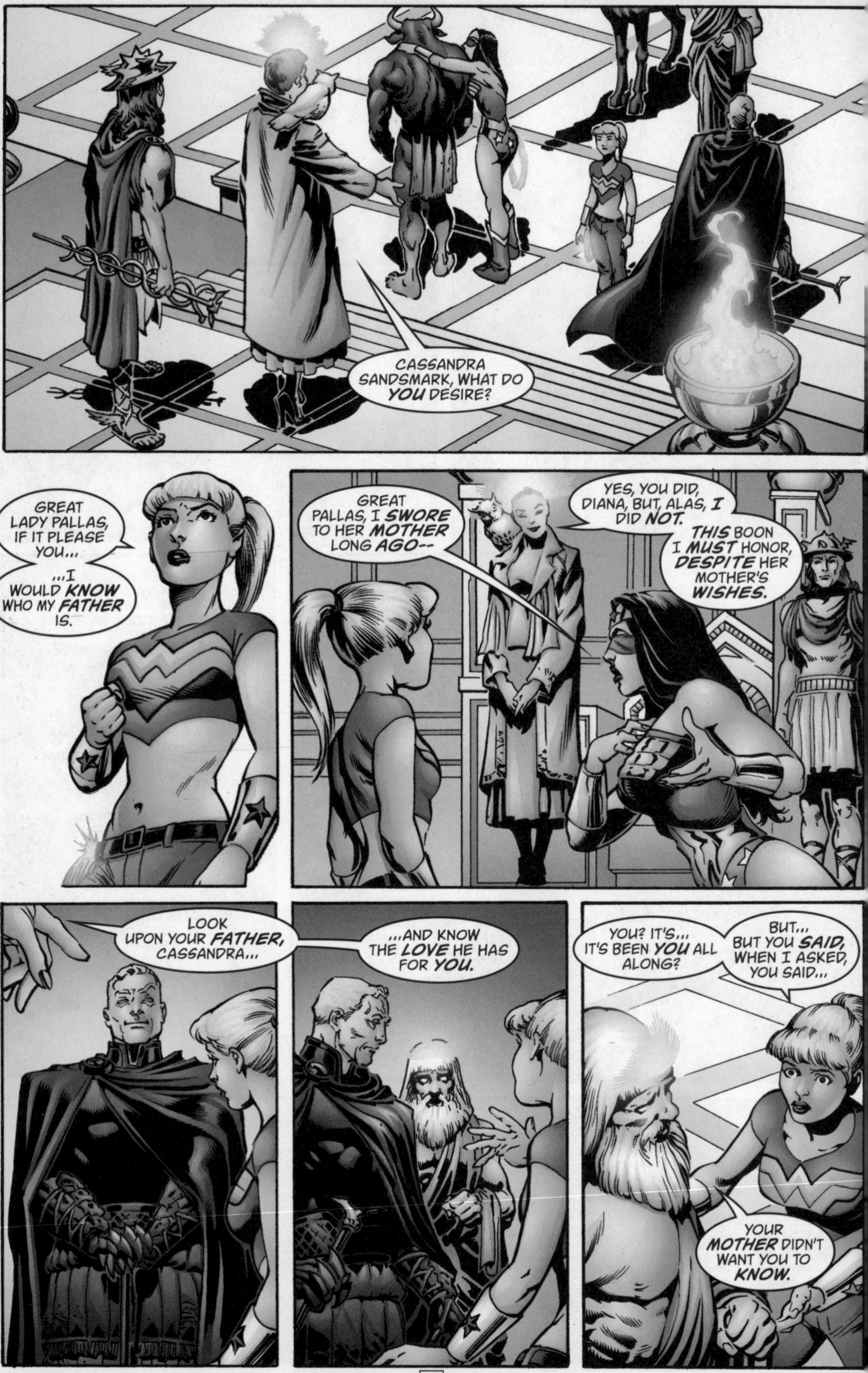
CASSANDRA SANDSMARK, WHAT DO YOU DESIRE?
GREAT LADY PALLAS, IF IT PLEASE YOU...
...I WOULD KNOW WHO MY FATHER IS.
GREAT PALLAS, I SWORE TO HER MOTHER LONG AGO--
YES, YOU DID, DIANA, BUT, ALAS, I DID NOT.
THIS BOON I MUST HONOR, DESPITE HER MOTHER'S WISHES.
LOOK UPON YOUR FATHER, CASSANDRA...
...AND KNOW THE LOVE HE HAS FOR YOU.
YOU? IT'S... IT'S BEEN YOU ALL ALONG?
BUT... BUT YOU SAID, WHEN I ASKED, YOU SAID...
YOUR MOTHER DIDN'T WANT YOU TO KNOW.

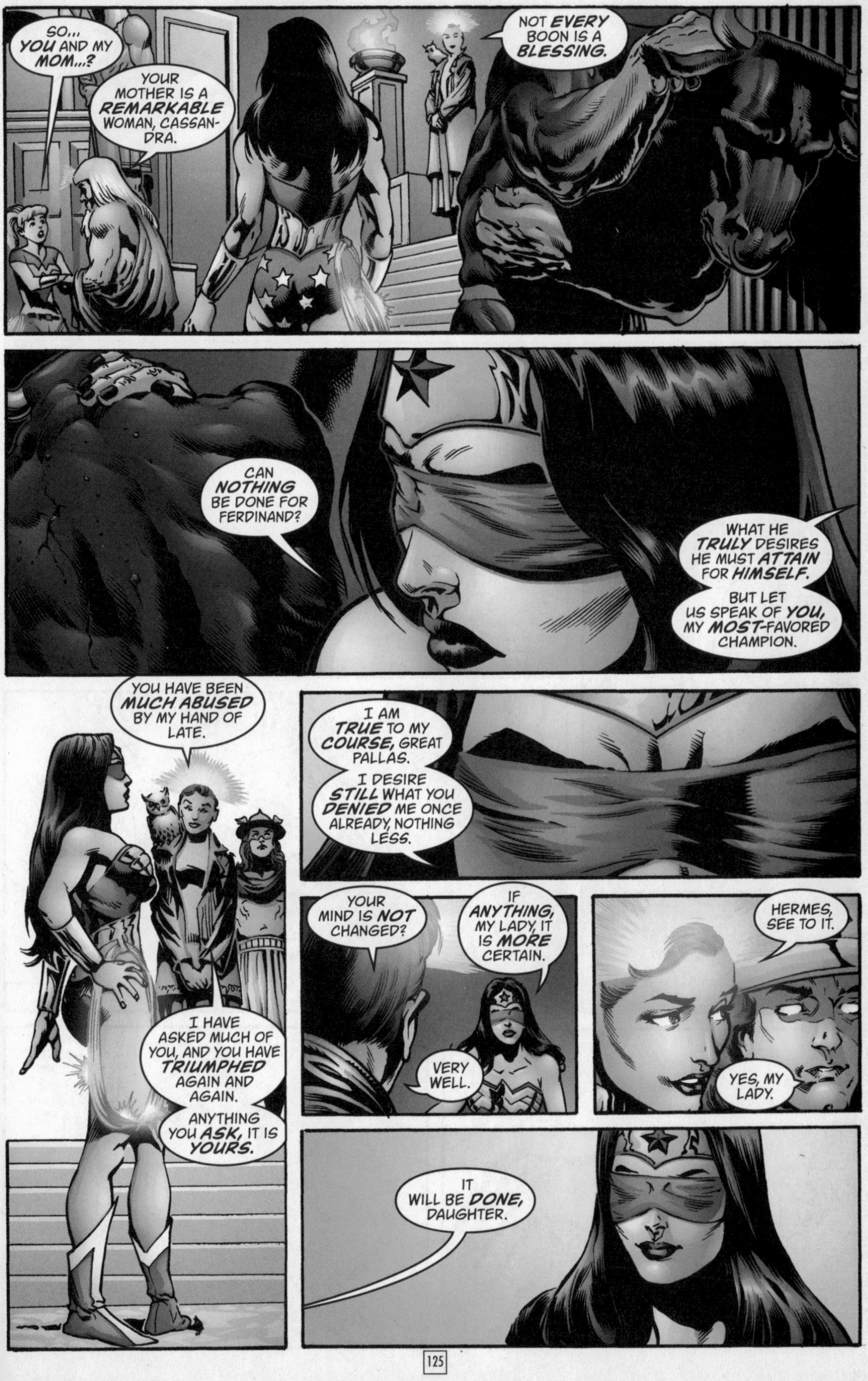
SO... YOU AND MY MOM...?
YOUR MOTHER IS A REMARKABLE WOMAN, CASSANDRA.
NOT EVERY BOON IS A BLESSING.
CAN NOTHING BE DONE FOR FERDINAND?
WHAT HE TRULY DESIRES HE MUST ATTAIN FOR HIMSELF.
BUT LET US SPEAK OF YOU, MY MOST-FAVORED CHAMPION.
YOU HAVE BEEN MUCH ABUSED BY MY HAND OF LATE.
I HAVE ASKED MUCH OF YOU, AND YOU HAVE TRIUMPHED AGAIN AND AGAIN.
ANYTHING YOU ASK, IT IS YOURS.
I AM TRUE TO MY COURSE, GREAT PALLAS.
I DESIRE STILL WHAT YOU DENIED ME ONCE ALREADY, NOTHING LESS.
YOUR MIND IS NOT CHANGED?
IF ANYTHING, MY LADY, IT IS MORE CERTAIN.
VERY WELL.
HERMES, SEE TO IT.
YES, MY LADY.
IT WILL BE DONE, DAUGHTER.

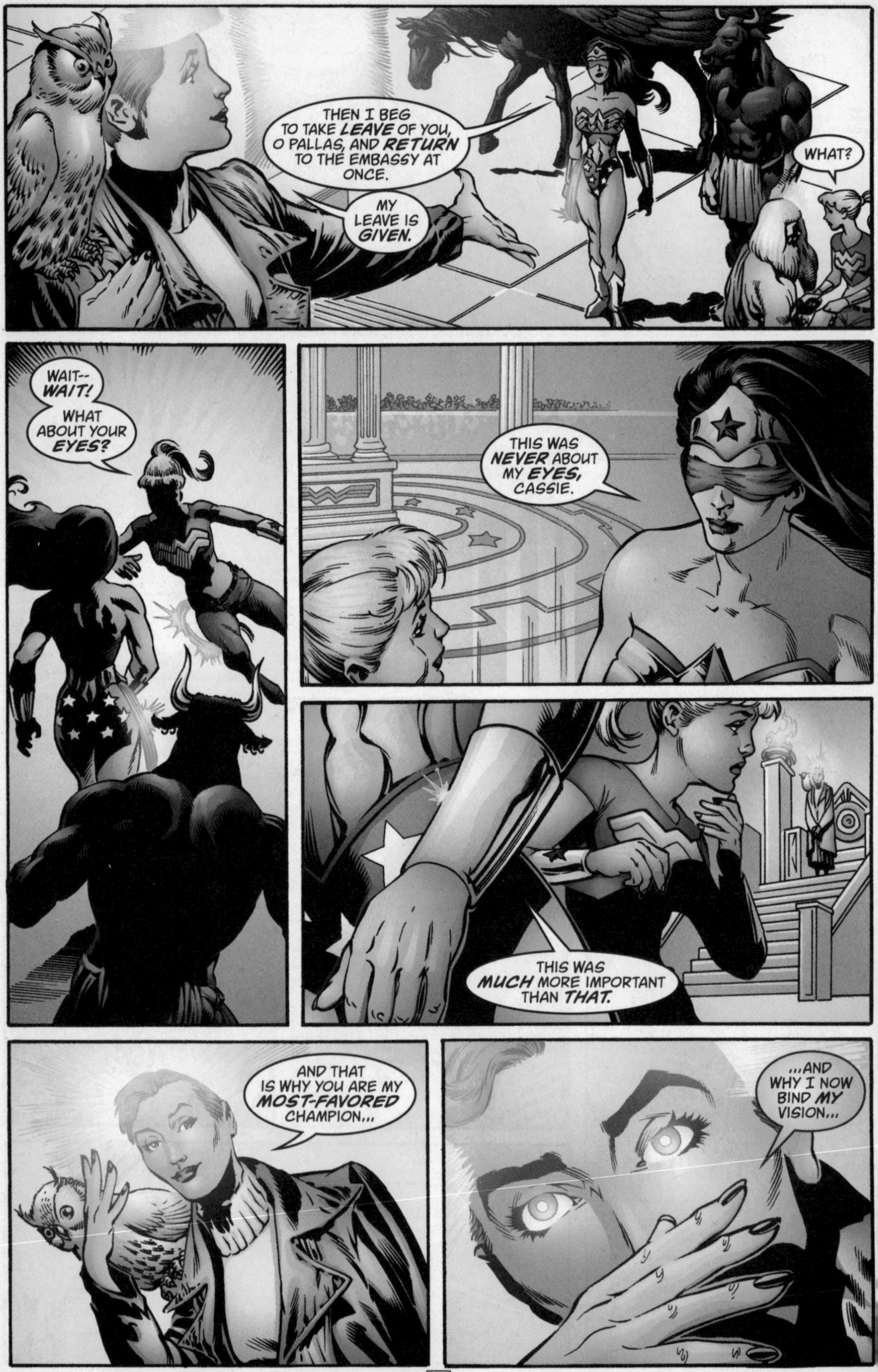

THEN I BEG TO TAKE LEAVE OF YOU, O PALLAS, AND RETURN TO THE EMBASSY AT ONCE.
MY LEAVE IS GIVEN.
WHAT?
WAIT-- WAIT!
WHAT ABOUT YOUR EYES?
THIS WAS NEVER ABOUT MY EYES, CASSIE.
THIS WAS MUCH MORE IMPORTANT THAN THAT.
AND THAT IS WHY YOU ARE MY MOST-FAVORED CHAMPION...
...AND WHY I NOW BIND MY VISION...

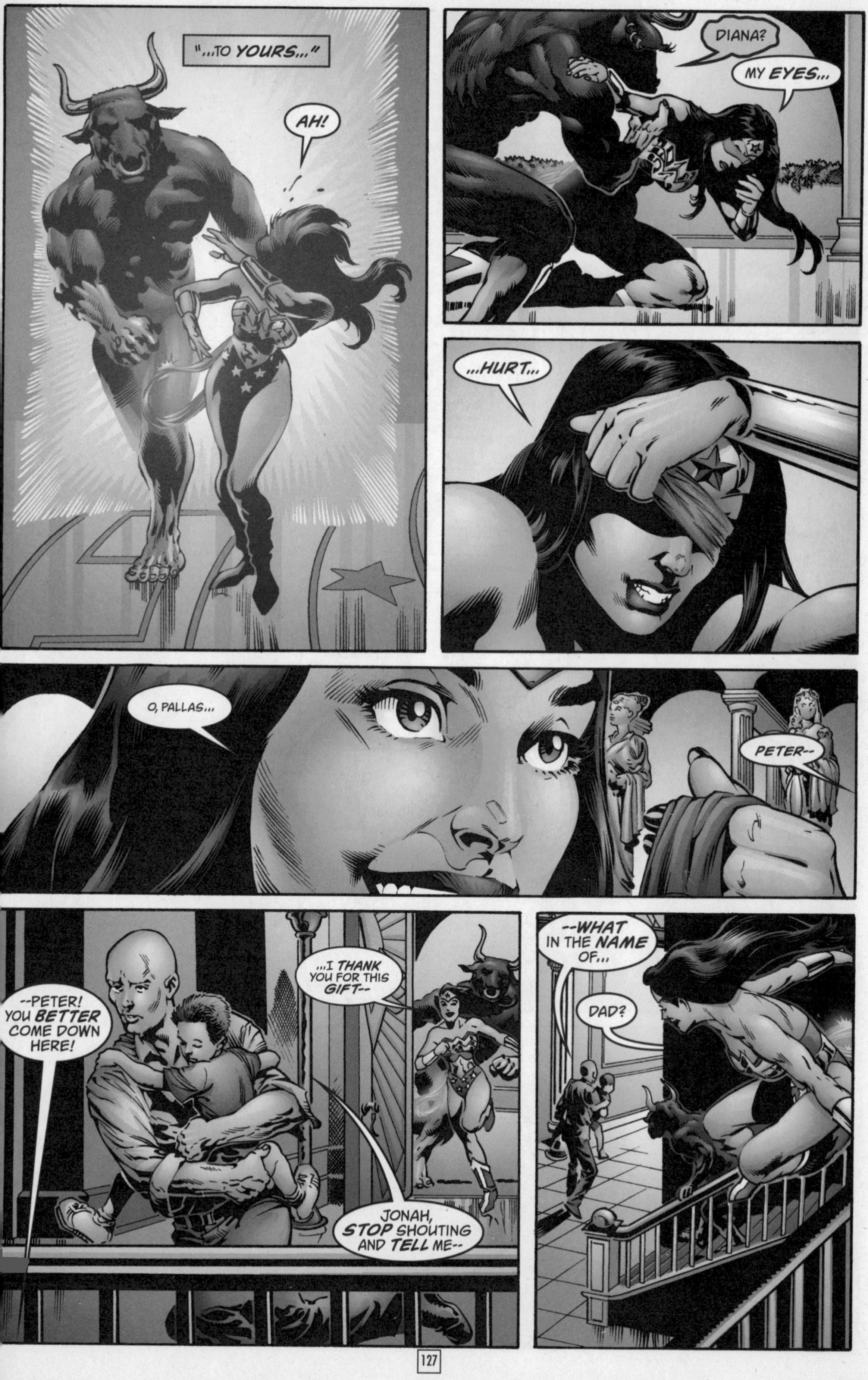
"...TO YOURS..."
AH!
DIANA?
MY EYES...
...HURT...
O, PALLAS...
PETER--
--PETER! YOU BETTER COME DOWN HERE!
...I THANK YOU FOR THIS GIFT--
JONAH, STOP SHOUTING AND TELL ME--
--WHAT IN THE NAME OF...
DAD?

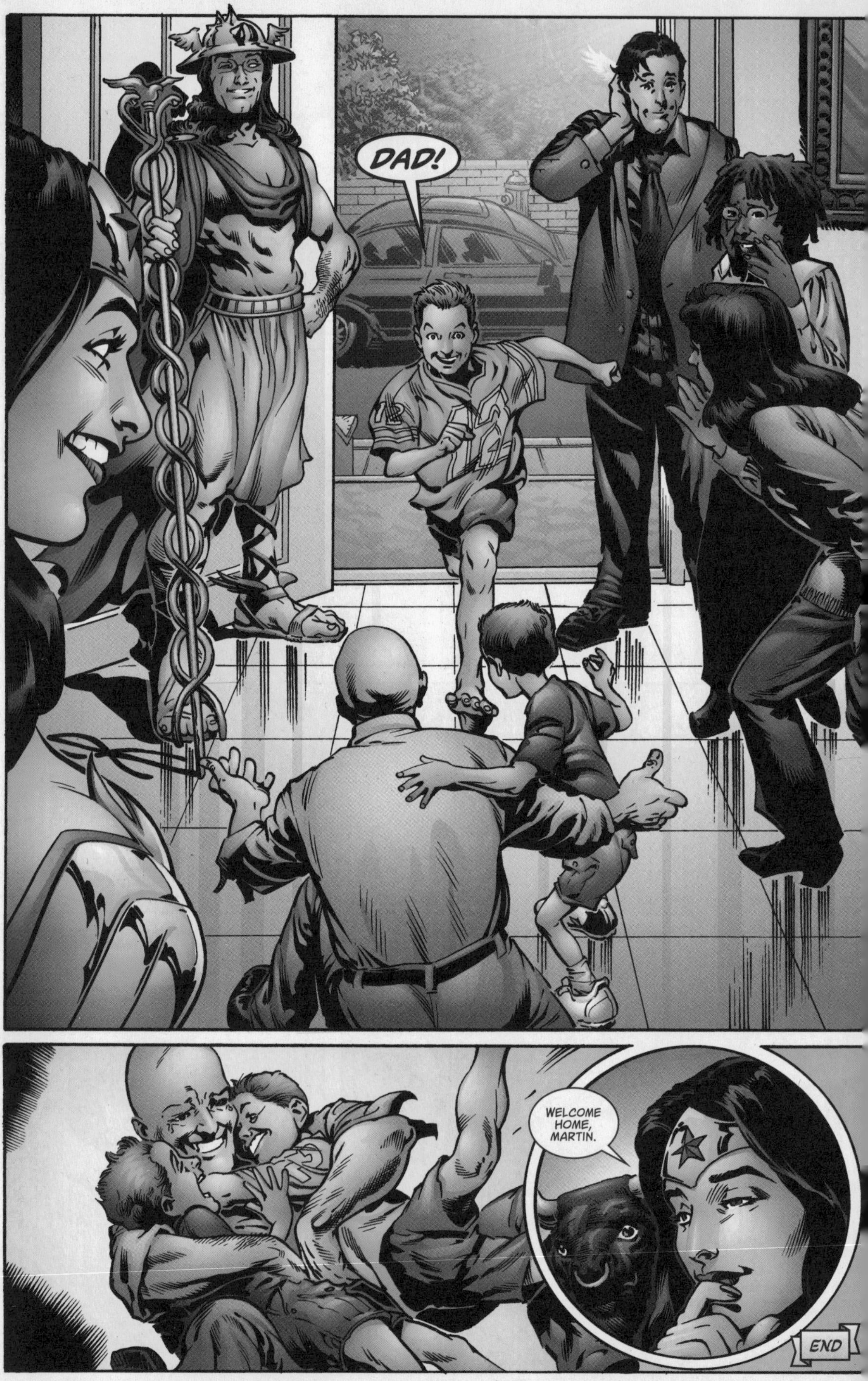
DAD!
WELCOME HOME, MARTIN.
END